CLOSE READING OF INFORMATIONAL SOURCES

Assessment-Driven Instruction in Grades 3–8

SECOND EDITION

SUNDAY CUMMINS

THE GUILFORD PRESS
New York   London

Copyright © 2019 The Guilford Press
A Division of Guilford Publications, Inc.
370 Seventh Avenue, Suite 1200, New York, NY 10001
www.guilford.com

Printed in the United States of America

This book is printed on acid-free paper.

Last digit is print number: 9   8   7   6   5   4   3   2   1

Library of Congress Cataloging-in-Publication Data

Names: Cummins, Sunday, author.
Title: Close reading of informational sources : assessment-driven instruction in grades
3–8
    / Sunday Cummins
Other titles: Close reading of informational texts
Description: Second edition. | New York : Guilford Press, [2019] | Includes
    bibliographical references and index.
Identifiers: LCCN 2018041448| ISBN 9781462539390 (hardcover)
    | ISBN 9781462539451 (pbk.)
Subjects: LCSH: Language arts (Elementary) | English language—Composition and
    exercises—Study and teaching (Elementary) | Exposition (Rhetoric)—Study and
    teaching (Elementary)
Classification: LCC LB1576 .C854 2019 | DDC 372.6—dc23
LC record available at *https://lccn.loc.gov/2018041448*

CLOSE READING OF INFORMATIONAL SOURCES

Also by Sunday Cummins

Unpacking Complexity in Informational Texts:
Principles and Practices for Grades 2–8

About the Author

Sunday Cummins, PhD, is a literacy consultant and author of professional books on assessment-driven instruction with informational sources. Formerly, she was Assistant Professor in the Reading and Language Department at National Louis University, before which she worked in public schools for 10 years as a middle school and third-grade teacher and as a literacy coach. Dr. Cummins teaches and learns alongside educators and students as a consultant and researcher, with a focus on the power of informational sources to transform students' thinking. She shares her experiences by presenting at state and national conferences, writing articles for numerous publications, and blogging regularly. Her website is *www.sunday-cummins.com*.

Acknowledgments

I want to extend a huge thank-you to the teachers and students who worked with me on the content for the first and second editions of this book. These teachers opened their classroom doors wide, and hundreds of students shared their learning with me. A special thank-you as well to Kelli, Amanda, Beth, Lori, and the countless educators in the Champaign Unit 4 Schools, North Kansas City Schools, and San José Unified School District for hosting my visits. Through our work with students, I have learned a great deal that has been incorporated into the new edition of this book.

A special thank-you to another group of peers who have read drafts, listened intently, and provided constructive feedback as well as an endless amount of encouragement—Catherine Stallmeyer-Gerard, Rachel Powell, Zoila Esquivel Moreno, Lisa Friesen, and Nicole Ballew. I am looking forward to continuing to learn alongside you!

I am also grateful to Jan Richardson, my professional mentor. Watching Jan work with teachers has also nudged me to, like her, create even more clarity for teachers whose instructional plates are extremely full. This has become a big goal for the new edition of this book.

A thank-you to my editor, Craig Thomas, and the production team at The Guilford Press. This book has *a lot* of figures of student work, informational sources, and other critical items that required persistent attention to detail and the development of a reader-friendly design and layout. I am super grateful for your patience and perseverance in making this book happen!

And then there's my family.

In this book, you will see a photograph of my father, Bruce Murray, with my daughter, Anna. For almost 30 years, my dad has called me on Sunday evening to check in about life, about what I'm writing, and about where I'll be that next week. In the last 5 years, he has added checking in on me when I'm traveling, sending thoughtful texts like "Are you home yet?" Thanks, Dad.

Anna, who is now 16 years old, has only ever known me as an avid reader of informational sources. She pretty much knows that when we talk about a nonfiction topic, I will probably say, "I have a book about that!" She embraces this—and will probably have these words engraved on my tombstone. Even more encouraging, though, is that she knows me as a writer. She understands that sometimes writing is tough and that sometimes it's exhilarating. She knows how to hold on during the ride, providing hugs as needed as well as space to think and write (frequently at a coffee shop with her there to keep me on task).

Finally, there's Stephen. When this book comes out, we will be close to celebrating our 20th wedding anniversary. His presence in my life, as a think partner and soul mate, is part of my identity as an educator and author. When you meet me, you are also meeting Stephen, the best friend who lifts me up in so many ways every single day.

Contents

Introduction   1

Overview of Chapters   3

Closing Thoughts   5

CHAPTER ONE Strategic Close Reading of Informational Sources   7

What Does Strategic Close Reading of a Traditional Text Look Like?   8

What Does Strategic Close Viewing–Listening to a Video Look Like?   9

What Does Strategic Close Reading of an Infographic Look Like?   11

How Do We Sum Up Strategic Close Reading–Viewing–Listening?   13

Closing Thoughts   15

CHAPTER TWO A Repertoire of Strategies Needed
for Close Reading   16

Being Clear about the Purpose   17

Tapping Prior Knowledge Related to the Topic of the Source   19

Tapping Prior Knowledge Related to How Sources Work   22

Monitoring for Meaning   24

Determining What Is Important (That Is, Identifying Key Details)   25

Synthesis   28

Closing Thoughts   30

CHAPTER THREE An Assessment-Driven, Three-Phase Plan
for Learning   31

How Do We Implement This Plan Effectively?   35

How Does the Three-Phase Plan for Learning Meet the Needs
of Different Learners?   42

Closing Thoughts   46

Contents

CHAPTER FOUR Selecting Sources 47

Key Questions to Guide Source Selection 48
"Leveled" Sources Can Be Problematic 54
On Selecting Sources to Read Aloud 55
Develop "Go-To" Resources for Sources 58
Closing Thoughts 58

CHAPTER FIVE Introducing Sources and Teaching Students 61
to Make *Informed* Predictions

Planning Purposeful Introductions 63
Releasing Responsibility for Previewing and Predicting
    with THIEVES 72
Closing Thoughts 81

CHAPTER SIX Synthesis and Identifying Main Ideas 82

What Do We Mean by "Identify a Main Idea" and "Synthesis"? 84
Do Your Students Need to Work at Identifying Main Ideas? 88
Where to Start? Introduce the Framed Photograph Analogy 89
How Do We Plan and Teach for Identifying a Main Idea? 92
How Do We Assess? 97
What Does Follow-Up Instruction Look Like? 99
Closing Thoughts 106

CHAPTER SEVEN Monitoring for Meaning 108

What Do We Mean by "Monitoring for Meaning"? 109
Do Your Students Need to Work on Monitoring for Meaning? 112
Where to Start? Introduce the Coding Strategy 113
How Do We Plan and Teach for Monitoring for Meaning? 116
How Do We Assess? 121
What Does Follow-Up Instruction Look Like? 121
Closing Thoughts 129

CHAPTER EIGHT Identifying and Explaining Key Details 132

What Do We Mean by "Determine What Is Important"
    or "Identify Key Details"? 134
Do Your Students Need to Work on This? 137
Where to Start? Identify Key Details 137
How Do We Plan and Teach for Identifying Key Details? 149
How Do We Assess? 154
What Does Follow-Up Instruction Look Like? 156
Closing Thoughts 158

CHAPTER NINE Learning from a Source's Visual Images   162
and Other Features

What Do We Mean by "Learning from a Source's Features"?   164
Do Your Students Need to Work on This?   167
Where to Start? Introduce Key Questions and Relevant Language   168
How Do We Plan and Teach for Learning from Visual Images?   174
How Do We Assess?   178
What Does Follow-Up Instruction Look Like?   182
Closing Thoughts   188

CHAPTER TEN Using Context Clues to Make Sense   190
of Unfamiliar Vocabulary

What Do We Mean by "Use Context Clues to Make Sense
     of Unfamiliar Vocabulary"?   191
Do Your Students Need to Work on This?   194
Where to Start? Explicitly Teach Types of Clues   195
How Do We Plan and Teach for Identifying Context Clues?   197
How Do We Assess?   198
What Does Follow-Up Instruction Look Like?   204
Closing Thoughts   205

CHAPTER ELEVEN Synthesis of Information from Multiple Sources   207

What Do We Mean by "Synthesis across Sources"?   208
Do Your Students Need to Work at Synthesizing Information
     from Multiple Sources?   210
Where to Start? Introduce Inquiry Charts with Guiding Questions   211
How Do We Plan and Teach for Learning from Multiple Sources?   213
How Do We Assess?   223
What Does Follow-Up Instruction Look Like?   224
Closing Thoughts   226

APPENDIX A Lessons for Phase 2— Meet the Strategies   227

1 Synthesis and Identifying Main Ideas Using the Framed Photo Analogy   229
2 Monitoring for Meaning Using the Coding Strategy   230
3 Identifying Key Details Using the Pasta Analogy   231
4 Recognizing the Types of Details Authors Use   232
5 Explaining Key Details with "Explode to Explain"   233
6 Recognizing a Source's Structure   234
7 Learning from the Features in a Source   235
8 Using Context Clues to Figure Out the Meaning of New Vocabulary   236
9 Identifying an Author's Purpose   237
10 Synthesizing Information from Two Sources   238

Contents

APPENDIX B Study Guide   239

References   247

Index   253

Introduction

During the past 15 years, the number of high-quality informational sources available to students and educators has risen exponentially. Sources are available in a wide variety of formats, both in our schools and on the Internet. Our students can read hard copies of printed texts or texts available online. They can watch videos and listen to audio clips. They can look at *infographics*—sources that are made up primarily of statistics and visual images—and they can browse through images of primary sources related to content-area instruction available online. The list of sources available can seem endless.

The demands on educators to teach with informational sources have also increased. State and national standards require that students be able to examine sources in different formats *closely* for a variety of purposes, including identifying the author's main ideas and point of view (National Governors Association Center for Best Practices & Council of Chief State School Officers, 2010; Massachusetts Department of Elementary and Secondary Education, 2017; Missouri Department of Education, n.d.). On state and national assessments, students are being assessed on their ability to comprehend texts; to glean meaning from features, including photographs, diagrams, and maps; and to make sense of information presented in video clips (California Department of Education, n.d.; Illinois State Board of Education, n.d.).

Given the number of well-developed informational sources available to educators and students and the focus of departments of education on learning from these sources, there is so much potential for students to grow as critical consumers of information. There is room for students to fall in love with learning about topics they are curious about and to develop a depth of knowledge on these topics. Being able to read informational sources closely or watch and listen to sources carefully—across all content areas—creates a path for being able to understand the world better and to engage in creation, innovation, and problem solving, as well as communication and collaboration—all essential skills in college and career success.

And yet there continues to be a pervasive problem. Many students are not able to engage deeply with informational sources—determining what is important and summarizing and synthesizing information (ACT, Inc., 2006, 2017). Some students get only the "gist" of a source, while others remember only the last detail they read. Many students are familiar with how to skim texts to locate answers to specific questions. But when you ask them to identify an author's main ideas and supporting evidence from the source or to tell you how they decided which details were important and which were not, they falter in their responses.

Does this sound familiar?

This problem was all too familiar for me as an intermediate and middle grade teacher, and it continues to be the case in many of the schools I visit as a consultant. In the Introduction to the first edition of this book, I wrote about my "long-term professional inquiry" into how to teach for higher-level understanding of informational sources. I am still engaged in that inquiry. Every time I plan and teach with an informational source, my learning grows—about how sources work, about how students make sense of sources, and about how the instructional moves I make can impact or hinder student learning.

More than ever before, *close reading* has become an essential approach in my work with students and the informational sources they are attempting to understand. My understanding of close reading has also expanded. As described in this book, close reading results when the reader analyzes any given *source* at the word or phrase level, at the paragraph or section level, and at the visual image level. Close "reading" can occur with video and audio sources as well as with traditional printed texts, meaning we have to teach students how to *watch* and *listen* closely too. As the reader, viewer, or listener analyzes the source, he or she determines which details are most important and how these fit together logically to convey an idea. As a result of closely examining a source or a part of a source, the student can begin to critically evaluate these ideas. Lots of different skills and strategies are required to engage in productive close reading–viewing–listening, including tapping prior knowledge, making inferences, and asking questions. These skills are essential for our students to cultivate in a world where they are constantly bombarded with information they need to understand in order to be active participants in society.

There are loads of professional books and resources on teaching close reading and the necessary skills and strategies students need to accomplish this task. There is also a plethora of books on teaching with informational sources in the various content areas. These books cover a great deal of information that gives educators a quick peek at what instruction "looks like" when teaching a variety of lessons. These books may be appropriate, given your particular purpose in reading them. Several years ago, however, my response to these texts became a series of questions like:

- What happens after the first lesson?
- What do students reveal in their written responses and oral comments about their ability to learn from informational sources through close reading?
- How do we teach and assess continuously in a way that moves students forward in their thinking and learning?

I am still asking these questions. This book represents what I, along with colleagues in the field, have learned so far.

For some of you, this is the second edition of this book that you have read. When my editor at The Guilford Press asked me to write the second edition, I warned him that I had learned a tremendous amount and would be rewriting the *whole* book. (He did not believe me at first!) The ideas in this edition are mostly the same. I'm still a firm believer in explicit instruction and the gradual release of responsibility. However, I have integrated some new thinking. For example, in addition to addressing instruction with traditional printed texts, I address how to teach for understanding of content in videos and infographics. I have also developed a three-phase plan for learning and a matching template for lesson planning. There are several new chapters too, including one on locating and vetting informational sources and one on teaching students how to figure out the meaning of unfamiliar vocabulary by using context clues. And because I have been in hundreds of schools since I wrote the last edition, I have also included a lot of new anecdotes about students and the learning I have experienced in my work with them.

OVERVIEW OF CHAPTERS

Chapter 1 examines what it means to engage in a close reading or examination of three types of sources: traditional printed texts, infographics, and videos. In this and other chapters, I provide links to sources on the Internet that I discuss in detail. I recommend making time to watch or look at these sources carefully as you read this book.

Chapter 2 describes some of the many strategies students need to be aware of when they engage in making sense of informational sources:

- Being clear about the purposes for reading–viewing–listening
- Tapping prior knowledge related to the topic of the source
- Tapping prior knowledge related to how sources work
- Monitoring for meaning
- Determining what is important
- Synthesizing

An important point in this chapter is that as readers–viewers–listeners, we do not use just one strategy to make sense of a source. For example, only asking questions will not help you identify an author's main ideas. You may have to ask questions, activate related prior knowledge, make connections between key details, and so forth to draw conclusions about an author's main idea. Instead, we use a repertoire of strategies flexibly and at the point of need. In other words, we engage in *strategic processing* as we make sense of the information in a source.

Chapter 3 sets forth an assessment-driven, three-phase plan for learning that looks like the following:

- **Phase 1—Meet the Source**
  - Introduce source and preview
  - Read–view–listen with coaching
  - Discuss
- **Phase 2—Meet the Strategies**
  - Introduce strategies and model
  - Guided and independent practice
  - Discuss
- **Phase 3—Meet the Response**
  - Introduce prompt and plan
  - Write with coaching
  - Share

In this chapter, I discuss the components of each phase of the plan, and then I delve into the instructional practices that are essential to implementing this plan successfully.

- Continuously assessing
- Carefully selecting and introducing sources
- Explaining and modeling strategic processing
- Engaging students in guided practice
- Incorporating opportunities to write in response to sources
- Providing opportunities for independent practice

We know that text or source-related factors, like the topic, the quality of the author's writing, and the layout and design of the source, play a significant role in what the student will take away from a source. **Chapter 4** offers guidance for selecting and vetting sources from the wide array that are currently available in schools and on the Internet. Examples of websites and materials from specific publishers are critiqued. Suggestions for how to introduce sources and how to teach students to make informed predictions before engaging with sources are provided in **Chapter 5**.

Chapters 6–11 each focus on a particular goal or purpose for closely reading–viewing–listening to an informational source or part of a source.

- Engaging in synthesis to identify main ideas
- Becoming aware of what we do to monitor for understanding

- Identifying and explaining key details (including identifying a source's structure)
- Learning from visual images (including graphics)
- Figuring out the meaning of unfamiliar vocabulary by using context clues
- Synthesizing information from multiple sources

Each chapter describes simple ways we can help students begin to think about what it takes to meet these goals and the strategies they may need to use along the way. The chapters are structured in a similar format, and most include the following components:

- Suggestions for informally assessing students
- Explanations of how to introduce the goal to students and the strategies they will need to employ to meet that goal
- Description of a sample three-phase lesson
- Guidelines for planning lessons
- Suggestions for what to notice and how to respond during conferences with individual students
- Stages of development you might observe in students' oral and written responses
- Analyses of students' written responses
- Recommendations for follow-up instruction

Appendix A serves as a quick and easy review of the content that is discussed in more detail in Chapters 6–11. Each page in this appendix describes one purpose for close reading (e.g., identifying a main idea or identifying a source's structure); lists student-friendly explanations of the *what, why,* and *how* related to strategic processing of the information in sources; and provides short descriptions of what Phase 2—Meet the Strategies lessons might look like over time. Take a look at page 227 now to get a quick preview.

Appendix B presents a study guide for each chapter with suggestions for how to enhance your understanding of the ideas in this book. Ideally, this guide should be used in conjunction with other educators in a "professional learning community" that provides opportunities to look at students' work samples and engage in meaningful conversations that serve to advance our understanding of effective instructional practices.

CLOSING THOUGHTS

Teaching students to closely read, view, or listen to sources is tricky, requiring a lot of perseverance on the part of both teachers and students. My goal is not to provide quick answers, but rather to suggest ideas to contemplate as you reflect on your own instructional practices and techniques in this area of teaching. You know your own students, and you have had experiences in teaching with informational sources that you can draw upon as you read this book; as you probably realize, your background knowledge will significantly affect how you understand and use the ideas in this book. So, consider this reading experience as an ongoing dialogue with me as a colleague as we both undertake this inquiry. You can also visit my website at *www.Sunday-Cummins.com* to keep track of how I'm continuing on this extended journey and to contribute to the knowledge base that a whole community of educators is helping to create there.

CHAPTER ONE

Strategic Close Reading of Informational Sources

I remember a lesson with a group of intermediate grade students reading an article that describes the similarities and differences between life on Earth and life on the International Space Station. As the students began to read, they seemed excited about what they might learn. When I leaned in to confer with individuals, though, I noticed they were only comprehending the content at a superficial level. One student told me she had learned that astronauts use "liquid salt and pepper" on their food (May, 2015). When I asked her to tell me more about that, she was not able to tell me why they used *liquid* salt—an important point the author addresses. Another student told me he learned that toilets on the space station are different. When I asked him to tell me more, he was not able to explain how they are different—another important point the author includes. These conversations revealed to me that while the students were making some sense of simple details in the source, they were not grappling with the more difficult information. This gap in understanding would hinder their ability to think about the bigger ideas in the article.

What do we do when we notice this lack of critical thinking? Teaching for strategic close reading may be helpful. Strategic close reading involves reading a source or part of a source multiple times to develop a deeper understanding of the content. The goal of the first read is to gain a basic understanding of the source. Then strategic close reading occurs when a reader carefully analyzes the entire source or a part of it as she reads the source again (Brummett, 2010). The reader looks closely at the pieces (e.g., words, phrases, an image), thinking about the value of these pieces and how they relate or connect to one another. As the reader engages in this process, she may employ the use of multiple strategies, or deliberate actions, that help her make sense of the source. Examples of these strategies include asking specific types of questions or tapping background

7

knowledge about how sources are structured. As a result, the reader can begin to think critically about different aspects of the source like the author's central ideas, writing craft, or point of view.

Strategic close reading is driven by a clear purpose. The purpose, or goal, is a reason, intention, or motivation for engaging in this experience (Almasi & Fullerton, 2012). The purpose acts as a guide. There are a wide variety of purposes a reader might have. The purpose, stated as a question, might simply be "What is important to learn from this source?" or "What is the author's message?" The purpose might be related to the craft of writing like "How does the author's word choice reveal his or her point of view?" The purpose may be related to the content in the source like "How did the social activists exhibit courage during this period?" or "How are chemical and physical reactions a part of our everyday lives?" In school settings some purposes for close reading may be set by the students and some may be set by the teacher.

In today's world, there are so many informational sources that our students need to learn to engage with mindfully. Strategic close reading can be done with any type of source, including traditional texts that consist primarily of written words as well as videos, audio clips, and infographics. For the purposes of this book, then, the term *strategic close reading* means *strategic close reading–viewing–listening.*

Before we get into how to teach students strategic close reading, let's take a moment to think about what strategic close reading looks like with three types of sources: an excerpt from a traditional text, a short video, and an infographic. In this case, our purpose for analysis will be to identify some of the main ideas in each source. I've provided the text or a link for each. I encourage you to give yourself a moment to engage in reading or watching these sources multiple times. As you do, begin to notice what you do—the strategies you use, as a proficient reader–viewer–listener—to make sense of these sources and to identify main ideas in each.

WHAT DOES STRATEGIC CLOSE READING OF A TRADITIONAL TEXT LOOK LIKE?

 As you read the following excerpt from the children's book *Frogs* (Bishop, 2008), begin to consider this question: What is one of the author's main ideas?

> Some frogs seek out their food. A toad hops around after dark, snapping up moths, beetles, and crickets. It may eat more than 5,000 insects during a single summer. Other frogs ambush their prey. A horned frog hides among leaves on the rain forest floor in South America. It stays absolutely still, day after day. When an animal comes by, the frog watches attentively, waiting until it moves closer. Then it seizes the prey with a loud snap of its huge mouth. The horned frog is not a fussy eater. It gulps down cockroaches, lizards, mice, and even other horned frogs. (p. 17)

After a first read, you might simply say, "This paragraph is about how frogs like the toad and horned frog seek out their food." But let's consider how our understanding of content in this paragraph might deepen if we read this excerpt again, pausing at the end of each sentence or so to consider what the author is trying to say? We might begin to realize that the author has used a variety of details to create a much richer picture.

Let's closely review the paragraph, sentence by sentence. The first sentence introduces the primary topic—how "frogs seek out their food." The second and third sentences describe how the toad finds its food—"hops around"—and even state how many insects it can eat in just one summer—"5,000." The fourth sentence begins with "Other frogs," which signals to the reader that a contrast is about to be made. The fifth sentence introduces the "horned frog" and proceeds into a four-sentence descriptive sequence of the horned frog's ambush of its prey. This is followed by a sentence that describes the horned frog as "not a fussy eater." In the last sentence, the author gives examples of what it eats. This list of examples is different from the foods for the toad listed earlier, so it can be inferred that the toad and frog eat different things. Students engaging in the act of close reading to identify the author's main idea might say:

> The author is describing how both the toad and the horned frog seek out their food. But he doesn't just give information about one and then the other. He describes these creatures' habits in such a way that I noticed the contrast between the two. They are very different in how they seek their food and in what they eat. I think this idea ties back to the theme in the book that frogs are highly diverse creatures.

By considering the weight of meaning of particular phrases or sentences in a section of text and by tapping prior knowledge about frogs and animals, we begin to see how important details fit together to support the author's central idea or message in a particular section of text. This kind of understanding can help our students analyze and then critique the author's ideas at the whole text level as well.

WHAT DOES STRATEGIC CLOSE VIEWING–LISTENING TO A VIDEO LOOK LIKE?

 Next, let's consider a National Science Foundation (NSF) video titled *Food and Fear* (2016) about the pygmy rabbit, a species that lives in the high desert sagebrush steppe of eastern Idaho. If possible, take a few moments to watch this 3-minute video.*

https://bit.ly/2Enm3J8

The first time you watch this video, you will probably notice that in the first minute the narrator clearly states a main idea—scientists are trying to understand this habitat by

---

*Links to this and all other QR codes in this book can be accessed at the companion website (see the box at the end of the table of contents).

taking the perspective of an animal that has lived there for a long time. This statement provides a clue about what information will be important to pay attention to in the video. As you continue watching, you make sense of who the people are, where they are, and what they are trying to do. You finish the video with a basic understanding of the content in this video. Your summary might sound something like the following:

> This video is about scientists who are studying the pygmy rabbit, which lives in the Lemhi Valley in eastern Idaho. What they learn from their research on the rabbit is helping them understand the ecosystem of this area. For example, they are beginning to understand how the sagebrush landscape provides nutrition for the rabbits as well as safe places to hide from predators.

This video has a lot more to offer, though. Try watching the video a second time. As you do, ask yourself these questions: "What does this video reveal about the work of scientists in the field?" and "How does the creator of this video develop this idea?" As you watch with this purpose in mind, you might notice how the creator of the video includes several examples of how scientists gather data systematically, using multiple methods:

- The scientists go out into the field and observe for rabbits.
- Then they catch rabbits to place tracking collars on them.
- Scientists also use drones to take photographs of the landscape.
- The data are used to create maps that document where the rabbits go and when.

Combined, these details reveal another main idea—that scientists are systematically investigating the life of the pygmy rabbit, using multiple methods. As a result of this systematic investigation, the scientists understand what the rabbit requires of the habitat it lives in. These details are conveyed through the images shown (see Figure 1.1) and the choice of words used in the narration.

FIGURE 1.1. Pygmy rabbit from the NSF video *Food and Fear.*

Close watching of this video a second time with a clear purpose can help us develop a deeper understanding of the ideas presented. Through careful analysis that involves identifying important details and thinking about how they are connected (i.e., synthesis), we begin to identify some of the central ideas in this video. Tapping prior knowledge (if available) about concepts like scientific investigation and the basic elements of a healthy habitat also helps in this endeavor.

WHAT DOES STRATEGIC CLOSE READING OF AN INFOGRAPHIC LOOK LIKE?

 An infographic is a visual image used to represent information or an idea. An infographic may be just one graphic, like a diagram, chart, or map, or it may be a compilation of graphics. Figure 1.2 on the next page is an example of the latter type of infographic created by the National Aeronautics and Space Administration (NASA) and titled "#suitup for safety." Take a moment to look at this infographic. Consider this your first "read."

Now let's do a close read. Our purpose for close reading is to answer the questions "How have space suits changed over time?" and "Why?" Around the edges of this infographic, you probably noticed that there are images of several space suits that NASA has created over time. Look carefully at the first three images of the space suits. What do you notice? You might notice details that show how the suits changed over the years to increase the capacity of what an astronaut could do. The first, the Mercury Suit, was less bulky but could only be worn inside the spacecraft. The second, the Gemini Suit, allowed the astronaut to leave the spacecraft while still connected by a line that provides oxygen. The third, the Apollo Suit, was the bulkiest of the three, but allowed the astronaut to be independent of the spacecraft and included a portable oxygen system. These details are conveyed in the images and captions that accompany them. You may have noticed this information when you first looked at the infographic, but what happened when you slowed down and considered the images and the words in just this part of the infographic? Hopefully, you furthered your initial understanding of the content and can walk away able to explain more easily the changes that occurred in these space suits.

Now take time to notice the wheel with spokes at the center of this infographic. Take a moment to "closely read" the details in this part of the infographic. What's a main idea that emerges for you? The center of the wheel is labeled "key capabilities" and each spoke lists a capability like "life support," "communications," and "long-term durability." Again, we can glean a main idea by considering each of these details—the wheel and spokes as well as the text or words—and how they are connected. If we think about how these details are related while tapping our background knowledge related to what it means to be safe, we may conclude that when NASA designs space suits, there are certain requirements for those suits or essential components that contribute to the safety and success of space exploration.

FIGURE 1.2. Infographic created by NASA and titled "#suitup for safety." This infographic can be found at *www.nasa.gov/content/suitup-for-safety-infographic.*

HOW DO WE SUM UP
STRATEGIC CLOSE READING–VIEWING–LISTENING?

What did you have to do to engage in the mindful analysis of these three sources? Hopefully you noticed a process emerging.

- You got a sense of the source the first time you read or watched it.
- You slowed down and strategically engaged with the source a second time.
- You kept a clear purpose for this experience in mind (e.g., to glean a main idea or answer a question related to a main idea).
- You used various strategies, such as making connections between details and tapping prior knowledge about the world and how sources are structured.
- You monitored for learning—adjusting or adding new information to what you already knew about the world.

These elements of strategic close reading–viewing–listening are critical for our students to experience with our guidance and eventually on their own. What do we need to teach our students in order to help them reach this level of proficiency?

Read Closely, Out of Habit, to Gain a Deeper Understanding

The first experience with a source—reading, viewing, and/or listening—is generally not enough to foster deeper understanding. While actively monitoring for meaning making, students must get in the habit of looking and then looking again; reading a chunk of text and then reading it again; listening to a dozen seconds of an audio clip and then listening again; viewing an infographic, then viewing it again, section by section.

Keep a Clear Purpose in Mind

Our students need to recognize that reading is driven by the reader's purpose or goal. The same applies to viewing or listening to a source. In the descriptions I wrote for close reading–viewing–listening, the purpose of identifying an author's main idea or the question I posed drove the analysis of these sources. With a different purpose, the reader–viewer–listener might arrive at a different answer. For example, if the student read the text about frogs with the question "How does the author compare and contrast the frog and toad?" in mind, he might arrive at a different answer.

Use a Repertoire of Skills and Strategies to Make Meaning

To make progress toward our purpose or goal for reading–viewing–listening, our students have to use skills and strategies at the point of need. Skills are "automatic actions that result in decoding and comprehension with speed, efficiency, and fluency and usually occur without awareness of the components or control involved" (Afflerbach, Pearson, &

Paris, 2008, p. 368). Strategies are "deliberate actions" a reader–viewer–listener takes to achieve a goal or purpose (Almasi & Fullerton, 2012, p. 1). As they think about their purpose for reading, our students may make sense of parts of sources effortlessly because, at some level, they are skilled readers–viewers–listeners. With more complex parts of sources, though, they may need to be more intentional in what they do to construct understanding. They may have to be strategic, employing the use of multiples strategies that will move them closer to achieving their goal for reading–viewing–listening. These strategies include (but are not limited to) the following:

- Maintaining clarity about the purposes or goals for reading–viewing–listening
- Tapping schemas related to content-area topics or issues (e.g., habitats, cells, civil rights)
- Tapping schemas related to how sources work (e.g., structure, purpose of text features, types of context clues, types of details authors use)
- Monitoring for when progress is or is not being made toward the goal for reading–viewing–listening
- Determining what is important by identifying key details
- Thinking about how key details are connected to reveal bigger ideas in the source (synthesis)

Our students may also have to use supporting strategies like the following:

- Jotting codes to mark their thinking
- Referring to anchor charts or bookmarks to help them remember how sources work
- Using analogies to help them conceptualize what they have to do as readers–viewers–listeners
- Underlining key words
- Annotating their thinking in the margins
- Taking notes that will trigger recall of important information

Our students need to be aware of these strategies and how proficient readers use strategies flexibly in a coordinated way that leads to understanding.

Construct Knowledge about the World

While our students are learning how to make sense of complex sources, they are also learning about the world around them. As we teach for strategic close reading, we need to remind students that this is *why* we are engaging in this process. We need to constantly ask the students, "What did you just learn about the world because you slowed down to closely read this source?" This can be a transformative experience for students as they realize that engaging actively in mindful reading of a source results in the construction of new knowledge. For some students, strategic close reading may simply help them state the facts they learned about a topic. For other students, strategic close reading may help them talk knowledgeably about their synthesis of details in a source (or multiple sources they have read or viewed closely) in order to formulate hypotheses about a particular concept based on what they learned through close reading.

CLOSING THOUGHTS

Our ultimate goal is for students to become self-regulated learners who, as the need arises, engage in strategic close reading, viewing, and listening to sources and, as a result, construct meaning. Students who engage in this deliberate and mindful analysis of sources are more likely to recall details from the source and to make connections between details to arrive at bigger ideas (e.g., the author's purpose, point of view, main idea) (Paris & Winograd, 1990). Knowing that they are capable of doing this can increase motivation and a sense of personal agency as they tackle making meaning from complex sources on their own (Johnston, 2004).

Remember the students I described at the beginning of this chapter who read the article about life on the International Space Station? Over the course of several lessons, I had the honor of teaching them how to strategically read parts of this source a second and third time and respond orally and in writing. I taught them how texts like this work and how authors frequently use particular types of details to share information. Through strategic close reading, they began to recognize details that explained how and why and ask questions that helped them determine what was important. As a result, they were able to talk more fluently about what they had learned and why what they had learned was important to understanding the world. As a result, I noticed a difference when they came to me for later lessons. Their body language and comments like "Let's do this!" revealed a sense of "I know how to tackle complex sources!"

CHAPTER TWO

A Repertoire of Strategies Needed for Close Reading

As we engage in reading, viewing, or listening to a source, we are *constantly thinking*. We make connections to what we already know about the source's topic. We make inferences about what the author is trying to say. We notice when information is unfamiliar or new to us.

Our thinking is *strategic*. We have a clear purpose or goal for engaging with that source—some type of understanding we are seeking. As we work our way through the information in a source, we monitor for whether we are understanding the source's information or not and whether we are making progress toward our goal. If some aspect of the source is getting in the way of our comprehension, then we problem-solve in order to get back on track.

Depending on the information that presents itself, our prior experiences with informational sources, and our knowledge of the topic, we determine when we need to use particular *strategies*. We may ask a question. We may notice the similarity in several details throughout parts of the source. We may identify a particular piece of information as important to remember. Sometimes we make these decisions automatically, with hardly a thought. Sometimes we make these decisions consciously, with intention.

Strategic thinking requires us to *use strategies flexibly* in a coordinated way that facilitates meaning making. For example, if we notice an unfamiliar word, we may look for a context clue to figure out its meaning. Similarly, with video or audio clips, we may notice a term we do not know and, as a result, begin to pay attention to whether the clip includes visual or verbal cues as to the meaning of that term. In both cases we are using at least three strategies—asking a question (i.e., "What does this word mean?"), searching for clues, and making sense of the clue.

Many of our students are early in their journey toward becoming proficient readers–viewers–listeners and are not in full control of what it means to process information strategically. Some students do not realize they need to be thinking while they read, view, or listen to a source. Some students simply decode the words or are word callers. Some students are proficient in making sense of information in one genre (e.g., narrative, cause–effect, problem–solution) or format (e.g., written text, video, audio clips) but not in another. In any of these cases, the students may not know what they need to do to make sense of informational sources for particular purposes.

Our students may need us to unpack this process—teasing out and explaining specific strategies and then demonstrating for them how to use these strategies during a careful analysis of a source in conjunction with other strategies. This type of instruction can serve them in many ways. They can develop an awareness of the thinking and strategic processing that need to happen while reading–viewing–listening. They can begin to develop a repertoire of strategies to tap as needed. As educators, we need to have clarity for ourselves about what these strategies are and how they work together in service of comprehension (Paris & Winograd, 2001). Strategies that we might highlight for students include, but are not limited to, the following:

- Being clear about the purposes for reading–viewing–listening
- Tapping prior knowledge related to the topic of the source
- Tapping prior knowledge related to how sources work
- Monitoring for meaning
- Determining what is important
- Synthesizing

The rest of this chapter describes these strategies and the role they play in making meaning of a variety of types of sources.

BEING CLEAR ABOUT THE PURPOSE

> ▶ A purpose is the reason why we read–view–listen to a particular source.
>
> ▶ A purpose acts as a guide for helping us determine what is important.
>
> ▶ Purposes can shift or change as we read–view–listen.

Various purposes for reading informational sources have long been listed in professional books and are even readily available on made-for-classroom wall posters. Examples of these purposes include to be informed, to be entertained, and to learn how to do something. While there is some value in sharing these particular purposes with students, we have to be careful that they don't then begin to use these purposes mindlessly. During one lesson, for example, I asked a fifth-grade student about his purpose for reading an assigned article on the dramatic impact of a volcano's explosion on the surrounding community. Instantly, he replied, "I am reading for information on volcanoes." I was surprised at this response, given the gravity of the content in the article and the fact that the article was not simply about volcanoes. There appeared to be no ownership or enthusiasm behind the student's answer; rather, he seemed to simply regurgitate what he had been taught. The challenge is to broaden students' understanding of how we can utilize "purpose" to make meaning as we read–view–listen.

Anytime we read, view, or listen to a source, we have a purpose. A purpose is a reason for doing something, an intention, a motivation (Almasi & Fullerton, 2012). We may read a news app to learn more about current political events or what is happening locally over the weekend. We may watch a video on YouTube to figure out how to fix a plumbing issue. We may look carefully at a table or chart to figure out how many calories are in a portion of our favorite snack. Our purposes vary depending on the type of source we are interacting with and our interests or needs. A purpose acts as a guide in helping us determine what is important in a source. If you are reading to find out about local events in your community, then you are going to notice details that give you information about these events. You will not pay as much attention to the details that do not.

A purpose for reading is not static. Purposes can shift or change. For example, problem solving may emerge as an in-the-moment purpose. Let's say the student reading about volcanoes initially has the purpose of learning about the impact of this volcano explosion. As he reads, he notices a word in the text for which he does not know the meaning. When he notices this, his purpose for reading changes. He shifts to the purpose of problem solving. He looks for and finds a context clue to help him figure out the meaning of the word. Once he does this and feels as though he has some understanding of the word, he returns to his initial purpose for reading. In this scenario, in a matter of seconds, he shifts from one purpose to another and then back again. Each of these purposes drove what he did to make sense of the information in the text.

Purposes may also change as we develop a better understanding of the source's topic. I remember working with a group of fifth-grade students who were reading an article titled "Thirsty Planet" (Geiger, 2010b). I asked the students to preview the article to make predictions about what they would be learning and to set a purpose for reading based on those predictions. At the beginning of the article, there is a close-up photograph of villagers from Marsabit, Kenya, filling up jugs with water from a well. One student thought the water in the well looked dirty. She wrote as her prediction, "Pollution is overruling the planet so bad [that] people can't even drink clean water" and set a purpose of reading to find out about water pollution. Actually, there is no mention of pollution at all in this article. The article focuses instead on how water is a finite resource, and we have to be careful about how we use it. The student had assumed (without any textual evidence to support the assumption) that the water in the well was dirty. As she read though, she realized that this was not the topic of the article. Although this student would benefit from instruction on how to make informed predictions, at the moment, what she needed to know how to do was adjust her predictions and change her purpose for reading.

In school, purposes may be student determined or teacher determined. Even though it is important for students to learn how to identify and set their own purposes for reading, we must remember that many have not had an abundance of meaningful experiences with complex informational sources—the type of experiences that lead them to a deeper understanding. By setting the purpose, the teacher can broaden students' understanding of types of purposes as well as how these purposes can be used to drive meaning making. Consider the fifth-grade student reading about the impact of the volcano explosion. Left on his own to set a purpose, he may only comprehend the content in the article at a superficial level. But what if his teacher set the purpose of noticing how the author uses a cause–effect structure to develop ideas in the article? The student might develop a much deeper understanding of the content in the article, while also learning how a source can be structured to convey meaning. He can tap this knowledge later as he sets purposes for thinking through other informational sources.

Another teacher-determined purpose may be related to learning content or developing depth of knowledge related to a specific content-area unit of study. For example, if this student's class was engaged in a unit of study on the Earth's systems, teacher-determined purposes for reading this article might be "What causes a volcano to erupt?" and "How do volcano eruptions impact surrounding communities?"

Because purposes are central to any reading–viewing–listening we do, the concept of "purpose" needs to be considered carefully whenever we think about how to teach for close analysis of informational sources. In Chapter 5, I share advice on how to help students make informed predictions that they can turn into purposes for reading. In Chapters 6–12, reading texts and infographics and viewing videos for specific purposes such as "to identify a main idea" are addressed in the lessons; these lessons can easily be adapted to include content area–driven purposes for interacting with sources as well.

TAPPING PRIOR KNOWLEDGE
RELATED TO THE TOPIC OF THE SOURCE

> ▶ Tapping prior knowledge on a topic helps us make connections between old information and new information.
>
> ▶ Prior knowledge about a topic has to be actively accessed and monitored in order for it to be helpful.
>
> ▶ Prior knowledge about a topic can be unhelpful, leading to confusion or misunderstanding.

As we read–view–listen to a source, we search, with hardly a thought, for any related prior knowledge on the topic of the source that we already have (Pearson & Cervetti, 2017). If we realize we have prior knowledge that can be used to help us, we activate that knowledge. For our students this knowledge may have been developed during their life outside of school (more commonly referred to as "background knowledge") or knowledge that they have developed in a school or learning environment. Once we have activated this knowledge, we make linkages between the new information in the source and what we already know or have experienced. If we can link new information to what we already know, we are more likely to understand (and be able to recall) the content in the source.

To illustrate this point, take a moment to look at the infographic "What Is a Sounding Rocket?" (NASA, n.d.) in Figure 2.1. As you absorb the information in this infographic, notice how you use what you already know to help you think about the information presented.

For me, when I first read the title, "What Is a Sounding Rocket?," I immediately thought about toy rockets I've seen set off in the past. A visualization of a toy rocket shooting up in the air popped into my mind with hardly a thought. Then I noticed the illustrations and photographs in the infographic and noted that I had seen these pictures or similar ones before. I also know a little bit about NASA and the work the agency does, so I started thinking that these rockets must be used to explore space in some way. At almost the same time this thinking occurred, I was also trying to process what *sounding* means in the term *sounding rocket*. I knew the word *sound* means vibrations that travel through the air and that we can hear. So, I thought maybe *sounding* has something to do with the same concept, but I was not sure. As I continued reading, I knew I would search for clues to gain some clarity on the meaning of this word.

What did I just do to make sense of only the title and a few images in this infographic? I used multiple types of prior knowledge—knowledge from what I have experienced in life, knowledge from what I have read previously, and knowledge about vocabulary. And I did all of this in just a few seconds with hardly a thought. We do this type of thinking constantly as we engage or interact with sources—including as we watch videos and listen to audio clips.

Tapping prior knowledge is important, but we also have to monitor for whether that knowledge is helpful (Almasi & Fullerton, 2012). What does this monitoring look like? Let's return to my lack of clarity about the meaning of the word *sounding* in the term *sounding rockets*. Notice how *sounding* is defined in this sentence (in the outlined box in the first section of the infographic).

> Known as sounding rockets for the nautical term "to sound," meaning to measure, these rockets reach a region between 30 and 800 miles above the Earth's surface.

In this sentence we learn that the word *sounding* in the term *sounding rockets* is related to the concept of *measurement*. Remember when I read *sounding* in the title and thought about the concept of *sound* or vibrations traveling through the air that we hear? When I read "meaning to measure" in this sentence a little later, I realized that this new information contradicted what I initially thought. I quickly adjusted my thinking. I no longer wondered how the concept of "sound" fits the content of this source. Instead, I began tapping what I know about measurement to help me make sense of the details of this source. What did I do here? I noticed that the prior knowledge I tapped initially was not helpful or appropriate. When I determined it was not, I began tapping prior knowledge related to the new information I had just learned.

What do we do if our students do not have prior knowledge on the topic of the source? Sometimes we can help students quickly develop prior knowledge during our source introductions, and suggestions for how to do so are discussed in Chapter 5, "Introducing Sources and Teaching Students to Make *Informed* Predictions." What if our students are

FIGURE 2.1. Infographic created by Jet Propulsion Laboratory, a partnership between NASA and the California Institute of Technology. Available at *www.jpl.nasa.gov/infographics/infographic.view.php?id=11445.*

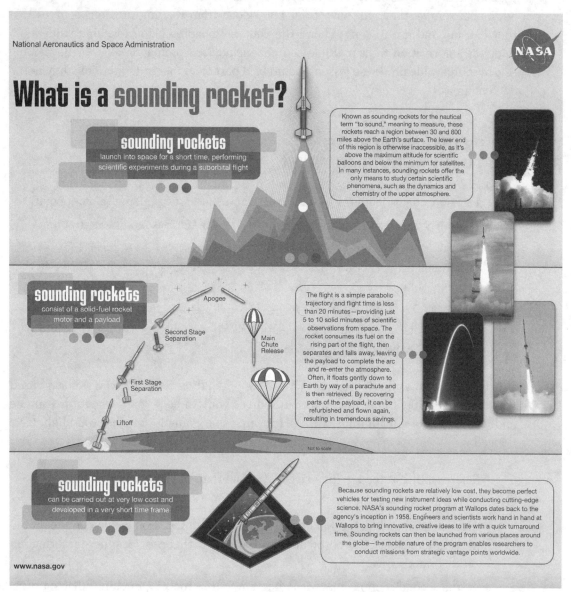

not activating prior knowledge? Chapter 5 also includes recommendations for teaching students how to make informed predictions as they read, view, or listen to sources. What if a student's lack of vocabulary is getting in the way? In Chapter 5, I explain simple steps for introducing vocabulary; in Chapter 10, I explore teaching the different types of context clues that can help students figure out the meaning of unfamiliar words.

Another response to these questions would be to use *sets of sources* on the same topic. In other words, over the course of several lessons, students have the opportunity to read–view–listen to several sources on the same topic. Then as they engage with each additional source, they will have prior knowledge from reading previous sources that they can tap and use to comprehend the content. Chapter 11 on teaching students to integrate information from multiple sources includes recommendations for developing sets of sources. Ideally, these lessons would be a part of an integrated unit of study in the content areas.

TAPPING PRIOR KNOWLEDGE RELATED TO HOW SOURCES WORK

> ▶ Prior knowledge about how sources work can include recognizing the following:
> ▷ The purpose of features like titles, illustrations, diagrams, and photographs
> ▷ How authors design or lay out information
> ▷ Traditional text structures (i.e., descriptive, sequence, comparison, cause–effect, problem–solution)
> ▷ Text structures used at the macro and micro levels
> ▶ Prior knowledge about how sources work has to be actively accessed and monitored in order for it to be helpful.

When you looked at the infographic "What Is a Sounding Rocket?," you probably used what you know about how informational sources work to help you navigate this source and make sense of it (Cummins, 2015). Here are some examples of what you might have noticed.

- There's a title at the top (in a larger-size font than the rest of the content).
- There are three main sections.
- Each section includes a shaded box with a brief description of some aspect of the sounding rocket, followed by another box of text that provides more information on that same aspect.
- In the second section, there is a diagram (of the rocket launching) that supports the meaning conveyed in the box of text to the right.
- There are additional illustrations and photographs that help you visualize sounding rockets.

We notice these aspects of the infographic because we are aware of the features that authors include to organize and convey meaning in informational sources. We also have prior knowledge about how infographics are designed.

Did you notice that this infographic also has a descriptive or enumerative text structure? Typically, sources with a descriptive structure are divided into sections that each describe a different aspect of the topic. In this case, the subtopics are primarily the following: what region above Earth a sounding rocket can reach, what happens when a rocket launches, and why and how these rockets are useful.

While the macrostructure or structure of the whole infographic appears to be descriptive, the author employs text structures at the micro level (e.g., at the sentence, paragraph, or graphic levels) as well. Notice the diagram of the sounding rocket launching that illustrates the events that occur. What's the structure of this diagram? You could say it fits into the category of sequence structures. Sources with a sequence structure describe a series of steps in a process or episodes related to an event. The text in the box just to the right of the diagram includes more information structured in a sequence.

> The rocket consumes its fuel on the rising part of the flight, then separates and falls away, leaving the payload to complete the arc and re-enter the atmosphere. Often, it floats gently down to Earth by way of a parachute and is then retrieved.

Take a moment to read the text in the outlined box in the third section that begins with this sentence:

> Because sounding rockets are relatively low cost, they become perfect vehicles for testing new instrument ideas while conducting cutting-edge science.

Notice how this short part of the text has a cause–effect microstructure. Authors use the cause–effect structure to explain why something occurs. In this case, the author relates that because the sounding rockets are affordable and can easily be moved (cause), scientists have been able to complete this work for many decades and from many places around the world (effect). It is important to note then that although the author of this infographic has created a source with a descriptive structure at the macro level, he or she has also employed the use of other structures at the micro level. Teaching students how to identify traditional text structures will have limited value unless we also help them to understand how the structures are used flexibly by authors to convey certain points.

There are many aspects of how sources work that our students need to understand in order to make sense of informational sources. If you have students who lack knowledge about how sources work or are not effectively tapping and using this knowledge, consider the recommendations for instruction on teaching students to recognize text structures in Chapter 8 and on teaching students how to learn from a source's features in Chapter 9.

> ▶ When we monitor for meaning, we notice when we do and do not understand the information in a source.
>
> ▶ When information is unclear or confusing, we employ the use of fix-up strategies to help us make better sense of the content in a source.

Self-monitoring is about knowing when we understand the content we are reading, viewing, or hearing and knowing what to do when our meaning breaks down (Baker, DeWyngaert, & Zeliger-Kandasamy, 2015). This monitoring happens at the word, sentence or image, and section or whole-source levels. Take a moment to look again at the infographic "What Is a Sounding Rocket?" As you do, ask yourself the following questions:

- What is information in this source that you already knew?
- What are you learning that is less familiar?
- What are questions you have?
- If there is a part you did not understand, what did you do to make better sense of that part?

What do you notice about your thinking?

Remember the earlier discussion about how I made sense of the title and information at the beginning of the NASA infographic in Figure 1.2? In that discussion, I shared information in the infographic that felt familiar—NASA's space experiments and the concept of a rocket. I described what was less familiar—the concept of a "sounding rocket." I also described a quandary I had about the author's use of the word *sounding* and how I resolved questions around that word when I read the definition "meaning to measure." What was I doing as I thought about what was familiar and unfamiliar and what I did not understand? I was monitoring for meaning. In other words, I noticed when there was meaning making occurring and when meaning was breaking down. When meaning began to break down, I kept a question in mind (i.e., "What does the word *sounding* mean?"). A little later I used a fix-up strategy (i.e., used a context clue) to figure out the meaning of the word.

Another example of being unclear when reading this infographic occurred when I saw the word *apogee* in the diagram of the rocket launching. Here's how I thought through this.

Apogee. What does this mean? Let me look at the diagram carefully and think about this. I notice that the author has labeled different parts of the launch "liftoff" and "first stage separation" and "second stage separation." I'm thinking that *apogee* must be a word that has something to do with what part of the launch the rocket is in. Visually, it looks like the rocket or part of the rocket called the payload is at the highest point of the launch. Maybe that's what *apogee* means.

What did I do here? Again, I noticed when meaning was breaking down, and then I used clues in the diagram to help me figure out the meaning of the word.

As proficient readers–viewers–listeners, we are constantly monitoring for whether we understand information in a source or not. If we do not understand, then we try to help ourselves in some way. Many students do not monitor in this way. Some are word callers who simply read words without thinking much about the meaning. Some notice when they do not understand, but they are not sure what to do next. We need to explicitly teach students to ask questions like "What information is familiar and unfamiliar?", "What do I understand or not understand?", and "What can I do to make better sense of this information?" Chapter 7 explains how to help students become aware of their thinking and actively begin to repair meaning when it breaks down.

DETERMINING WHAT IS IMPORTANT (THAT IS, IDENTIFYING KEY DETAILS)

▶ Your purpose for reading–viewing–listening acts as a guide in determining what is important.

▶ Recognition of the types of details an author uses, like *why, how, when, example, function, cause,* and *effect*, can help us understand the type of detail better and, as a result, determine if it is important.

When we read, view, or listen to informational sources, our purpose acts as a guide for determining what is important. For example, when I asked you earlier to reread the infographic "What Is a Sounding Rocket?," your purpose was to monitor for understanding by thinking about which pieces of information were new, which were unfamiliar, and which led you to ask questions. This purpose acted as a guide for what you would pay attention to while reading. If your purpose had been different, you might have identified different information as being important. For example, what if your purpose had been to learn what happens when a rocket is launched? You would probably have spent more energy looking at the second section of this infographic, examining the diagram and rereading the text in the outlined box to determine what was important.

Let's think about determining importance with another source. The excerpt of text on the next page is from a short book that discusses the early founding years of the United States (Finkelman, 2006). In the first chapter, the author is trying to convey the idea that the national government as described in the Articles of Confederation (ratified by the Second Continental Congress in 1777) was too weak. The text is on a two-page spread, along with a painting depicting George Washington and an illustration showing various examples of paper money, accompanied by short captions repeating information provided in the text (i.e., not supplying any additional information).

As you read this excerpt, consider this question or purpose for reading, "What is the author's central or main idea?"

Title of Chapter 1: "First Government"

Deck (the text immediately below the title): By 1783, the American Revolution was over. The United States had won. However, our new national government was dangerously weak.

Section Heading: "Too Little Power"

Text: This national government had been set up during the Revolution. It was based on a plan called the *Articles of Confederation*. The Confederation was a loose union of 13 states. In this plan the national government was weak. The state governments held most of the power. The states wanted it that way. They had just fought a war with Great Britain to escape from a strong central government.

The Confederation government had so little power it could not do many of the basic things a government needs to do. The Confederation government was run by a Congress. However, there was no president to carry out the laws passed by this Congress. There were no courts to settle disagreements between citizens or between states. Congress could not collect taxes and had no money to pay its debts.

An example of this weakness occurred near the end of the Revolution. A group of army officers was angry because Congress had not paid them or their soldiers. They were ready to march on the government and take it over. George Washington, commander of the American army, stopped them with a speech in which he appealed to their love of country.

The 13 states ignored many of the laws the Confederation government passed. There were also conflicts between states. Some states charged taxes on things for sale from other states, just as if they were imported from foreign countries. Each state had its own form of money. Almost no one wanted to take the "continental dollars" printed by the national government. So, farmers did not know what they could get for their crops. People with goods to sell did not know what kind of money to accept. Trade between people in different states was complicated and difficult.

After reading this passage a first time, you probably gathered that the new national government was weak or vulnerable. (The main idea is basically stated in the deck or information under the title.) Now take a moment to closely read this excerpt again and think about key details that support this idea. You probably noticed several during your first read. This second read will confirm the key details.

When I read this excerpt for a second time with this purpose in mind, I noticed several details that are important. Figure 2.2 shows the same text excerpt, but with the words I chose to highlight or underline as key details and my annotations about why I chose to underline particular details. My notes reveal how I justify that these are key details that support the main idea. For example, I underlined the phrase "could not do many of the basic things a government needs to do" because this detail told me "why" the new government was weak. Then I underlined "no president to carry out the laws passed" because that was an example of a "basic thing" the national government could not do. Both of these details support the idea that the Confederation was weak at this point in its history.

You might choose to underline different details than I did. What's important is that you can justify why you chose certain details over others. Returning to the purpose—to

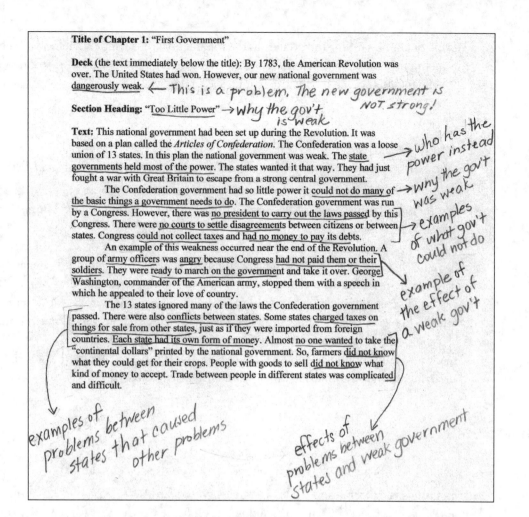

FIGURE 2.2. Excerpt from *The Constitution* (Finkelman, 2006), with key details underlined and annotations. From National Geographic Learning. *Reading Expeditions (Social Studies: Documents of Freedom): The Constitution, 1E.* © 2004 South-Western, a part of Cengage, Inc. Reproduced by permission.

identify key details that support the idea that the new government was weak—can help us (and our students) think about why a detail is important or not.

The language in my annotations reveals why I underlined certain details and what I noticed about those details that made me think they were important. Notice that I wrote words like *problem, why, who, examples, cause,* and *effect.* These are types of details authors of informational sources use to convey meaning (Anderson & Armbruster, 1984). To illustrate further what I mean here, consider this excerpt from the book *Simple Machines: Wheels, Levers, and Pulleys* (Adler, 2015).

A slide is an inclined plan, sometimes called a ramp. It's a flat surface with one end higher than the other. An inclined plane makes it easier to climb up and down. It makes it easier to carry things up or down.

In this book, the author introduces and explains different simple machines, including the inclined plane. What are the types of details the author uses to introduce the reader to the inclined plane in this excerpt?

- *Slide* is an *example* of an inclined plane.
- *Ramp* is a *synonym* for inclined plane.
- *Flat surface with one end higher than the other* describes the *physical features* and *structure*.
- *An inclined plane makes it easier to climb up and down* and *makes it easier to carry things up and down* are both *functions* or *purposes*.

My point here is that identifying key details involves understanding what type of information is revealed in a detail. This is key to helping a reader determine what is important. Recognizing types of details also helps us explain why these details are important and how they are connected. Then we can draw conclusions about the main ideas in a source or an author's point of view or position more easily as well.

Chapter 8 examines how to support students in identifying and explaining key details and then using them to summarize and evaluate their learning.

SYNTHESIS

▸ Synthesis occurs when we think about how key details are connected.

▸ We synthesize information to draw conclusions regarding main ideas, an author's point of view, a source's structure, and more.

Synthesis can be difficult to explain to students. When we read, view, or listen to an informational source and synthesize its content, we sift through an extraordinary number of details. If we are reading to identify an author's main idea, we determine what details seem important and how they are connected. The connection between these details might reveal one of the author's main ideas. For example, think about the connection between some of the key details I identified in the excerpt from *The Constitution* (Finkelman, 2006).

- Could not do many basic things.
- No president to carry out laws.
- No courts to settle disagreements.
- Could not collect taxes.
- No money to pay debts.

All of these details are problems that would make a government not as strong and effective as it should be. Recognizing these details as problems, then connecting them to each other, and tapping our prior knowledge about the purpose of governments and how they function lead us closer to inferring the author's main idea. In other words, if we consider this group of key details and the connections among them—using information from the source and our prior knowledge—a main idea emerges: that the new national government, the Confederation, was indeed weak, even vulnerable. This is synthesis.

Synthesis is a complicated process. It's even more difficult to unpack because as proficient readers, we intuit what a main idea might be as we read further and further into a source. It's as though we are determining what is important along the way. To do this we make connections to prior knowledge. We make inferences. We make predictions (e.g., the author is going to share more problems that the Confederation faced and then maybe a solution). We monitor for understanding. When we finish reading, we have a sense of what the author's main idea is. We do not do much of this work consciously. We do not think, "To understand the main idea, first I must do this . . . then I must do this."

We also synthesize for a variety of purposes, not just when we are looking for main ideas. For example, we synthesize information when we are trying to determine an author's point of view. Let's think about the author's point of view in the excerpt from *The Constitution* (Finkelman, 2006). Close to the beginning of the passage, the author states that the new national government was "dangerously weak." As a reader, we know the meaning of these words, and we also recognize that combined, they have a negative connotation.

We know how sources work too. We know that an author's word choice can reveal his point of view. Notice the thread of negative language in the same key details listed earlier.

- **Could not** do many basic things.
- **No** president to carry out laws.
- **No** courts to settle disagreements.
- **Could not** collect taxes.
- **No** money to pay debts.

If we consider how the author states these facts, his point of view seems to be that the government was at a disadvantage because of all of the things it could not do or that it lacked. Although this point may be commonly accepted by historians, it is still a point of view. Again, as a reader, early in this passage we had a clue as to what the author's point of view is (i.e., the phrase *dangerously weak*) and then as we read, we began to notice other similar details. When we think about the connections between these details—how they are all stated as negative factors—we have synthesized information to draw a conclusion about the author's point of view.

What we learn through synthesis may simply affirm or add to what we already know about the topic, or it may transform our thinking. For example, before reading this passage, some students may have thought, "The colonists won the American Revolution! Hooray! The world was a better place!" After reading this passage, they may have had to adjust their thinking. They might think instead, "Well, winning the American Revolution was good for the colonists, but then there were new problems, and these problems made the country's future uncertain."

How do we make this process clear to students? This is not a "strategy" we save for the end of the year or after we teach other strategies. Students should be introduced to the concept of synthesis from the very beginning of any kind of reading instruction because it reveals the power of reading–viewing–listening, which is a better understanding of the content in the source, an understanding that may transform how we see the world or what we know about the world. In Chapter 6, I discuss introducing the concept of synthesis to students. The role of synthesis in meaning making is revisited in Chapters 7–11.

CLOSING THOUGHTS

You have probably noticed that I have not discussed every possible strategy we use to help us make sense of informational sources. That doesn't mean that other strategies aren't important. Making, checking, and adjusting predictions are critical. Asking relevant questions like "Do I understand this?" is crucial. Visualizing can be helpful. And so on. What's important to consider here is that we used each of these strategies (i.e., predicting, asking questions, visualizing) as well as others when we engage in practicing the featured strategies. For example, I visualized when I was tapping prior knowledge of the topic of "sounding rockets." I asked questions when I was monitoring for understanding, trying to determine the meaning of the word *sounding*. With the passage from *The Constitution* (Finkelman, 2006), I made inferences when I was determining what was important as part of my synthesis.

This returns us to a point I made at the beginning of the chapter: We never use just one strategy to make sense of a source. Instead, we use a repertoire of strategies in a flexible and coordinated way to facilitate comprehension. In other words, we are *strategic*. This is what we have to teach our students—how to be strategic processors of informational sources. This kind of knowledge has the power to nurture in our students a sense of agency and identity as proficient readers–viewers–listeners (Johnston, 2004). Chapter 3 describes what instruction in pursuit of this goal looks like.

CHAPTER THREE

An Assessment-Driven, Three-Phase Plan for Learning

If we want to nurture a sense of "I can do this!" in our students as they tackle complex informational sources, then we have to create a learning environment that is designed to support them. Creating this environment begins with an assessment of how students already go about processing information. What are our students' strengths? And needs? Are they able to process information in a way that leads to deeper understanding? Or do their responses reveal superficial thinking or a lack of thinking while reading–viewing–listening? Are there specific purposes or goals for reading–viewing–listening like "identify a main idea" or "learn from visual images" that your students might need to learn how to achieve? What are the strategies you might need to explore with them in the service of reaching these goals? Through formal and informal assessment, objectives for teaching or "what" we need to teach will emerge (Afflerbach, 2012).

Once we have determined objectives for teaching, we can design lessons in response. We know that many students benefit from an explicit teaching of strategies (Allington & McGill-Franzen, 2017; Baker et al., 2015). This instruction includes the teacher explaining a strategy or multiple strategies and then modeling how to use those strategies *strategically*, in pursuit of a particular goal like "identifying a main idea" or "comparing the moth and the butterfly" (Almasi & Fullerton, 2012). Over the course of one or several lessons, the observant teacher gradually releases responsibility to the students (Pearson & Gallagher, 1983). This involves helping students *take control* of being strategic through guided and independent practice. The individual student determines when and where he will use the strategies that have been modeled, as well as any other strategies he has in his repertoire. He does this while keeping in mind the ultimate goal: developing knowledge.

There are numerous factors that influence the success of the instruction I just described, including the fact that this type of instruction has to happen on a regular basis over time to be effective (Cummins & Stallmeyer-Gerard, 2011; Pressley, 2000). The three-phase plan for learning in Figure 3.1 is a model for how we might think about regular instruction with informational sources. Each phase in the plan occurs during one or more 20- to 40-minute lessons. In Phase 1, students are introduced to the source and read, view, or listen to it for the first time. In Phase 2, students have an opportunity to engage in revisiting the source or a part of the source for a closer analysis. Phase 3 provides an opportunity for students to formulate a written response to the source. All three phases incorporate the use of assessment to drive instructional decisions—prior to teaching and in the moment of teaching. This model can be used as part of larger units of study in the content areas or during language arts instruction. It can be used with small or large groups. What follows is a brief introduction to each phase.

The objective of Phase 1 is for students to get the gist of the source as a whole before they engage in close reading, viewing, or listening to expand their understanding of the source. The teacher provides a purposeful introduction to the source and then confers with students as they read, view, or listen to it. As she confers with individuals, she observes what the student is doing to make sense of the source. She affirms the student in some way and also coaches at the point of need. This may include helping students self-monitor, word-solve, or comprehend. The teacher may adjust the focus of strategic processing students will try out in Phase 2 based on what she notices during these conferences. To sum up, during Phase 1, the following activities occur:

- The teacher introduces the source.
- The students preview the source and make predictions.
- The teacher and/or students set a purpose for reading–viewing–listening to the source.
- As the students tackle the source, the teacher leans in to confer with individuals.
- The teacher closes with a discussion related to the content the students learned and the problem solving she noticed the students engaging in as they grappled with the source.

The objective of Phase 2 is for students to gain a deeper understanding of the ideas in the source or part of the source by closely reading, viewing, or listening for a specific purpose. Students practice particular strategies for which the teacher has determined

Phase 1— *Meet the Source*	Phase 2— *Meet the Strategies*	Phase 3— *Meet the Response*
• Introduce source and preview. • Read–view–listen with coaching. • Discuss.	• Introduce strategies and model. • Provide guided and independent practice. • Discuss.	• Introduce prompt and plan. • Write with coaching. • Share.

FIGURE 3.1. Three-phase plan for learning.

they need support. They also practice using supporting strategies like underlining, annotating, or taking notes. The learning they do during Phase 2 will support their work during Phase 3. A Phase 2 lesson includes the following activities:

- The teacher states the goal or purpose for reading (e.g., identify a main idea, learn from graphics, or figure out the meaning of unfamiliar words).
- The teacher explains and then models how to use one or more strategies to meet the stated goal.
- The students engage in guided and independent practice.
- The students take notes or annotate the source as they practice the strategies.
- The teacher and students close with a discussion about what strategic close reading–viewing–listening looks like and how their understanding of the source expanded as a result.

The objective of Phase 3 is for students to strengthen their understanding of the source's content and their ability to communicate what they have learned through writing. After sharing a prompt for writing, the teacher guides the students in using their notes or annotations from Phase 2 to develop a plan for writing. Based on the students' needs, the teacher might provide scaffolds that support writing, such as asking the students to orally rehearse a sentence before they write or engaging the group in shared writing of a portion of the response before they continue on their own. During Phase 3, the following activities occur:

- The teacher provides a prompt for writing related to the learning done during Phase 2.
- The students plan for writing a response with the notes or annotations written during Phase 2.
- If needed, the teacher engages the students in oral rehearsal and/or shared writing before they begin to write.
- The students write a response and the teacher leans in to coach individuals.

This three-phase plan for learning can be turned into a template for writing lesson plans (see Figure 3.2) or it can be used simply as a guide. Ideally the three phases are tied together. The learning done in Phases 1 and 2 prepares students for the writing that will be done in Phase 3. Chapters 6–11 each focus on teaching strategies students can use to meet a particular goal or purpose. These chapters include examples of lessons and suggestions for how to plan by using this model as a guide.

What's critical to effective use of this plan is *how* we implement it. We know that students learn when they are challenged to do something they have not already mastered and, at the same time, are provided with just the right amount of support from a more knowledgeable person. In other words, students learn best when they are in their zone of proximal development and a supportive learning environment is present (Vygotsky, 1978).

FIGURE 3.2. Lesson planning template for the three-phase plan.

Three-Phase Plan for Learning

Title of Source:

Objectives:

Phase 1— *Meet the Source*	Phase 2— *Meet the Strategies*	Phase 3— *Meet the Response*
1. Introduce source and preview. Choose one or more: ☐ Language objectives ☐ Discuss structure ☐ Content objectives ☐ Predict with THIEVES ☐ Synopsis ☐ Purpose ☐ New vocabulary ☐ Other: Notes:	**1. Introduce strategies and model.** Comprehension strategies: Supporting strategy: ☐ Underlining and annotating ☐ Note taking ☐ Other: Explanation and think-aloud notes:	**1. Introduce prompt and plan.** Writing prompt: Notes about how students will plan: ☐ Key words on sticky notes ☐ Outline ☐ Oral rehearsal ☐ Other:
2. Read–view–listen with coaching. Notes:	**2. Guided and independent practice.** Notes:	**2. Write with coaching.** Notes about shared writing (if needed):
3. Discuss. Prompt: Teaching point (if needed):	**3. Discuss.** Prompt:	**3. Share.** Prompt:

In order to teach in this zone, we have to know our students' strengths and needs. We have to listen to students and watch them closely, responding as needed (Turbill & Bean, 2006). What does this look like when we assess, plan, and teach with this three-phase plan as a guide? What follows is an explanation of instructional practices that are critical to the effective implementation of the three-phase plan for learning.

HOW DO WE IMPLEMENT THIS PLAN EFFECTIVELY?

Our role as the teacher, or more knowledgeable other, is to support students in a way that moves them forward in their learning (Vygotsky, 1978). Ideally, the students can do more with the supports we provide than they can do on their own. This does not mean that students should breeze through reading–viewing–listening and responding. There needs to be a *productive struggle*. The key is providing just enough support so that students can actively engage in problem solving to make sense of the content in a source and communicate what they learned. When teaching for careful analysis of informational sources, the following practices support students in this kind of problem solving:

- Continuously assessing
- Carefully selecting and introducing sources
- Explaining and modeling strategic processing
- Engaging students in guided practice
- Incorporating opportunities to write in response with support
- Providing opportunities for independent practice

Continuously Assessing

As explained in Chapter 1, we orchestrate the use of many skills and strategies to help us make sense of informational sources. How do we begin to determine which skills our students have mastered and which strategies we may need to teach? There are many qualitative reading inventories available, including the *Fountas & Pinnell Benchmark Assessment System 2* (Fountas & Pinnell, 2017) and the *Next Step Guided Reading Assessment* (Richardson & Walther, 2013), that can reveal what students are doing to make sense of informational sources. These sources include informational passages that students read and questions you ask that assess literal, inferential, and analytical thinking on the part of the student. What you notice during the assessment can help you determine what to teach (International Literacy Association, 2017).

Another suggestion is to simply observe students as they engage with informational sources. Leaning in to confer with students as they read a source can reveal what they are understanding as far as the content in a source and what they are doing strategically to make sense of that source (Johnston, 2010). What we say in response can nurture our students' identity and sense of agency ("I can do this") as problem solvers (Johnston, 2004). Opportunities to assess and then coach in-the-moment are a key part of all three phases of the plan for learning. During Phase 1, when the students read the source for the first time, you can lean in to check for monitoring, word solving, or comprehension issues. Based on what you notice, you can affirm the student in some way and then provide a teaching point. There's a similar opportunity in Phase 2 when you guide the students in practicing the strategies you have explained and demonstrated. Assessing and coaching can also happen when students write responses during Phase 3.

Critical to the practice of assessment is the teacher's knowledge of what the students should be able to do as proficient strategic processors of informational sources. Just as important is knowing how students' development should take shape as they work toward proficiency. So, when we talk about a student beginning to self-monitor or to identify an author's main ideas while analyzing a source, we need to know specifically what to look for. In other words, we have to know what patterns of interaction would reveal students' growth toward proficiency in close reading–viewing–listening. Chapters 6–11 include the following tools to support you in noticing students' strengths and needs and in responding:

- Quick tips for assessing students' understanding of different purposes or goals for reading and the strategies needed to meet those goals.
- Notes about what to observe for when you lean in to confer with individual students.
- Descriptions of what students' written responses might look like at four different stages on a continuum of learning—attempting, approaching, meeting, and exceeding.

Carefully Selecting and Introducing Sources

Just as we have to set up our students to do well, we also have to set up ourselves to teach well. The careful selection of sources and our analysis of sources will make our teaching easier and our students' learning experience more rewarding. When selecting a source, there are three important factors to consider:

- The purpose for strategic processing during Phase 2
- Students' prior knowledge related to the topic and structure of the source
- Students' interest in the topic of the source

A potential focus for strategic processing during Phase 2 (e.g., identifying a main idea, becoming aware of monitoring for understanding, learning from visual images or graphics) should be kept in mind as you consider various sources. So, if you have determined that your students need to work on identifying a main idea, then you need to choose a source or sources that have clear main ideas or main ideas worthy of identifying, discussing, and then writing in response to. Remember too that it is not always necessary to use all parts of a source. While the students may read or view an entire source or large part of a source during Phase 1 of the learning plan, they may only engage with a part of the source during Phase 2. As you consider sources, notice parts of the source that would lend themselves to a demonstration of strategic processing by you and to an opportunity for students to practice this type of processing with your support and independently.

We know that the more a student knows about the topic of a source or how that source is structured the better she will understand it (Pearson & Cervetti, 2017). Interest in the topic also plays a role in how willing a student will be to engage in the productive struggle necessary for making meaning of that source (Springer, Dole, & Hacker, 2017). This may be a topic that students of certain ages find interesting, a topic for which we have nurtured interest during the hands-on part of a unit of study in the content areas, or an area of interest we spark through our introduction to the source. What is critical is that the teacher *knows the source*. We have to read, view, and listen to that source for ourselves. As we do, we can consider what we might need to do to help students access a source or *want to* engage in learning from a source. Sometimes a quick introduction to a source may be enough. At other times, we may need to provide introductions that make the source more accessible to our students.

Based on what we know about our students, there are a variety of elements we can include in a purposeful introduction.

- Content and language objectives
- Brief introduction to the topic of the source
- Purpose for reading–viewing–listening to the source
- Introduction to a few key vocabulary words or unfamiliar language structures
- Opportunity to view and briefly discuss additional sources that activate or build background knowledge (e.g., photographs, maps, short video clips)
- Opportunity to preview the source using a mnemonic like THIEVES as a guide to make informed predictions

Chapter 4 provides recommendations for how to select sources, and Chapter 5 explains further what you might consider when planning an engaging, but also helpful, introduction.

Explaining and Modeling Strategic Processing

What do we mean when we use terms like *monitor for meaning* or *tap schema* or *identify key details*? When and how do we use these strategies? And why are these strategies important? For many students these concepts may not be clear even when we have engaged them in strategic close reading numerous times. During Phase 2 of the plan for learning, the language we use to define and explain these terms can begin to clear the way for students to make meaning from a source efficiently and effectively (Almasi & Fullerton, 2012). For example, when a teacher is introducing what monitoring for meaning is, she might say the following:

We know that some parts of sources will be harder to understand than others. As we read–view–listen to a source, we need to be aware of when we are understanding information and when we are not. This means we need to monitor for meaning.

Monitoring for meaning will help you remember information in the source. It will also help you notice when you need to stop and figure out a tricky part of a source so that you understand the rest of the source better.

You can monitor for meaning by asking questions like

- Is this new information?
- Do I understand this information?

When you don't understand, you need to use a fix-up strategy to help!

This language introduces students to the what (the strategy), the why, and the how. I provide examples of this type of explanation in Chapters 6–11.

Many students also need to see what strategic reading–viewing–listening looks and sounds like. This means we need to think aloud for students about what we are doing in our heads as we make sense of a source. This is different from explaining what students should do. When we model by thinking aloud, we use *I* statements and minimize *you* statements. Consider the difference between these two statements made by a teacher:

- Wow! Right here I was confused, and I needed to go back and listen to the last 10 seconds of that video again. Let's see what happens for me when I do.
- When you get confused, you need to go back and listen to that part again.

There's something about the first statement that resonates with students more emphatically than the second statement. In the first statement, you, the teacher, are putting yourself out there as a meaning maker for the students to observe. You are showing how you are vulnerable to challenging content in a source and yet strategically oriented toward trying to make sense of content when meaning breaks down. Students can readily connect with your plight because they have faced the same difficulty many times. This experience may serve to motivate students to engage in strategic analysis of a source— not only because they have gained some clarity, but also because they have connected with you as a reader–viewer–listener. Examples of teachers thinking aloud and suggestions for planning these think-alouds are incorporated into Chapters 6–11.

Engaging Students in Guided Practice

Procedurally, guided practice involves the teacher being fully present and knowing when to step in and step back. During Phase 2 of the plan for learning, after I have demonstrated strategic processing with a set of strategies, I assign a portion of the source for students to "try out" what I have just modeled. I assign just a portion because I do not want students to become overwhelmed but instead to view the task at hand as manageable. I confer with individual students for a few minutes, while the others read and take notes or mark the text, and then I regroup with all of the students to discuss what they did to make sense of that part of the source. (This exercise may look a bit different with a video or audio clip unless students are each accessing this source on their own device.)

Next, depending on what I have observed, I may assign another (perhaps longer) section of the source for the students to analyze, or I may decide to think aloud about another portion of the source if I have noticed some frustration or roadblocks. This stepping-in and stepping-back approach gives me the flexibility to gauge students' needs, determining whether they need less or more support as they engage in closely reading–viewing–listening.

How do we know in-the-moment what to do in response to what we observe? Which scaffolds do we offer? The strongest support we can offer students is carefully crafted language that encourages them to think more deeply about what they are understanding and not understanding in the source (Clay, 1993; Cummins, 2011; Johnston, 2004). Examples of prompts we can use include:

- "Tell me more."
- "What made you think that?"
- "What can you do to solve that problem?"

If students are unable to problem-solve or elaborate on their thinking after we offer a prompt like those listed above, we may need to help a student by together returning to the source at hand and engaging in a shared think-aloud. This involves the teacher and the student thinking aloud together about what they are doing to make sense of the source and what they are learning as a result.

Opportunities for students to share their thinking—how they were being strategic as they made sense of a source or how they were confused and problem-solved and what they learned as a result—are a critical aspect of reading instruction. Verbalization (and hearing their peers verbalize their thinking) can help students become aware of the "covert thought processes" we engage in as we read–view–listen to informational sources, which in turn increases their comprehension of sources (Almasi & Fullerton, 2012; Pressley et al., 1992). This verbalization can happen during conferences with individuals, when students think–pair–share with a peer, or even in a quick note they write to you at the end of a lesson. A few examples of what we might hear students say are:

- "I realized that this part wasn't making sense so I . . ."
- "I stopped and looked carefully at the bold words in the diagram, and this helped me understand . . ."
- "I didn't know what this word meant, but I thought it was important so I reread to look for clues about what it means . . ."
- "I started to notice how these details are connected, and that made me think the author's main idea is . . ."

Ideally, this thinking becomes part of the inner conversation students engage in when they grapple with making meaning on their own.

When we provide opportunities for guided practice, we are, in a sense, nurturing a community of practice in which students see themselves as active members. Membership in this learning community can be an intrinsically motivating force for students—as they witness you, their peers, and themselves engaged in productive processing of informational sources and, more important, in the construction of knowledge about the world (Guthrie & Winfield, 2000). Chapters 6–11 feature descriptions of lessons in which guided practice is implemented, as well as charts that list possible scenarios that might develop when conferring with students and suggestions for the language you might use to nurture students' thinking.

Incorporating Regular Opportunities to Write in Response with Support

Writing in response to what students have just read, viewed, or listened to is a powerful way to deepen their comprehension of the source (Armbruster, McCarthey, & Cummins, 2005; Headley, 2008). Writing in the form of annotating or note taking while we read–view–listen can help us keep track of our thinking and start to determine what is important. Writing after we read–view–listen to a source requires us to consider the content of the source and/or our notes and to ponder what we really understand about this content.

Students too frequently write mindlessly about what they have read, just simply regurgitating the same words used in the source. Mindful writing, though, includes the following features:

- Considering what is important to share
- Planning what will be shared, so that our writing is coherent and concise
- Elaborating and revising this thinking as we put pen to paper

During the three-phase plan for learning, students have the opportunity to take notes of some kind or to annotate their source during Phase 2—Meet the Strategies. They also have an opportunity to write in response to the source during Phase 3—Meet the Response.

Whether the students are taking notes, annotating a source, or writing a response, the teacher plays a key role in helping the students write (Graham, Harris, & Chambers, 2016). During Phase 2, depending on students' needs, the teacher may need to model thinking about what she will write in her notes or in the margins of a source and why. During Phase 3, the teacher may need to engage the students in conversations about what they will write or how they will plan for writing. She may need to demonstrate making a plan for writing. In addition, some students may need to see the teacher engage in writing part of a response, or they may need to write collaboratively with the teacher as a way to launch them into their own writing. Figure 3.3 is an example of shared writing I did with a group of students. I was the scribe; I wrote down the sentences they composed orally. Notice that I also wrote the name of the student who contributed the sentence. This small move on my part can nurture a student's sense of "I can do this!" After the shared writing experience, the students finished the rest of the response on their own. Chapters 6–11 include some suggestions about how to support students as they write as well as suggestions for written responses.

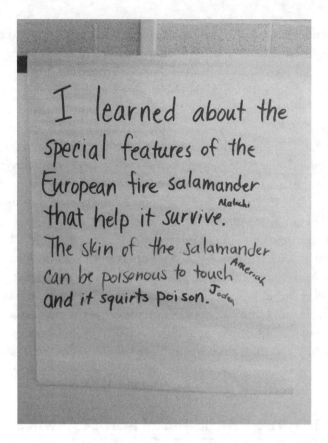

FIGURE 3.3. The shared writing of the beginning of a response I completed with a small group of students.

Providing Opportunities for Independent Practice

We develop a supportive learning environment because our ultimate goal is for students to take on their own learning of content. The tricky part of the gradual release process is that it does not necessarily occur in a linear fashion (i.e., I do–we do–you do). Always cognizant of the students' needs and the complexities of the source, the teacher has to engage in a dance of stepping in and stepping back to support students along the way (Englert, Mariage, & Dunsmore, 2006). For example, during Phase 2 of the learning plan, after a teacher models strategic processing for students and observes them during guided practice, she may determine that she can step back and release them to work more independently. If she observes frustration, though, she may decide to step back in by regrouping with the students to continue making sense of a source together for a while.

Anytime you step back and are not providing support, students are working independently. An important question to consider, though, is whether we provide enough time for independent practice. If we want them to grow as readers and writers, students need to be given countless opportunities to engage with and then respond to challenging sources on their own. Ten minutes of independent practice here and there are not enough for students to really learn or master what we are trying to teach. This is a common pitfall of instruction: Students do not get sufficient time to practice extensively what we have invested heavily in both modeling and coaching during guided practice. As a result, students stand little chance of becoming the skilled readers we want them to be, and they come up short in learning the content we are teaching in a particular subject area (Allington, 2009).

What might this independent learning look like? Here's one example. Let's say you have implemented several three-phase lessons focused on identifying a main idea and explaining supporting textual evidence. Students might engage in self-selecting sources and chewing on the main ideas in these sources on their own. This activity might occur in a student-led group or individually while you meet with other students. It might occur as part of homework. Or it might occur several times during each unit of study in science or social studies. In a sense, these opportunities are a "Phase 4" of this plan for learning—a phase that, while not addressed in detail in this book, is essential, with the end goal of developing independent learners. In addition, students need lots of opportunities to engage with informational sources during the school day for a variety of purposes, including reading or viewing self-selected sources. Chances are the learning they have done with you during close reading–viewing–listening will be tapped during these experiences as well.

HOW DOES THE THREE-PHASE PLAN FOR LEARNING MEET THE NEEDS OF DIFFERENT LEARNERS?

When we are continuously assessing students and stepping in and back to offer support that has generative value, the potential for individuals with diverse needs to grow as learners is enormous. What follows is an explanation of how this plan for learning can meet the needs of three groups in particular: students with learning disabilities, students who are learning English, and students who are "reading above grade level."

Students with Learning Disabilities

My first position as a teacher was in a middle school as a special education reading teacher. I quickly found that I was in over my head as young adolescents (most of them taller than me) filled the classroom on the first day of school, many with a defeated look on their faces. They had been struggling with reading for years and did not see any way out of their predicament. They were completely unmotivated, and some were even defiant. What saved me from despondency myself was a professional development opportunity my principal offered early in the school year. I spent several days "training" on a reading program that incorporated a systematic and sequential multisensory approach to teaching reading comprehension. I quickly began implementing the program when I returned to the classroom, and my students—some for the first time in years—began to experience success almost immediately.

Then we reached an impasse. The problem was that I was using only the controlled texts from the program manuals, and, as a result, the students were only successful when they were reading the program's texts. When the students left me to go to a regular science or social studies class, their ability to read fell short, so they continued to be frustrated. A major pitfall of many "programs" for students with learning disabilities is a lack of instruction on how to bridge from the controlled texts provided by the program to the uncontrolled texts students face in every other part of their day. With my students' patience, we spent a lot of time trying to figure out what this kind of instruction looks like. What I eventually realized was that I had to learn how to *teach the reader* versus how to teach the program.

Students with learning disabilities exhibit noticeable characteristics related to attention, memory, sense of agency, and coordinated use of strategies (Reid, Lienemann, & Hagaman, 2013). With respect to attention, they frequently struggle to stay focused on a task or a source. They may not recognize when meaning is breaking down during their reading, and even when they do, they tend to give up easily, exhibiting a lack of agency. When we confer with these students, their initial response may be "I'm done" or "I read it," not wishing to admit to their frustration right away; when we probe further, however, their response may become "I don't know what to do" or "I can't do this!" After years of perceived failure, their obvious lack of motivation only serves to perpetuate the problem.

So, how do we teach *these* readers? As noted in Chapter 1, a reader has to be equipped with a variety of strategies that can help in comprehending informational sources and then be prepared to monitor one's understanding while engaging in a multistep, frequently repeatable process. Many of these students' struggles have to do with an inability to recall strategies for successful reading and an inability to engage in coordinated use of these strategies while they are reading (Reid et al., 2013). Instruction that focuses on making strategic reading clear and accessible to students automatically benefits every student (Allington & McGill-Franzen, 2017; Swanson & Hoskyn, 2001; Swanson, Kehler, & Jerman, 2010; Swanson & Sachse-Lee, 2000). This type of instruction possesses some or all of the following characteristics:

- Systematic, explicit explanations of strategies and steps for strategic reading.
- Strategy cuing that includes the teacher modeling or thinking aloud, the teacher explaining the benefits of using particular strategies, and the teacher prompting for the use of particular strategies.
- Segmentation, or breaking a task into smaller parts.
- Distributed practice and review, that is, providing frequent opportunities to use the strategy multiple times when first learned and over time with regular feedback.
- Dialogue between the teacher and the student that is purposeful, providing teacher assistance at the point of need.
- Small interactive groups.

These characteristics correspond well with the approach to instruction described in this chapter and the specific lessons described elsewhere in the book. With my former students in mind, I would also recommend linking the instruction that occurs with the special education teacher and general education teachers.

English Learners

The demographics of our classroom participants have changed dramatically during the past two decades, and the chances are high that you work with English learners in your classroom. Also, the English learners in our classrooms do not always have the same language proficiencies—in either their native or home language or in English (Echevarría, Vogt, & Short, 2017; Fu, 2009). Some students come to us with formal schooling in their native language and can achieve in content-area learning with native language materials. Other students' formal education has been interrupted in some way, and, as a result, they do not have a strong grasp of reading and writing even in their own native language. Many students were born in the United States, but speak a different language at home and have not yet developed academic skills in either their home language or in English. Since these students' experiences with their native language and English vary so greatly, their needs vary as well.

For these students to achieve success in either content areas or academic literacy, they need to tap into at least three areas of knowledge: their knowledge of the English language, their knowledge of the content area, and their knowledge of how to facilitate accomplishment of the tasks confronting them (Short, 2002). For example, when we ask a student to annotate important details that support a main idea in a source about chemical reactions, he has to use knowledge of the English language to understand the content in the source. He has to make connections to his background knowledge related to chemical reactions, and then he has to figure out how to go about using his annotations. In addition, English learners need to understand how to interact socially with both teachers and peers. When we ask students to think–pair–share (turn and talk with a partner) about their annotations, this task requires some understanding of how a conversation should be conducted in this particular context for learning (Gibbons, 2015).

For students who are English learners to experience some success during the instruction described in this book, several elements of the sheltered instruction approach to teaching (Echevarría & Graves, 2015) are incorporated into the lessons that I describe. Sheltered instruction approaches are based on the idea that language is acquired through meaningful opportunities to read, write, speak, and listen during content-area learning. The primary ways in which the instruction described here serve to support English learners as well as other students include:

- Clearly stating the objectives.
- Activating students' knowledge of how sources are structured (as developed across the lessons in this book) and linking what English learners already know to what they are either going to learn or continue to learn in the current lesson.

- Modeling for students with teacher think-alouds that include projecting visual images of the source and the teacher's notations.

- Chunking tasks into smaller segments during guided practice, so that they are still supported through scaffolding but also increasingly challenged.

- Using analogies to promote conceptual understanding of higher-level thinking skills, such as determining what is important and synthesizing.

- Linking lessons, that is, making explicit connections between them.

- Using manipulatives and mnemonics.

In addition, the language we use with English learners is important. We have to pay attention to their language proficiency and adjust our own language accordingly. So, for example, during a conversation about chemical reactions, the teacher might paraphrase, give examples, provide analogies, or elaborate on a student's response (Echevarría et al., 2017). This kind of language is incorporated into the examples of teacher think-alouds described in subsequent chapters and also into the conferencing scenarios and language prompts suggested for one-on-one coaching with individual students.

Students "Reading above Grade Level"

Students who "read above grade level" typically read avidly and can tell you every single detail about every single book in a popular fiction series, for example. They easily complete assigned reading tasks in class and always have their hands held aloft whenever you ask a question of the group. When teachers ask me how to support these students who seem to be reading above grade level and who seem hardly challenged by grade-level materials, my first response is always: "What has this student revealed about his [or her] ability to read–view–listen to informational sources closely? Can this student synthesize the content in individual sources and across sources for multiple purposes?"

My own experience is that there is a noticeable gap for many high-achieving students in their capacity to think deeply about a fiction text versus an informational source. They are smart or savvy enough to readily locate answers to questions in a source, fill in two-column notes and other cool graphic organizers we push their way, and complete content-area projects that include creating infographics or PowerPoint presentations. But what happens when you sit down with these students to talk informally about the informational sources they are reading or writing? Frequently, they rely on prior knowledge and share what they already knew. Sometimes they reveal to you the loss they feel when it comes to determining what is really important or synthesizing one or more sources. A couple of key questions you can ask to get at how deeply the student is thinking about the source are "Tell me about what you are reading–viewing–listening to—what do you think the author is trying to say?" and then "What evidence in the source supports your point of view? Why do you think that's evidence?" The key takeaway point is to proceed with caution before concluding that these students are really proficient in understanding informational sources.

CLOSING THOUGHTS

I was visiting a school district not long ago and had the honor of teaching the same students for several days in a row. On the last day, Malachi walked in. No, he *marched* in, pulled up a chair to the reading table, and said, "Let's do this!" In just a few lessons (using the three-phase plan for learning), this student had gone from reading and learning from a source at a superficial level to being able to talk about the topic of this source in detail. Later in the lesson, when I asked students if any of them had told someone about what they'd learned from the source in previous lessons, Malachi's hand shot up. "I told my dad!" The instructional approaches described in this chapter have that kind of power— the power to nurture students' sense of agency, their sense of "I can do this," and their identity or sense of "I am a reader!"

Selecting Sources

If we want to engage students in meaningful close reading, viewing, or listening, then we need to find informational sources that are worthy of returning to multiple times. These sources are worth talking about with peers and in writing responses and are engaging and pique students' curiosity. The source might be an excerpt from a book or an article in the *Los Angeles Times*, or a video produced by National Geographic, or an infographic published by NASA. Primary sources—letters, government documents, and photographs—can also be worthy of our students' close analysis. The sources we select need to be diverse in genre (e.g., persuasive, narrative, explanatory, descriptive, and instructive). They also need to include a variety of formats (e.g. traditional texts, video and audio clips, and infographics).

Now more than ever, many informational resources are available for classroom use, and sometimes the sheer number of choices can feel overwhelming as we plan for instruction. Identifying clear objectives for teaching can help us begin the process of selecting sources. Ideally, the sources we choose should be part of a content-area unit of study or a set of sources on the same topic. When students read–view–listen to multiple sources on a topic, their understanding of that topic expands. They can use knowledge they develop reading a first source to help them comprehend the information in a second and third source. As discussed in Chapter 2, essential questions from units of study can inform our objectives for teaching and can also be adapted easily to serve as purposes for reading, viewing, and listening.

Use your assessment of the students' strengths and needs to drive your selection of sources as well. So, if you want to start teaching a group of students how to identify the main ideas in a source, then pick a source with clear main ideas. If you want to teach students how to identify context clues that help them figure out the meaning of unfamiliar vocabulary words, then pick a source that has unfamiliar words and a variety of context clues.

The length of a source should contribute to your decision as well. Short sources work better for close reading during Phase 2 of the three-phase plan for learning. When students engage in careful analysis of a source, they can only analyze so much and still retain the information. A short clip of video, say 20 seconds, can contain a lot of information for students to process auditorily and visually. Some infographics- are complex enough to warrant careful analysis as part of a three-phase lesson. Sometimes just one paragraph of a printed text can have a lot of details that students need quality time to think through. As you look for sources, then, consider the length or amount of information in the source.

Thoughtful selection of a source can make a huge difference in our students' work with that source. Here I have just begun to touch the surface of what we might consider when selecting sources. The rest of this chapter focuses on exploring questions you might ask yourself as you search for sources and issues I have noticed in the field.

KEY QUESTIONS TO GUIDE SOURCE SELECTION

As you locate and select sources, there are two questions you might keep in mind:

1. Is this source worthy of close reading–viewing–listening?
2. Does the source lend itself to reading–viewing–listening for a particular purpose or in service of a particular objective for teaching?

What follows is an explanation of how we can use these questions as a guide when considering sources for instruction.

Is the Source Worthy of Use during Instruction?

Five criteria, frequently referred to as the "five A's," can help you think through the merits of a source (Moss, 2003; Moss & Loh-Hagan, 2016):

1. *Authority*
2. *Accuracy*
3. *Appropriateness*
4. *Literary and Visual Artistry*
5. *Kid Appeal*

Figure 4.1 lists questions for each of these criteria that you can use to help you determine if a source merits close reading–viewing–listening.

Criteria	Questions to consider
Authority	• What is the author or creator's expertise on this topic? • Is there an authors' note at the end of the book or an "about us" page on the website that explains their expertise? • Are reliable sources cited somewhere in the source? • Does the author distinguish between facts and theory?
Accuracy	• Is the content (printed word and visual images) accurate to the best of your knowledge or compared with other accurate sources? • Does the author identify opinions or conclusions drawn with qualifiers like *may have, potentially,* and *could*?
Appropriateness	• Will the students, with some support, be able to make sense of the ideas in the source? • Are there features that make this source student friendly or easy to navigate or learn from?
Literary and Visual Artistry	• Is this source well developed? • Does the author or creator employ literary devices like metaphors, similes, or analogies? • For video, does the creator use a variety of visuals to support the narration or the content? • For infographics and some texts, are the layout and design kid friendly or easy to navigate with some guidance?
Kid Appeal	• Will the students be interested in the topic of this source? • Does the source have aesthetic appeal? • Will students want to visit this source again on their own?

FIGURE 4.1. Criteria for determining a source's merit. Adapted from Moss and Loh-Hagan (2016).

AUTHORITY

When I think about *authority,* I want to know what the author's expertise is on the topic of the source or about the research that was done. For example, at the end of the book *Big Top Burning: The True Story of an Arsonist, a Missing Girl, and the Greatest Show on Earth* (Woollett, 2015), the author includes the following description of her research:

> In researching the Hartford circus fire, I consulted many sources, including books, documentaries, and newspaper and magazine articles about the fire. I conducted personal interviews, and I dug through the boxes and boxes of material on the circus fire collected by the outstanding librarians at the Connecticut State Library Archives. As my research progressed, it became clearer to me than ever that the word of one person may not hold the truth. In fact, the words of many people may still leave questions unanswered. I believe the best way to decide for yourself just how close you can get to the truth is to ask questions of as many people as possible. I hope that I have done justice to this effort. (p. 136)

In this short note, Woollett reveals how she engaged in extensive research. She also includes a list of the names of the people she interviewed and an extensive bibliography of sources she consulted, including primary sources from the Connecticut State Archives.

Another suggestion is to lean on government agencies like NASA and the NSF for sources because of the expertise of these agencies. The infographic "What Is a Sounding Rocket?," discussed in Chapter 2, was created through a partnership between NASA and the Jet Propulsion Laboratory at the California Institute of Technology. This partnership focuses on research that carries out robotic space and Earth science missions. In other words, there is an abundance of expertise in this partnership on the topic of sounding rockets.

Frequently, sources feature quotes from or interviews with experts in the field. For example, in the NSF video *Food and Fear* (2016) discussed in Chapter 1, two experts are featured—University of Idaho mammalian ecologist Janet Rachlow and Washington State University foraging ecologist Lisa Shipley. The expertise of these two scientists lends authority to the video's content.

Traditional texts, videos, and infographics frequently include a bibliography at the end of the material. When I am considering an infographic that is not developed by members of a group with significant expertise on the topic or by a group I am familiar with, I always look for a list of resources consulted by the creator of the infographic. There are a lot of infographics or visual images currently on the Internet that are just "out there," with no documentation of who developed them. For example, you might find a source on Pinterest with no author identified and no bibliography. This can be problematic. My recommendation is to at least know who developed the source and which resources were used to inform the content. If you have time, I'd also recommend cross-checking the information in the infographic with the source material listed.

ACCURACY

Accuracy means that the content of the source is free from error and up-to-date. Some authors acknowledge the experts who helped them or who fact-checked the content of their sources. For example, in *Giant Squid*, Fleming (2016) includes the following "acknowledgment" in the notes at the end of the book:

> I am especially grateful to Dr. Edith Widder of ORCA (Ocean Research & Conservation Association), marine biologist, deep-sea explorer, and bioluminescence expert for sharing her time, expertise, and enthusiasm for the giant squid and by fact-checking this book. I am also obliged to Richard Ellis, author of *The Search for the Giant Squid*, who helpfully answered my squid questions.

Notice how in this acknowledgment the author also makes clear the expertise of her fact-checkers.

If you are familiar with the topic of an informational source, you can also rely on your own expertise to determine the accuracy of the information or you can compare the source to other sources available on the topic. One benefit of developing a set of sources on a topic is that you will begin to notice information that is consistently portrayed among sources. You may also notice discrepancies, and then have a reason for questioning the accuracy of a source. This discovery does not mean that this source should not be used.

Instead, it may be an opportunity for students to do a close analysis of multiple sources to compare and contrast content and to check an author's sources. The important point is that you are aware of discrepancies or errors before sharing the source with students.

Another aspect of accuracy to consider is whether the author of a source distinguishes between facts, theories, and opinions (Moss, 2003). Authors should be clear when they are engaging in supposition, or supposing something based on what they believe or have learned. They should inform the reader when they are engaged in conjecture or drawing conclusions based on incomplete information by using qualifying phrases with words like *probably, almost,* and *nearly.* Notice the qualifying language (in italics) the author uses in the following excerpt from an online article titled "A New 'Spin' on Concussions" (Stevens, 2015):

> The crunch of a tackle *may* indicate more than just the end of a football play. It *could* trigger a concussion. That's a *potentially* serious brain injury that can lead to headaches, dizziness or forgetfulness. Scientists have long known that rapid forward, backwards or side-to-side movements *could* damage the brain. A new study finds signs that the worst damage *may* stem from rotational forces deep within the brain.

The author makes it clear that the research on concussions does not say "this will happen," but instead qualifies her message with words like *may* and *potentially.*

APPROPRIATENESS

As you consider whether a source is *appropriate,* keep in mind its youth-friendly aspects. Is the source well structured, with features the students can use to easily (or with support) navigate it? For example, most infographics are structured to be read or looked at from left to right and top to bottom like the NASA (n.d.) infographic "What Is a Sounding Rocket?" described in Chapter 2. This is also the way we navigate traditional texts—reading from left to right, starting at the top of a page and moving toward the bottom—so an infographic that is structured this way as well is easier for students to navigate.

If a source is intended for an audience other than your students, will they be able to make sense of it or some parts of it with and without support? The video *Food and Fear* (NSF, 2016) has some relatively straightforward information related to how the pygmy rabbit uses the landscape to meet its needs. It also has more sophisticated information related to how the pygmy rabbit shapes the landscape. Some students may be able to understand the first type of information, while others may be able to understand both types. Whether students can make enough sense of the content to make it worthy of close analysis may depend on how much they know about the topic—another consideration in judging the appropriateness of a source.

LITERARY AND VISUAL ARTISTRY

Informational sources that merit close reading–viewing–listening should not look or sound like old encyclopedia or textbook entries. Instead, the content should have a sense of *literary and visual artistry*. This means that the printed or spoken words and visual images keep the reader–viewer–listener interested and engaged in meaning making. Check out this sentence in the picture book *Giant Squid* (Fleming, 2016).

> With writhing arms and ghostly, lidless eyes they glide; some large as buses, some weighing a ton.

Notice how Fleming's language helps the reader create a vivid, moving image in his or her mind with descriptive words like *writhing, lidless eyes,* and *glide*. Fleming's choice of words and her craft as a writer also help the reader compare the size of the giant squid to a familiar concept, *buses*. Similar to Fleming, many authors of informational sources use literary devices, such as metaphors, similes, and analogies, not only to support the reader in making meaning, but also to nurture or nudge the reader to a sense of fascination.

Authors may also draw readers, viewers, or listeners in with interesting or playful language or entertaining images at the start. In the video *Food and Fear* (NSF, 2016), the narrator begins by saying the following:

> When your task is trapping a rabbit, you gotta be on the hop.

As the narrator speaks, a short video clip shows three research assistants surrounding a pygmy rabbit and then giving chase, precariously over sage brush, as the rabbit escapes.

As you consider a source's artistry, examine the visual images for aesthetic appeal as well. The clip just mentioned, of the research assistants chasing the rabbit, is exciting to watch. This NSF video has several up-close shots of the pygmy rabbit as it scurries through its habitat, as the research assistants handle it carefully to put a tracking collar on it, and as it disappears down a hole. The developer of this video has chosen clips that support the content *and* keep the reader entertained. In the book *Giant Squid* (Fleming, 2016), the illustrator's paintings of the squid portray an elusive, mysterious creature in murky blues and blacks with a hint of pink. Each illustration is a glimpse of just a part of the squid—an eye, a tentacle—until the finale when the squid squirts ink to escape a predator and a foldout reveals an image of the entire creature. The visual artistry of this source is stunning and worthy of closely viewing again and again.

KID APPEAL

The video clip just described and the illustrations of the giant squid also have *kid appeal*. That is, they are attractive enough so that kids want to watch the video or read the book. They want to engage with this source in a group and on their own. The bright colors and photographs of real-life rockets taking off in the NASA infographic "What Is a Sounding Rocket?" is another example of a source that would appeal to kids. When considering sources, keep this aspect in mind as well. Is this a visually appealing source your students would pick up or locate on their own? Is this a topic that interests students at particular grade levels?

If a source lacks aesthetic appeal, there are ways to draw the student in or to make it more appealing. You might tie the source to a content-area unit of study that includes other appealing sources as well as hands-on experiences. Frequently, if you can help the students develop curiosity about the topic during other parts of the day, they will find the topic itself and not hesitate when you present a source that is not exactly "eye-appealing." For example, with a fourth-grade class engaged in a unit of study on simple machines, the students had the opportunity to think through a project that required them to build simple machines. When they were presented with excerpts of texts about simple machines printed in black and white without illustrations, they were still excited to be reading these texts because they were familiar with the topic and wanted to build knowledge they could tap when they worked on their projects.

Does the Source Lend Itself to Reading–Viewing–Listening for a Particular Purpose?

When we select sources, we need to keep in mind the purpose the students will have for reading–viewing–listening to that source. As discussed earlier, a clear purpose can serve as a guide in determining what is important. This purpose may be related to a language arts objective. For example, you may be asking students to identify the author's point of view in a text and how that view is conveyed. The purpose may also be related to a content-area unit of study. In social studies, the students may be closely watching a video with interviews of civil rights activists in order to answer the question, "How can individuals or groups influence government policy?"

In the first chapter of this book, I described a lesson with a group of students reading an article titled "A Day in Space" (May, 2015) about daily life on the International Space Station (ISS). When I initially looked for an article to use with these students, I knew I needed to teach them strategies for recognizing and making sense of a source with a comparison text structure during Phase 2—Meet the Strategies of the three-phase plan for learning. This article lends itself to lots of discussion about the similarities and differences between life on Earth and life on the ISS. This article could be used for other purposes related to language arts standards too, including teaching students how to identify an author's main idea or teaching students how to learn from the visual images as well as the written text. I could also have used it as part of a study unit on engineering design processes with a question or purpose for reading like "What are the criteria and constraints of a successful solution?"

Once you think you've located an appropriate source, examine it closely to see if it has enough content or depth for close reading–viewing–listening. In my experience, I have found that there should be several parts of the source that call for students' careful analysis during Phase 2. When I was considering "A Day in Space" (May, 2015) as a candidate for teaching for recognition of a comparison structure, I looked for chunks or excerpts that described an aspect of the astronauts' life in enough depth that we could draw conclusions about how that aspect is similar to or different from life on Earth. I *did not* choose the following excerpt:

For example, astronauts wash their hair with a "rinseless" shampoo so they don't need to get their hair wet.

Why? The author only included this single sentence about the rinseless shampoo. There isn't enough content for students to really wrestle with as they closely read during a Phase 2 lesson. I *did* choose the following excerpt, though:

Salt and pepper are available, too, but only in a liquid form. Astronauts can't sprinkle salt and pepper on their food in space because the salt and pepper would simply float away. There is a danger they could clog air vents and contaminate equipment. The tiny bits could also get stuck in an astronaut's eyes, mouth, and nose.

Why did I choose this one? Because it has some depth. The author describes the salt and paper and shares three reasons why astronauts do not have salt and pepper in a solid form. There's room for the students to construct a literal understanding and to make inferences about how this is different from life on Earth. As you consider a source, start thinking about which chunks or parts you can use to demonstrate strategic processing during a think-aloud and which parts would be appropriate for guided and independent practice. With an infographic, you may think aloud about one section of this source and then provide support as students analyze the other sections. With a video, you may think aloud with a very short clip and then support students as they think through additional short clips.

"LEVELED" SOURCES CAN BE PROBLEMATIC

One hang-up in selecting sources might be determining if the source is the "right level" for a group of students. For students who are instructional, somewhere in a typical third-grade range and higher, I generally don't stress out about finding a particular level of text. Using what I know about the students, I look for a source with some content the students can access with some ease and other content that leaves room for problem solving or strategic processing. The students reading the article about life on the ISS were instructional at a typical mid-third-grade range. I knew this article was written in that range. As I read through the article, I noticed parts I thought the students would easily understand. The author includes facts about familiar ideas, like how the astronauts have to stay clean and healthy by washing their hair and brushing their teeth just like people on Earth. Then there were other parts of this source I thought the students might have to slow down and be strategic to make sense of, such as an explanation of how the toilet on the ISS is different from a toilet they have at home. In a nutshell, I look for sources that have some content that will come easily and some content the students can chew on.

If you are examining sources that have been leveled, be sure to consider what the publisher has done to "level" those sources. Some resources that have "leveled" texts for students have used an algorithm that subtracts or uses substitutions for difficult words. Sometimes the adjustments to a text—in an effort to lower the Lexile of that text—actually make it harder to understand. This is revealed in the following two excerpts. The first is from an original article in *The Guardian* titled "How Do You Stop a Wildfire?" (Saner, 2016b). The second is an adaptation of the article to a lower Lexile posted on the site *Newsela.com*.

Excerpt from article in *The Guardian*

Bruce Malamud, professor of natural and environmental hazards at King's College London says: "To stop a wildfire, you need to remove one of the following: the heat of the fire, the fuel that feeds the fire [such as vegetation] or the oxygen that allows the combustion to take place." (Saner, 2016b)

Excerpt from the adapted version (Lexile 730)

Bruce Malamud is a professor who studies events like these. He says that to stop a fire, you need to remove one of three things. You need to remove heat, oxygen, and dry plants. Without them, the fire cannot spread. (Saner, 2016a)

The adaptation is supposed to be at an easier reading level. But is it really easier to understand, or is it confusing? Heat from what? Why oxygen? And why dry plants? Notice how each of these questions is clearly answered in the excerpt from the original article.

If you are working with sources that have been leveled, my recommendation is to look for and read the highest-level source in the set. For example, when you find an article at *www.newsela.com,* you have a choice of Lexiles with which you would like to read the source. Some publishers, like McGraw-Hill, level their books using labels like "Approaching," "ELL," "On," and "Beyond" to reveal the complexity of the text. In both cases, read the highest-level source. Then when you read the source at a lower level, you will know what has been left out or adjusted and can more easily determine if the information in the source is still clear.

ON SELECTING SOURCES TO READ ALOUD

One of the easiest ways to increase students' familiarity or comfort with informational texts is to read aloud these texts as part of your instruction. While there are times when a read-aloud should be just for the students' enjoyment, an interactive read-aloud can also be a great teaching and learning experience (Cummins & Stallmeyer-Gerard, 2011). Using the three-phase plan for learning, on Day 1, read the source aloud or only parts of the source, if it's a longer one. Then on Day 2, reread aloud parts for the students to listen to carefully and discuss or provide copies of excerpts from the source for the students to read and annotate. In Chapter 6, there is a description of a three-phase lesson that incorporates an interactive read-aloud with the book *The Wolves Are Back* (George, 2008). Because the text's content is made accessible (to some extent) for all learners to grapple with during conversation, interactive read-aloud experiences also help create the feeling that all students are acting as meaning makers. Basically, by reading aloud to students, we are easing the cognitive load they must bear. Students can thus focus on thinking more deeply about the content being presented without having to worry about reading the text themselves.

In the beginning, you might choose shorter and less challenging texts until your students develop some stamina for listening to more complex ones. Plan, though, for continually increasing the complexity of the texts being read aloud. For example, in September in a third-grade classroom of one of my colleagues, we read aloud *What Do You Do with a Tail Like This?* (Jenkins & Paige, 2008), which is written at a late third-grade level. My colleague continued reading aloud various informational texts, and when I came to visit in January, I observed the students fully engaged in a read-aloud of Simon's (2018) *Icebergs and Glaciers,* written at a mid-fourth-grade level. My recommendation is not to spend a lot of time thinking about the levels of texts, but rather to just keep an eye on the rigor (and length) of the texts you are reading aloud.

I would also not shy away from reading aloud from longer, more complex sources. The beauty of most informational texts is that you do not have to read the entire text in order to identify the author's central ideas or engage in close analysis for a different purpose. As a result, we do not have to shy away from sharing a text with students simply because of its length. Instead, we can read aloud several excerpts from the text. When you go about choosing the particular excerpts and features to share with students, keep the students' purpose for listening in mind. I read aloud excerpts from *The Prairie Builders* (Collard, 2005) to a group of fourth graders while beginning a content-area unit on the prairie habitat. Our focus was on identifying the main ideas in this source. Collard's central idea in this text is that, while the tall grass prairies in the American Midwest have been mostly decimated by farming, there is at least one hope-inspiring community project in place to restore and conserve prairie land. The text, in a large picture-book format, is about 70 pages long. I selected enough excerpts to fill 15–20 minutes of reading-aloud time. I chose three excerpts to convey Collard's central ideas: introducing how the project began when U.S. Congressman Neal Smith located land and wrote a bill for the state to purchase the land; explaining the process for turning farmland back into prairie, including a "burn method" implemented by Native Americans to stimulate prairie plant growth; and vividly describing the flora and fauna of the restored prairie. I also selected some key accompanying features to share, including a map of the United States indicating where there were once prairies in the Midwest; photographs of scientists and volunteers growing seedlings and planting seeds; photographs showing the farmland burning process; and related captions highlighting the flora and fauna. This process of studying and selecting generally enables me to select complex texts with rigorous content that wouldn't otherwise be accessible if I chose to read the text from start to finish.

Choosing the best informational texts to read aloud can sometimes be a tricky undertaking. The following are a few suggestions for selecting "just-right" texts:

1. Choose texts written at the students' listening comprehension level, which is typically higher than what they can read on their own.

2. As you do for other sources, check for *authority, accuracy, artistry, appropriateness,* and *aesthetic* or *kid appeal.*

3. Practice reading aloud from the text to see if the sound of the text read aloud is appealing or will be easy for students to follow while listening.

4. Plan for reading aloud *sections* of longer sources.

5. Choose from a variety of formats like trade books, news articles, and nonfiction poetry.

6. Choose from a variety of genres, including *narratives* recounting experiences or events that occurred, *descriptions* or *explanations* of various concepts, and *persuasive* texts.

Figure 4.2 includes some titles of trade books that lend themselves to being read aloud. You might choose some of these titles to read or just use them as key exemplars of the kinds of texts you need to locate for your own instruction.

Science Content

Lower Grades (3–5)

Adler, D. A. *Simple Machines: Wheels, Levers and Pulleys.*
Fyvie, E. *Trash Revolution: Breaking the Waste Cycle.*
Jenkins, S. *Trickiest: 19 Sneaky Animals.*
McNulty, F. *If You Decide to Go to the Moon.*
Strauss, R. *One Well: The Story of Water on Earth.*

Middle Grades (6–8)

Burns, L. G. *Citizen Scientists: Be a Part of Scientific Discovery from Your Own Backyard.*
Castaldo, N. F. *Sniffer Dogs: How Dogs (and Their Noses) Save the World.*
Collard, S. B. *Fire Birds: Valuing Natural Wildfires and Burned Forests.*
Montgomery, S., & Bishop, N. *The Hyena Scientist.*

History/Social Studies

Lower Grades (3–5)

Bragg, G. *How They Croaked: The Awful Ends of the Awfully Famous.*
Burcaw, S. *Not So Different: What You Really Want to Ask About Having a Disability.*
Goodman, S. E. *See How They Run: Campaign Dreams, Election Schemes, and the Race to the White House.*
Plimoth Plantation. *Mayflower 1620: A New Look at a Pilgrim Voyage.*

Middle Grades (6–8)

Aronson, M. *Trapped: How the World Rescued 33 Miners from 2,000 Feet Below the Chilean Desert.*
Deem, J. M. *Bodies from the Ice: Melting Glaciers and the Recovery of the Past.*
McClafferty, C. K. *The Many Faces of George Washington: Remaking a Presidential Icon.*
Walker, S. M. *Blizzard of Glass: The Halifax Explosion of 1917.*

FIGURE 4.2. Examples of trade book titles to read aloud.

DEVELOP "GO-TO" RESOURCES FOR SOURCES

What I have found over the years is that there are some go-to authors and go-to resources I continually return to when looking for sources. This makes searching for sources more manageable. For example, if I'm looking for a book about animals to read aloud, I check to see if Nic Bishop or Steve Jenkins has written one that would work. If I am looking for current events articles in science for middle school students, I visit the website *www.sciencenewsforstudents.org*. If I am looking for a video on a historical figure, I check websites like *www.biography.com* and *www.history.com*. If I am looking for an infographic on health and nutrition, I search on the National Institutes for Health site. Figure 4.3 includes suggestions for resources you might consider as you develop your own list of "go-to" sources; the authors whose books I listed previously in Figure 4.2 tend to be "go-to" authors when I am looking for sources I am going to read aloud as well.

If I am looking for sources on a topic for which I do not have a "go-to" resource, then I research a lot of potential sources and spend time reading–viewing–listening to them and weeding. Once, a teacher and I were locating sources for a unit of study with the essential question "How can water and wind change a landscape over time?" We started by collecting books we found in a closet and some miscellaneous library books and just skimming to find excerpts or graphics that might be worthy of our students' time and energy. We never found a "whole" source that we could use, but we did find several excerpts and visual images that would work. The essential question and the five A's criteria (listed earlier in this chapter) served as a guide for our decision making. After the unit of study, these sources were tucked away carefully to be pulled out again the next year.

CLOSING THOUGHTS

We seem to have access to more sources than ever through our schools or on the Internet. Many of these sources, though, are poorly written or are written for an audience that may not include our students. In reality, sometimes we are also required to teach with sources that may not be that well written or developed. Getting to know the strengths and pitfalls of a source can help us be aware of where we might need to step in and support students' comprehension. For example, if I think that a sentence or graphic in a source is unclear, I think aloud for students about how I couldn't make sense of that part of a source. I think aloud about specific words or phrases that confused me and how, as a result, I decided to read on or continue listening. In their life beyond our classrooms, students will have to grapple with poorly written or badly developed sources. Thinking aloud for students about the strengths and weaknesses of a source works to their benefit.

As discussed earlier, another option is to only use parts of a source during a Phase 2—Meet the Strategies lesson. Sometimes there is a really well-written section in a text or a particularly helpful clip in a video that students would benefit from engaging with multiple times. There are parts of the article "A Day in Space" (May, 2015) that I think are well written and parts that I think are unclear or do not have enough depth. While the students read the whole source during Phase 1—Meet the Source—they only closely

FIGURE 4.3. Examples of resources.

Source	URL	Types of sources	Notes
Biography	*www.biography.com*	• Short texts • Video • Audio clips	Videos and short texts complement each other; could be used as a text set.
History	*www.history.com*	• Video • Audio clips • Infographics	Access to primary sources like audio clips of radio interviews from a certain period.
Jet Propulsion Laboratory at California Institute of Technology	*www.jpl.nasa.gov/ infographics/index.php*	• Infographics • Visual images	The JPL is managed for NASA by Caltech.
National Aeronautics and Space Administration	*www.nasa.gov/audience/ foreducators/index.html*	• Short articles • Video • Podcasts	This site was created for educators by NASA.
National Geographic	*www.nationalgeographic.com*	• Video • Visual images • Infographics	Search "infographics" on the site to find this type of source.
National Institutes of Health	*www.nih.gov*	• Short texts • Infographics	Search "infographics" on the site to find this type of source.
National Science Foundation	*www.nsf.gov/index.jsp*	• Short texts • Video	The NSF is an independent federal agency.
Newsela	*newsela.com*	• Short articles	Articles come from sources like the *Washington Post* and are available at multiple Lexile levels.
San Diego Zoo Kids	*kids.sandiegozoo.org*	• Short texts • Video	Videos are generally kid friendly and easy to glean information from.
Science News for Students	*www.sciencenewsforstudents. org*	• Short articles	Content frequently includes reference to current research and quotes from experts.
Smithsonian "Explore History & Culture"	*www.si.edu/explore/history*	• Short texts • Images of primary sources	Primary sources include photographs, printed materials, and images of objects from a particular period.

read three paragraphs during Phase 2. The paragraphs I chose for analysis were not consecutive, but were from three different parts of the source. During Phase 3—Meet the Response—the students only wrote about what they learned from those three parts of the article as well. In another case, I was planning a lesson with a 3-minute video about ecosystems. During Phase 1, the students watched the entire video, but during Phase 2, we only listened carefully and took notes from the first 30 seconds. In both cases, the amount of content we discussed during close reading and viewing was enough cognitively. In other words, the students could not hold onto more information and still explain well what they had learned.

During the lessons with this article and video, I talked with the students about how to notice and then choose parts of the source from which they could glean adequate knowledge. I encouraged them to also not try to learn everything a source has to offer because that might become overwhelming. Instead, they should look for a part that meets their purpose or goal for reading–viewing–listening and then spend quality time thinking about that part. In the real world, this is how our students will grapple with informational sources anyway. They may skim a source and figure out that only part of it is helpful or worthy of slowing down to consider; then they will closely read only those parts to construct new knowledge. It makes sense then that we start this conversation in the classroom as we work our way through complex and varied sources.

CHAPTER FIVE

Introducing Sources and Teaching Students to Make *Informed* Predictions

Picture this moment at the beginning of a reading lesson. With a small group of students, a teacher introduces a Scholastic news article titled "Invasion of the Drones" (Westrup, 2015). In this article, the author introduces interesting ways drones might be used—to deliver pizzas or an Amazon package—as well as some of the problems with the use of drones. The author also describes complex problems drones pose related to safety and privacy. As you read the transcript of the first part of this introduction, notice the content the teacher has chosen to include.

> TEACHER: In this article we are going to learn about drones, which are unmanned aerial vehicles. Before we read the article, let's think for a minute about the meaning of those words—*unmanned aerial vehicle.* (*Points to a piece of paper with the words* drone—unmanned aerial vehicle *written on it.*) We can use the photograph in the article to help us think about what that means. (*Students pause to look at a photograph of members of the National Guard gathered around a drone sitting in a field.*)

> JOHN: Maybe *unmanned* means there is no one riding on it.

> TEACHER: Yes! Let's jot down "no one" or "no person" next to the word *unmanned.* (*Pauses to write.*)

> SUSAN: What does *aerial* mean?

> TEACHER: Let's think about that word. What part of it sounds like or looks like a word you know?

61

DEON: Something about air?

TEACHER: Would that make sense that a drone is in the air? Or flies up in the air?

DEON: Yeah.

TEACHER: Let's jot down "in the air" on our definition. (*Pauses to write.*) What about the word *vehicle*?

SUSAN: That means it's like a car.

JOHN: Or a truck.

TEACHER: So you're saying that it's a form of transportation or it moves things around like a car or truck? Let's jot that down on our definition. (*Pauses to write.*) [See Figure 5.1.] Let's look at our notes on the definition of a drone. How can we use these notes to explain what a drone is? I want you to turn and talk to your partner about what you are thinking. Explain what a drone is.

What occurred during this exchange? The teacher introduces an unfamiliar term, *unmanned aerial vehicle*, and helps the students unpack its meaning with conversation. She also employs the use of a visual scaffold of the term and notes from their conversation written clearly on a piece of paper.

For the next part of the introduction, the teacher presents the vocabulary words *disadvantage* and *advantage*, sharing kid-friendly definitions and encouraging the students to briefly discuss the advantages and disadvantages of technology in their lives. Then the students preview the article. As they notice details in the photographs and headings, the teacher poses the question, "What do you think you'll be learning about the advantages and disadvantages of drones?" Finally, the teacher poses a clear purpose for reading: "As you read, I want you to think about what you are learning about the advantages and disadvantages of drones."

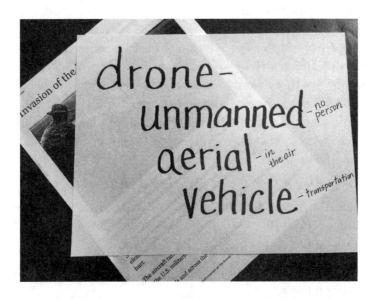

FIGURE 5.1. Visual scaffold created by a teacher and students.

The introduction to this source lasts about 8 minutes. The teacher chose this article because the content would be engaging, but also because it offered some challenging ideas for the students to comprehend. For example, while the students would easily understand that businesses like Amazon want to use drones to deliver packages, the students would have to be more strategic in making sense of a section that describes state regulations being developed in response to drone accidents. The teacher also knew that the students might get one of the author's main ideas (e.g., "there are good and bad things about drones"), but not have the vocabulary (like "advantages" and "disadvantages") to explain this idea in detail. The teacher's goal in planning this introduction was to make this source accessible to the students, but still leave room for them to grapple with making meaning.

PLANNING PURPOSEFUL INTRODUCTIONS

During Phase 1—Meet the Source, of the three-phase plan for learning, purposeful introductions can help students activate or build (quick) background knowledge. Sometimes an introduction may be lengthy (5–9 minutes), similar to the one just described. Sometimes, though, an introduction may be short or left to the students to lead. For example, if the group of students just described read or view additional sources about drones, they could use the knowledge they developed with this first source to help them make predictions as they preview each new source. The teacher would not need to provide as elaborate an introduction to these additional sources. When we plan introductions, our goal is to provide just enough support to help the students get started. "Just enough" means the students will still have complex content to productively wrestle with during reading or viewing.

How do we plan introductions? What you include in the source introduction will depend on what makes the source complex or harder to understand and the strengths and the needs of your students. One of the questions I ask myself when planning an introduction to a source is, "What small bit of background knowledge would be helpful in understanding this source?" In the scenario with the article about drones, the teacher believed that having a firmer grasp on the meaning of the term *unmanned aerial vehicle* would help the students grapple with key ideas in the source. In another lesson, which focused on an article about deforestation, the teacher showed the students an aerial photograph of an uncut forest and a cut forest. The author of the article had described this idea, but there was no visual image to support it. The visual image and the short discussion that ensued helped the students grasp a key concept that was integral to the article.

Here are some of the many components that you can include in an introduction to a source:

- A language and/or content objective for the three-phase lesson
- A brief statement about the topic of the source

- Introduction of key vocabulary or unfamiliar language structures
- An opportunity to view additional sources that provide some background knowledge (e.g., photographs, maps, short video clips)
- An opportunity to explore the structure or format of the source
- A stated purpose for reading–viewing–listening to the source
- An opportunity to preview the source

I'm not suggesting that you include all of these components. Students can get cognitively overwhelmed if we include too much information before they start to engage with the source. I pick and choose based on the needs of the students and the complexity of the source. I always share an objective, and I strongly recommend providing a clear purpose for reading–viewing–listening, whether it is student generated or teacher generated. The trick is to plan just enough to launch the students forward. We also need to help the students launch themselves forward—by previewing, activating prior knowledge, and predicting on their own. This chapter focuses on describing the components you might consider when planning introductions to sources, including how you can use mnemonics like THIEVES to help students make their own informed predictions.

Content and Language Objectives

While the three-phase plan for learning may have multiple language and content objectives, choosing a few key objectives to share with students can help them develop a vision of what they are going to experience and will also help them set goals for themselves. Stating objectives might be a part of the source introduction during Phase 1, or you might state objectives at the beginning of each phase.

Content objectives are what the students will learn about the topic of the source. For the three-phase plan with the article about drones, the objective might simply be a student-friendly statement like the following:

> You [the student] will be able to describe orally and in writing the advantages and disadvantages of drones.

Ideally, these objectives are part of a unit of study that integrates state or national content-area standards, such as the *Next Generation Science Standards* (NGSS Lead States, 2013) or the *College, Career, and Civic Life (3C) Framework for Social Studies and Standards* (National Council for the Social Studies, 2013). For example, if the lesson on the drones article was part of a civics unit of study, the content objective might be the following:

> You (the student) will be able to explain why people need to make rules to create responsibilities and protect freedoms.

The language objectives are what the student should be able to accomplish as a user of the English language (Echevarría et al., 2017). They can vary and change depending on which of the three phases of the learning plan you are in—meeting the source, meeting the strategies, or meeting the purpose for responding. During Phase 1, you might have a language objective related to the use of academic vocabulary.

Students will be able to define the words *advantage* and *disadvantage* and give examples of each using content from the article about drones.

You might have a language objective related to the comprehension strategy you are teaching during Phase 2—Meet the Strategy. For the article about drones, the teacher planned to teach the skill of identifying details that support a main idea. She planned to introduce an analogy and the strategy of underlining and annotating key details with a clear purpose in mind. (See Chapter 8 for an explanation of these strategies.) For these lessons her language objectives might be the following:

- Students will be able to explain why some details in a source are more important than others.
- Students will be able to identify details that support a main idea in a source.

A Topic Statement

There are multiple points in the introduction when the topic of the source may become clear. You may allude to the topic of the source through the content objective, or the topic may be clear when you state the purpose for reading–viewing–listening to the source. The topic may become clear as the students preview the source and make predictions. Sometimes, though, it's helpful to prepare a brief statement about the source because your objective is a learning standard or essential question that is broader, like the NGSS example given earlier.

A topic statement might include some of the following points:

- Who or what (place, thing, idea) the source is about
- When (specific date or general period in history)
- Location
- The author or creator of the source
- The author or creator's purpose (e.g., to teach you how to . . . , tell the story of, persuade, explain, describe)
- One or more main ideas in the source

If a strong preview of the source can reveal any of this information, then you might narrow down your statement even further and leave the work of inferring the topic for the students to do as they preview the source.

Introduction of Key Vocabulary

There are usually several vocabulary words in a source that we may feel the need to discuss with students prior to reading–viewing–listening. Sometimes it's hard to choose. Here are a few tips for selecting words:

- Choose words that do not have a context clue present to help the student determine the meaning.
- Choose some words that you can define quickly (as part of the topic statement or when students preview a source and predict).
- Choose words that you will spend more time discussing because they might be helpful to the students in understanding a bigger part of the source or a main idea in the source.

The words in the last category may or may not be in the source. As stated earlier, during the lesson with the article about drones, the teacher introduced the words *advantage* and *disadvantage*. These words are not in the article, but instead are words the students can use to explain what they learned. Figure 5.2 is a photo of the kid-friendly definitions for these words the teacher wrote on a piece of paper and placed in front of the students.

In other cases, the words we choose for focused instruction may be in the source. During a lesson featuring a news article about how the government of Brazil was trying to clean up Rio de Janeiro's Guanabara Bay in preparation for hosting the Summer Olympics (Associated Press, 2014), a teacher introduced two words that were in the article: *sewage* and *waste*. (See Figure 5.3.) While there were some general context clues for students to guess the meanings of these words, the teacher thought that understanding the difference between these words would help the students understand the complexity

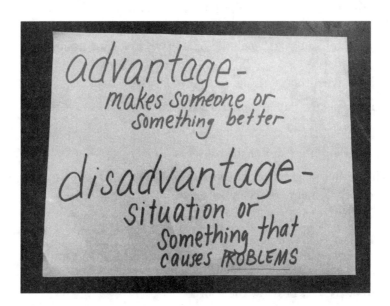

FIGURE 5.2. Student-friendly definitions for the words *advantage* and *disadvantage*.

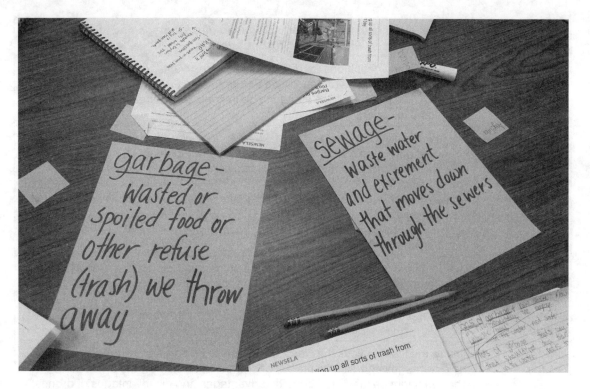

FIGURE 5.3. Student-friendly definitions for the words *sewage* and *garbage* that can be introduced during Phase 1—Meet the Source.

of the problem the government was trying to solve. The citizens of Rio de Janeiro were dumping waste (trash) into the bay, and the decrepit sewage system was releasing a lot of human excrement into the bay as well.

Based on the work of Beck, McKeown, and Kucan (2013), there are four quick steps that can be used to introduce unfamiliar vocabulary in a meaningful way:

1. Define.
2. Associate.
3. Turn and talk.
4. Link to the source.

Figure 5.4 on the next page is a description of how the teacher implemented these steps to introduce the words *disadvantage* and *advantage*.

When planning to introduce vocabulary, keep in mind how much your students can retain cognitively. There is always a temptation to "go over" several vocabulary words before students read–view–listen, but at some point, they will not remember what you said or discussed. It's too much. The students who had the lesson about the drones article are more likely to remember the words *disadvantage* and *advantage* because they engaged in the four steps and because the teacher limited the number of words she introduced.

Step	Explanation of how the teacher introduced *disadvantage* and *advantage* during the lesson with the article about drones
Define	The kid-friendly definitions for *disadvantage* and *advantage* were written on a piece of paper (see Figure 5.2) and placed in front of the students. The teacher reads aloud the definitions and then asks the students to read and think about them silently.
Associate	The teacher asks the students to make an association or connection to their own lives. She poses the following questions for their response: • *If you live far away from your school, would that be an advantage or a disadvantage?* • *If you have a pencil to do your math homework, would that be an advantage or a disadvantage?* • *If your mom or auntie works at an ice cream store, would that be an advantage or a disadvantage?*
Turn and Talk (Provide a prompt and, if needed, a language stem.)	Then the teacher provides a prompt for a student-led discussion. She asks partners to turn and talk about whether having a computer in your house is an advantage or disadvantage. For some of the students, she leans in and provides a language stem to help them get started: *Having a computer in your house is a/ an _____.*
Link to the Source	Finally, the teacher links the words to the article by saying, "This article is about the advantages and disadvantages of drones. Let's preview the article to see what we might be learning about the advantages and disadvantages of drones."

FIGURE 5.4. Steps for introducing key vocabulary. Based on the work of Beck et al. (2013).

Viewing Additional Sources

Sometimes our students need a quick chance to develop some helpful background knowledge before they preview a source. Maps, short videos, photographs, and other sources can be very helpful. For example, during the lesson on pollution in Rio de Janeiro's Guanabara Bay, the teacher used her smartphone to show a map of South America to the students. She wanted the students to understand where this bay is located, and this information is not provided in the article. She also shared a photograph (similar to the one in Figure 5.5) of a couch and other refuse sitting in the shallow waters of the bay. Although the text in the article focused on this problem, there was no strong supporting visual image. The concept of waste (as big as an old couch) floating in a bay of water might be a hard one for some students to grasp. But when the teacher presented the photo and asked, "What do you notice?," there was an audible gasp from the students, and they quickly began talking about what they saw. This brief experience provided knowledge the students could use to understand the source better and also piqued their curiosity. The discussion of the map and the photograph was very short, just long enough to develop some background knowledge the students could tap easily as they began to read the article.

FIGURE 5.5. Sometimes a quick discussion with visuals like this photograph of garbage floating in Guanabara Bay (a) and a map of South America (b) can make the content in a complex text more accessible.

Discussion of the Source's Structure

Informational sources come in all shapes and sizes. Some follow traditional structures (i.e., sequence or narrative, comparison, cause–effect, problem–solution, descriptive) and some are a blend of structures. For example, many news reports presented in a video or audio format begin with a narrative or a story about a particular person to draw the viewer or listener in before moving into an explanation of the focus of the report. In one narrative I listened to, the reporter began with a story about how a man discovered he had cancer. Then the reporter proceeded to explain new research that is exploring the gene that causes this man's cancer. He closed by returning to the story of the man and sharing the progress that he had made toward beating this disease. This news report has two structures—narrative and explanatory.

Some students may need a heads-up about the structure or format. With an audio clip, you might hint at the structure during the introduction to this source. You might say the following:

> As you listen to this news report, think about the different structures the reporter has chosen and why.

Or you might be more explicit and say:

> As you listen to this news report, notice how the reporter starts with a narrative structure and then moves into an explanatory structure. Think about why he chose those structures.

While we might have to be more explicit before listening to an audio clip, the structure of a traditional text or an infographic can frequently be addressed as students preview these sources. While students are looking at the source, ask the question, "What do you notice?" in a purposeful way or in a way that leads them to notice the source's structure. In the short book *Side by Side* (Pigdon, 2012), the author compares an impala and a lion. On one page he describes the birth of the impala, and on the following page he describes the birth of the lion. This layout begins a pattern where alternative two-page layouts describe a particular period in the lives of the lion and the impala. As the students previewed this source, the teacher asked the students, "What do you notice about the headings on the alternate pages?" With this prompt, the students noticed the structure of the source, which would help them make better sense of the author's ideas as they began to read.

Purpose for Reading–Viewing–Listening

During instruction, and depending on the objectives of the lesson, students might determine their own purpose for reading–viewing–listening or the teacher might set the purpose. A purpose for reading during Phase 1—Meet the Source might simply be one of the following:

> As you read, think about what you are learning about this topic.
> Or
> As you read, think about what one of the author's main ideas is.

Or a purpose might be more specific, like the one for the lesson about the drones article:

> As you read, I want you to think about the advantages and disadvantages of drones. What are you learning about the advantages and disadvantages of drones?

The purpose for reading acts as a guide for determining what is important. Setting the purpose also drives your conversation over the course of the lessons in the three-phase plan for learning. You can use this purpose to drive the strategic close reading during Phase 2—Meet the Strategies and as part of a prompt for writing during Phase 3—Meet the Response (for writing). In the article about drones, the purpose for close reading during Phase 2 was to be able to explain in detail one disadvantage of drones and what happened as a result. Then the writing prompt for Phase 3 involved giving advice about the advantages and disadvantages of drones to someone the students knew. I provide more guidance on developing purposes for reading–viewing–listening in Chapters 6–11.

Opportunity to Preview and Predict

We know that pausing to preview the source and then make an informed prediction can help students activate prior knowledge and set a purpose for reading–viewing–listening (Fisher & Frey, 2009). Activated prior knowledge can serve as a filter for helping us determine whether information in the source is new, unfamiliar, or confusing. A clear purpose can serve as a guide for thinking about what is important in a source. Previewing the source and making predictions are critical components of a Phase 1—Meet the Source lesson. We may facilitate this step early in the year by prompting students as they preview a source with questions like "What do you notice?" Or our questions might relate to another component of our introduction. For example, in the drones lesson, the teacher posed the question "What do you think you will be learning about the advantages and disadvantages of drones?" as students previewed the article.

Previewing a source to make *informed* predictions includes noticing the features (like titles, introductions, and visual images) and thinking about how the content in those features provide readers with clues about the information they will be encountering. As students think about the content in the features, they also need to activate any prior knowledge they have related to that content. As stated earlier, they can compare and contrast this knowledge as they read, view, or listen to the source, noting what information is new and what is not. Students who carefully preview sources with the intention of making helpful predictions are constantly amazed at the power of this process. One fourth-grade student bragged to his teacher, "I feel like I already know what the whole article is about!"

If your students tend to skip previewing and making predictions or they are not making thoughtful predictions based on their preview of the source, you might introduce a mnemonic like THIEVES (adapted from Manz, 2002). As students begin to use this mnemonic or another one effectively, you can release more and more responsibility to them for taking control of how they are introduced to a source during Phase 1 and at other points during the school day when they are working independently. There will still be Phase 1 lessons with sources that you keep some control over introducing—using some of the components described earlier in this chapter (e.g., new vocabulary, content objectives, etc.). We just need to keep in mind how we can give students more control over time or at various points. What follows is an explanation of the THIEVES mnemonic and suggestions for instruction.

RELEASING RESPONSIBILITY FOR PREVIEWING AND PREDICTING WITH THIEVES

Consider the metaphor of a thief. When a thief takes something that is not hers, what is she trying to do? She is trying to get ahead! In a sense, when we preview a source, we are trying to get ahead of the author or creator. THIEVES is a playful mnemonic that can be used to focus students' attention on the importance of previewing a source. Figure 5.6 is a bookmark and one student's sketch of a "thief." The letters in the word *thieves* form an acronym that reminds readers of the specific features in the source that they should study prior to close reading. Figure 5.7 identifies the features named in the acronym and the questions a reader–viewer might naturally ask in considering these features. (Please note that one of these features has changed since the first edition of this book was published; the second letter *e* now stands for "end of the source." I find that students rarely work with a source that has questions to answer at the end. Previewing the end of a source can be helpful, so I have made this adjustment in my practice. Create a variation that meets the needs of your students. You will see both in the examples I provide.) Initially, when you introduce this mnemonic or a similar one, you may need to step away from the three-phase plan and spend a lesson or two modeling how to use the mnemonic in a helpful way.

Introducing THIEVES

 I remember many years ago I had been talking with educators in the field for a while about using the THIEVES mnemonic as an activity for teaching students to preview and predict, but I had never actually taught the lessons I was suggesting. A small group of fourth-grade teachers invited me to come to their school to "walk the talk," and I jumped at the chance. I immediately started planning, using a science text on different types of severe weather, and then—oh, my—did I stumble! I soon realized there were just too many features in each chapter for students to manage. As a result, I modified my thinking drastically and created instead a lesson plan to use the THIEVES mnemonic with

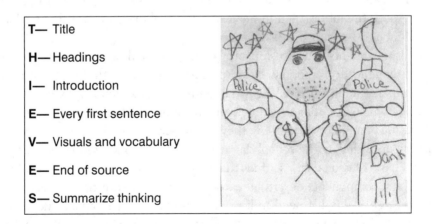

FIGURE 5.6. Example of the THIEVES bookmark and a student's sketch of a thief.

Feature or element of the text to be previewed	Questions the reader might ask when considering the named feature or element of the source
T—Title	• What does the title make me think the source will be about? • What might be a message the author is trying to communicate? • What do I already know about this topic?
H—Headings	• How has the author divided the content of this source into smaller topics? What are these smaller topics? • Based on these topics, what do I think I will learn about in each section? How does that relate to the larger ideas in the source?
I—Introduction	• What does the introduction do to make me curious about this subject?
E—Every first sentence in each section	• What additional details can I gather about the content of the source?
V—Visuals and vocabulary	• What do the accompanying features like figures, captions, and boxed information tell me about the content of this source? • Are there words in bold or italic type that I need to pay special attention to as I preview the source? What do they mean?
E—End-of-source	• How does the author wrap up?
S—Summarize thinking	• If I think about all of the information I have gathered, what do I predict I will be learning about? • What do I think the author's main ideas will be in this source?

FIGURE 5.7. The THIEVES mnemonic.

one two-page spread of the text only. These two pages included a title, two figures with captions, a map, and the main text. Previewing just a part of the source can still launch the students forward in making informed predictions that can serve as a guide while they read, view, or listen to a source.

In preparation for the lesson, I walked myself through how a reader might preview the two pages of text on "droughts." I not only thought about my predictions, but also how they tied into the author's central idea for this two-page spread. Going through this process for myself helped me articulate for the students during the think-aloud. On a copy of the bookmark, I even drew my own picture of a thief (my little brother sneaking away with my Halloween candy) to share with the students (see Figure 5.8 on the next page). For the lesson, I made transparencies of the two pages of text and the THIEVES bookmark. (This occurred before classrooms had document cameras and smart boards; nowadays, I would project the pages from the book and the bookmark in a different way.)

At the beginning of the lesson, I thought aloud in front of the students, introducing THIEVES and then demonstrating the use of this mnemonic to preview two pages in the source on droughts, activate my prior knowledge, and make predictions about what I would be learning. Figure 5.9 on page 75 is an example of what you might say during a similar introduction. During the lesson, I switched between the transparency of the THIEVES bookmark and transparencies of the text. I used the THIEVES bookmark

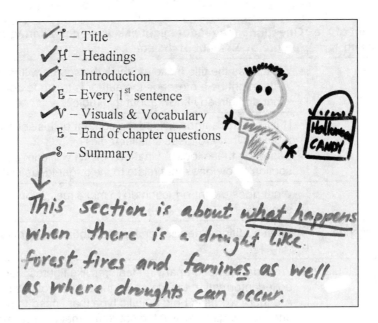

FIGURE 5.8. The notes I took in front of the students as I did the think-aloud.

as a way to keep track of my previewing and checked off each letter in the acronym as I previewed the text. I also marked the transparencies of the text as I thought aloud about each feature named in the THIEVES mnemonic. So, for example, when I read the title, I circled it. Seeing me mark the text as the students hear me think aloud serves as a visual support for the process I am modeling. At a certain point the students wanted to join in on the think-aloud. We finished by composing a summary sentence of what we thought the text would be about and also setting a purpose for reading. The students were amazed at how much they had learned about the topic of the book even before they read.

Then we read the two pages of text we had previewed (each student read silently) and regrouped to discuss what they had learned. Next, I moved into guided practice by asking the students to try out the THIEVES mnemonic with another two-page section of this text. After previewing, as they read, they took notes, and I walked around to confer with individual students. As each child finished one two-page section of text, I asked him or her to use the mnemonic to preview the next two-page section of text and predict and read until they were done with several sections. This introduction might be considered a Phase 1—Meet the Source lesson. Students could easily move into a Phase 2—Meet the Strategy lesson on the following day.

Using THIEVES with Infographics and Video

 What would using this mnemonic look like with other types of sources? Infographics have many of the same features as traditional texts, including titles, headings, and graphics. If you have introduced THIEVES with traditional texts, you might pose the question, "How can we use THIEVES to help us make predictions about what we will be learning

---

Introduction to Using THIEVES

Explain the "why" of previewing and predicting.

This might sound like the following:

> *When you read an informational article, do you ever just begin reading at the first paragraph? Or maybe you casually look through the article, but you are doing this mainly to see if it will be interesting? [Pauses for response.]*
>
> *When you want to really understand an informational source, you need to start by previewing the source. When you preview the source, you are in a sense getting ahead of the author or creator of that source. You are getting a sense of what the source is going to be about and starting to think about what you already know about some of the ideas that are in the source. When you pause after previewing and think about all of the information you have gathered, you can make thoughtful predictions about what the source is going to be about. This will prepare you for reading the actual source. You can think about the author's bigger ideas and set a purpose for engaging with that source. Then as you read, view, or listen to the source, you can use that purpose as a guide for thinking about what is important to remember.*

Introduce the THIEVES mnemonic.

Tell the students that you are going to share an activity that will help them practice previewing a source strategically in order to make thoughtful predictions. If you are using a bookmark, hand out sticky notes and ask the students to draw what they think about when they visualize the word *thief*. Give the students 2–3 minutes to sketch, and then ask them to share with their peers. If it would be helpful, share your own sketch. Then pose this question to the students: "What is the purpose of being a thief?" The students' replies may mention stealing, getting something that you want, or the like. I don't wish to focus unduly on "thievery" or "stealing," so I offer an alternate way of thinking about the subject by saying the following:

> *A thief is trying to get ahead. He or she feels that if one takes something in particular, one will be better off. We can be "thieves" when we read a new text or look at a new infographic in that we can get ahead and feel like we know more about what we will be learning from this source. [Refers to the bookmark or anchor chart with the THIEVES mnemonic.] When we preview a source, we can look at particular features or elements of that source to help us predict what we will be learning about. This mnemonic is a reminder of the features or elements of a source we might look at. Let me show you how I do this with a text that I am planning to read.*

Project the source and think aloud about a few features.

Using notes you prepared in advance, think aloud about the source you chose or a part of that source. Use language that positions you as an active reader. For example, for the article on drones, the teacher might have said the following:

> *When I look at the title, "Invasion of the Drones," that makes me think that drones might be a bad thing. I often think of the word "invasion" as having a negative connotation or meaning something bad is coming to take over, like aliens or bees! I'm using my prior experiences with the word "invasion" to help me predict that the author may be writing about the disadvantages of drones. I will be looking for information to support that as I read. Let's look at another feature and think aloud together about our background knowledge and predictions.*

from this infographic?" Infographics may look as if they do not have a lot of information and are not worthy of making predictions, but this is usually not the case. Infographics also may appear to students as though they just include bits and pieces of information that they can consume in isolation of each other. Think back to the "#suitup for safety" infographic by NASA described in Chapter 1. If students took a moment to look at the title and some of the headings in the largest fonts (e.g., "Key Capabilities" and "SAFER") and to notice the numbered suits, they could make a helpful prediction like "I am going to be learning about how space suits are built to be safe and how they have changed over time." This prediction can serve as a helpful guide in making sense of some of the more complex ideas in this infographic.

Many videos provide a good deal of information in the first 30 seconds that students can use to predict what they will be learning about. For example, in the NSF video described in Chapter 1 about the work of scientists studying the pygmy rabbit in Lemhi Valley, the narrative and images in the first 30 seconds include details about the where, the what, and the how. A thoughtful student may quickly predict what they will be learning about and be able to use this information as a guide. This short section of the video also includes the beginning of an interview with ecologist Janet Rachlow who works at the University of Idaho. A heading appears with her name and the university she works for, giving the student an idea of the type of experts he may be learning from in this video. While the student may not be working his way through the features named in the THIEVES mnemonic in the same way he would with a traditional text, he can still "get ahead" by listening to the first 30 seconds for the purpose of making a prediction about content in the rest of the video.

Whether the source is a traditional text, an infographic, or a video, the trick is to teach students how to preview the source with an awareness that the information presented can help them make predictions and guide their meaning making as they read, view, or listen to the rest of the source. Figure 5.10 offers suggestions for what to notice and how to respond as you confer with students about the predictions they are making.

Follow-Up Instruction with THIEVES

In Figure 5.11 on page 78, you will find a continuum that describes what you might look for as you observe students attempting to make thoughtful predictions based on their preview of a source. When I assessed the THIEVES notes written by a group of fifth graders who read the magazine article "Thirsty Planet" (Geiger, 2010b), I noticed that many of the students' notes were in the approaching stage or very listlike. The students did not always think *across* the content revealed in the headings, in every first sentence, and in all of the visuals to make their predictions. As a result, I planned a mini-lesson to model this skill. I used the same article from the first lesson and demonstrated reading and thinking about the information conveyed in each first sentence in each section. What follows are the first (and occasionally second) sentences in each section:

- Water covers 70 percent of Earth's surface.
- Water has been recycled like this for millions of years.

Scenario	How you can respond
The student is off-task.	Prompt: *Tell me about what you are doing to preview the source.* If needed, follow with *So, what do you need to do next?*
The student has looked at a feature or element in the source but has not been able to write notes yet.	Prompt: *When you looked at that feature or part of the source, what did you predict you would learn about? Why do you think so?* If needed, offer to write the first note for the student as he or she responds orally. Summarize aloud what you heard the student say, and then ask him or her to repeat it. Encourage the student to immediately write down what he or she just said.
The student has written notes easily, but only about features that are easily understood.	Possible prompts: • *When you looked at this diagram (or photograph or chart, etc.), what did you notice?* • *What does this make you think about that you already know?* • *So, what are you predicting you will be learning about from this diagram?*
The student is writing notes easily and may need a push to think more deeply about his or her predictions, perhaps by making connections between the features or elements of the source that was previewed.	Possible prompts: • *You have made several predictions in your notes. How are they all connected? What might be the author's big idea?* • *How do two of the features you have previewed (e.g., a heading and a diagram) seem connected?*

FIGURE 5.10. Common conferring scenarios and suggestions for coaching.

• Where there's water, animals can't be far behind.
• Animals don't just crawl, walk, slither, or fly to water. Many live in it.
• You need water, too.
• With so many demands on our fresh water supply, do we have enough?
• To solve some of these problems, people are getting creative.

Using a document camera, I turned to each page as I read aloud the first sentences and made the text accessible for viewing. The students each had a copy of the article as well. After I read aloud the sentences, my think-aloud sounded like the following:

As I was reading these sentences and sometimes rereading them, I began to think that this article is about how water is a precious resource. There's a lot of water because it covers 70% of Earth's surface, but I know we can't use it all because a lot of it is saltwater. Also, there's not an infinite amount of water—I want to know more about this, for sure.

FIGURE 5.11. Stages of development in previewing and predicting (before reading, viewing, or listening to a source).

Stage	Characteristics of oral and written responses
Attempting	• The student writes or states aloud predictions that are *not* based on evidence in the text; the student may be drawing too heavily from background knowledge. *Example from the student's notes:* Pollution is overruling the planet so bad, people can't even drink clean water. *Explanation:* The student wrote this prediction after looking at the title, deck, and photograph; there is no indication from the evidence in these features that the author will be discussing the issue of pollution. • The student veers away from writing about the content of the text to writing about the purpose of the feature or text referred to in the mnemonic. *Example from the student's notes:* The first sentences tell me what the story is going to be like or what it's about. *Explanation:* The student wrote this in his or her notes next to the first *E* in the mnemonic THIEVES for "every first sentence." He or she has stated the purpose of these sentences. Instead, he or she needs to read the first sentence of each section of the text and predict the content of the text.
Approaching	• The student writes or states aloud predictions that either restate the text or are very literal interpretations. *Example from the student's notes:* This will be about the wonders of water. *Explanation:* The student has simply restated the subheading "The Wonder of Water." The student may not be interpreting what the author means by "wonder of water" and therefore may not be making a real prediction. • The student's predictions are listed as though he or she is mindlessly filling in a blank. *Example from the student's notes:* This will be about how there is a lot of water on the Earth, how water has been around for millions of years, how every plant and animal needs water, and how people need water, too. *Explanation:* It is clear that the student has previewed the text because all of these ideas are addressed in the article. This response lacks depth; there is no indication from the student about the author's central idea and the reason the author might be putting all of these details into one text.
Meeting	• The student writes or states aloud responses tying the information gathered during the preview to a prediction about the author's central ideas. *Written example from the student's notes:* Reading every first sentence made me think it's about different creatures trying to survive with little water. *Explanation:* If you read the first two to three sentences in each section of the article, you could make this prediction. The student has synthesized the information and written a prediction about one of the author's central ideas.

(continued)

Stage	Characteristics of oral and written responses
Meeting (continued)	• The student's summary of what he or she predicts the text will be about reveals synthesis of the information gathered. *Written example from the student's notes:* I think that it will be about how people and animals need water, how they struggle for it, and what they use it for. *Explanation:* The student has identified three central ideas in the text. • The student identifies evidence in the text to support his or her predictions. *Written example from the student's notes:* I think this article is going to be about how hard it is to get water because there is a picture with a caption about people in Kenya walking really far to get their water and another picture of two girls sweeping mud from a watering trough. There's also a picture of Salton City, California, that looks like a desert and the people have to have their water pumped to them. *Explanation:* The student is beginning to rely on his or her own sense of agency when previewing and predicting; he or she is not limiting him- or herself to a lockstep application of the THIEVES steps.
Exceeding	• Without the aid of the THIEVES bookmark, the student previews the text fluently, sharing aloud what he or she is thinking and making references to information in the text that supports his or her predictions. The student's predictions are relevant and reveal a synthesis of the content gathered during the preview.

FIGURE 5.11. *(continued)*

It seems like if we are recycling water, then there is a limited amount. Yet animals need water, and we need water, and I know plants need water. I know what I do to save water, but I'm curious to see what the author shares. So, again, I think I'm going to be reading about how every living thing needs water, but there's only so much of it, and we have to figure out how to share and conserve water.

As I thought aloud in front of the students, I returned to different first sentences in the text and underlined key words that were part of my think-aloud. For example, I underlined "70% of Earth's surface" as I spoke. Then I discussed this process with the students before setting them off to give this a try. I posed the questions, "What did I just do to preview the text?" and "How did that help me start to think about the author's central ideas?"

Then I asked the students to meet in groups to engage in using THIEVES. Students can get tired of this approach to previewing a text if you ask them to write notes every time they use the mnemonic. I wanted them to think of THIEVES as a tool they could use flexibly, with the end goal of a thoughtful prediction related to the author's main idea. So, for this lesson, I asked the students to preview the text aloud in small groups. As a group, they would be collectively accountable for previewing strategically and then talking to one another about what they had noticed about similar features—in a way that was like the process I modeled with every first sentence.

After the students previewed and predicted what they would be reading as it related to the author's main idea, they each read the article silently and then got back together with their groups to talk about what they had learned. This particular class of students had been meeting in literature circles for several weeks, so they understood how to summarize what they read and then continue to share. If your students have not previously met in literature circles or in any kind of discussion group, you will need to instruct them in how to have a meaningful conversation before undertaking this lesson. Suggestions for follow-up instruction, based on your observations, are provided in Figure 5.12. For a quick overview of this chapter's discussion of THIEVES and additional suggestions for lessons, see Appendix A, page 227.

Since that first lesson with the source on droughts, I have learned a lot about using the THIEVES mnemonic with students. My main goal in using this mnemonic is to help

If . . .	Then . . .
Students are making predictions that are not supported by evidence in the elements or features of the sources they are previewing.	• Give a mini-lesson with a teacher think-aloud that models making supported and unsupported predictions. • When students discuss their predictions in small groups, ask them to prompt each other with the question *What's your evidence in the text?*
Students write about the purpose of the feature instead of about their predictions based on the content in the feature.	• During a mini-lesson, think aloud for students about the difference between predicting what the feature will do (e.g., *The photo will show me what the source is about*) and predicting what the source will be about based on the content in the feature (e.g., *In the photo, I noticed members of the National Guard preparing the drone. This made me think the article will have information about how groups like the National Guard use drones*). • When conferring with students, ask them to explain the difference between the purpose of the feature and the information or details learned from a feature.
Students' oral or written responses either restate the text or are literal interpretations.	• During a mini-lesson, share examples of students' written notes that reveal thoughtful interpretations of the information previewed. • Engage in a shared think-aloud about a particular feature in a source and then a shared writing of related thoughts and a prediction.

Students are thinking about the features they preview in isolation rather than looking for common threads that might reveal one of the author's main ideas.	• During a mini-lesson, specifically model how you made connections between two or more features. For example, with the article on drones, the teacher might say, "When I saw the subheading 'Warfare,' I thought back to the photo of the National Guard and wondered if that is one way they use drones, as part of their engagement in some type of conflict. Maybe that's what the author will be teaching me about."
	• As you confer with students, look for opportunities to help them see the connections between features. You might use prompts like:
	  ○ *What do both features reveal that you might be learning about?*
	  ○ *When you examined this feature, did it remind you of any other features you had already previewed?*

FIGURE 5.12. Suggestions for follow-up instruction.

students make informed predictions and move forward in making sense of the source. Students need to think flexibly about how to use this mnemonic as a reminder for what they need to do. This means they may not need (and we should not require them) to look at every feature listed in the mnemonic or to look at the features in a certain order (although the title is usually first). Some sources do not have all of the features listed in the mnemonic. Some sources have too many features to preview productively. Students need to make decisions about what is "just enough" of a preview to help them make an informed prediction that they can use as a guide while reading, viewing, or listening. Do not belabor instruction with this mnemonic; students will tire of THIEVES if its use becomes tedious. It is important to quickly move on to lessons in which you simply remind them of how they can be THIEVES as they preview the source. Eventually they should do this automatically.

CLOSING THOUGHTS

There's an art to planning a helpful introduction. We can provide too much information, and as a result the students know all there is to learn from the source before they even read–view–listen. We can give students more information than they can hold onto cognitively or that they can use productively. We can also create students who are dependent on us to help them preview sources productively. My advice is to consider the components discussed in this chapter. If they are not already a part of your Phase 1 instruction, then try a few out at a time and reflect on what seemed helpful to your students. Then continue to keep an eye on how you can help students to efficiently and effectively preview and predict on their own or, in a sense, introduce themselves to a source independently.

CHAPTER SIX

Synthesis and Identifying Main Ideas

In the book *The Wolves Are Back* (George, 2008), the author describes how the flora and fauna of Yellowstone National Park changed when wolves were removed from the ecosystem in the early 20th century. She also explains what happened when the wolves were returned to the park decades later. Take a moment to read one student's written response to this book in Figure 6.1. What do you notice about this student's grasp of the author's main idea?

You may have noticed that the student's response reveals a great deal of thinking about the content in *The Wolves Are Back* (George, 2008). In this short response, the student does the following:

- Names main ideas in general terms ("to show children cause [and effect]" and in more thematic terms ("the food [chain] was off [balance]" and "when the [wolves] were gone, everything was out of order").

- Provides general evidence to support these ideas ("some animals came [back] and some left" and "then everyone saw that we need [wolves]").

- Shares insight that serves to elaborate her point ("when your mom isn't [there]").

- States how her thinking changed as a result of this book.

- Emphasizes particular points with exclamation points and underlining.

- Exhibits passion for what she has learned.

While this response could be stronger, the student has clearly synthesized the information in this book. That is to say she has thought about how important details in this source are connected and drawn conclusions about what the author is trying to say. The passion

82

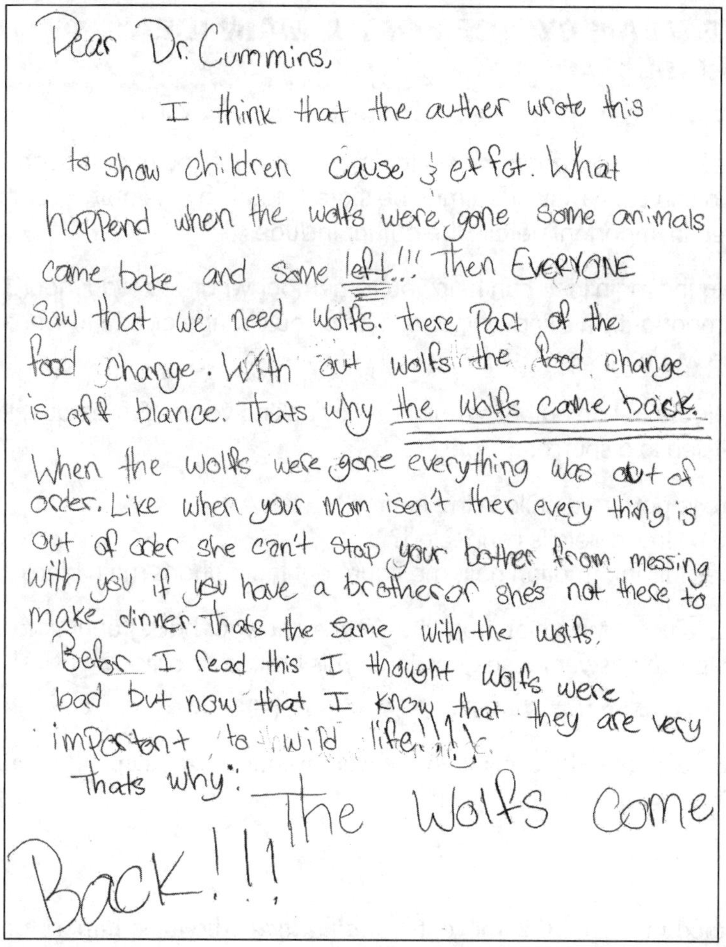

Dear Dr. Cummins,

I think that the auther wrote this to show children cause & effct. What happend when the wolfs were gone some animals came bake and some left!!! Then EVERYONE saw that we need wolfs. there Part of the food change. With out wolfs the food change is off blance. Thats why the wolfs come back.

When the wolfs were gone everything was out of order. Like when your mom isen't ther every thing is out of oder she can't stop your bother from messing with you if you have a brother or she's not there to make dinner. thats the same with the wolfs.

Befor I read this I thought wolfs were bad but now that I know that they are very important to wild life!!!

thats why: The Wolfs Come Back!!!

FIGURE 6.1. Maddie's response to *The Wolves Are Back* (George, 2008).

she exhibits reveals that somehow this information has resonated with her. This is what we want to happen for students as they read–view–listen to informational sources. Just like this student, we want our students to be able to:

- Identify important ideas in the source.
- Connect those ideas to their lives in relevant ways.
- Reflect on how this new knowledge has affected their understanding of the world.

Not all students are this engaged with sources, though. Some students do not understand how to interact with a source to identify a main or central idea; some do not realize that they need to consider how what they are learning resonates with what they already know. Others are not even clear on what we mean when we use terms like *main idea* and *synthesis* to describe what readers–viewers–listeners do. This chapter clarifies these terms for students and explores the strategies they can use to engage in this type of text analysis.

WHAT DO WE MEAN BY "IDENTIFY A MAIN IDEA" AND "SYNTHESIS"?

What: Readers know that a ***main idea*** is the most important point or thought in a source or a section of a source. A main idea may be stated clearly by the author, or the main idea may be revealed in important details the author includes.

Why: Identifying the main idea can help you remember what you read, heard, or saw in a source that is important. This knowledge can help you change or add to what you already know about the world.

How: You can figure out an author's main idea by asking yourself three questions as you read, view, or listen to a source:

- What are important details in this source?
- How are all these details connected?
- How does this information help me figure out the author's main idea?

You might have to use information from the source and your background knowledge about the world to help you answer these questions. This process is called **synthesis**!

FIGURE 6.2. Student-friendly explanation of what we mean by "identify a main idea" and "synthesis."

As described in Figure 6.2 above, the *main idea* is the most important point or thought in a source or a section of a source. There can be more than one main idea in a source. The following is an example of a main idea statement for *The Wolves Are Back* (George, 2008):

> When directors of the national parks removed the wolves from Yellowstone Park, the ecology of the park was changed. Many animals and plants disappeared as a result. When the wolves were reintroduced to the park, many animals and plants reappeared.

This example is very source-centered, meaning that it applies to this source in particular. A main idea could also be more global or thematic. A thematic statement for *The Wolves Are Back* might be:

> Removing an animal or plant can drastically change the ecology of an area.

Identifying the main ideas in a source requires the reader–listener–viewer to notice the relationships or connections between key details presented in a source. Consider how these details, presented at various points in *The Wolves Are Back* (George, 2008), are connected.

- When the wolves were removed, the elk overgrazed on the grasses the Vesper sparrow needed for food and nesting material, so the sparrow disappeared.
- When the wolves were removed, the mountain sheep moved into the valley and chewed the abundant wildflowers down to the ground, so bees and butterflies that fed on these flowers disappeared.
- When the wolves were removed, the bison overpopulated and trampled the young trees, leaving nowhere for the flycatcher to live.

Each of these details reveal an effect that occurred because the wolves were removed. As a reader begins to notice this connection, he can begin to glean a main idea. Noticing a connection requires the reader to use his own background knowledge as well as details in the source. In this case, the reader must have at least some background knowledge about the concept of cause and effect and some understanding of how a food chain works.

Identifying connections or relationships between details and using our background knowledge to help us do so is what we mean by **synthesis**. When we synthesize, we strengthen or transform our understanding of the source's topic.

 We synthesize information as we watch videos in a similar fashion. Take a look at the video produced by the NSF titled *Understanding the Ecological Role of Wolves in Yellowstone National Park* (2015). If you have a few moments to watch this short video, you can locate it with the QR code or link.

https://bit.ly/2qht3D7

The video focuses on how a team of ecologists in Yellowstone are researching the impact of the presence of wolves on the elk population. Notice how the following details, which are revealed visually and as part of the narration, are connected.

- The ecologists drive out into different parts of Yellowstone.
- They use binoculars to watch the landscape.
- Female elk are outfitted with radio collars to track their movements.
- When an elk has not moved for a while, the ecologists track it down.
- The ecologists investigate the deaths of elk to see if a wolf was responsible.

If we think about how these details are connected using our own background knowledge as well as the details from the source, we might decide that one main idea is that the team of ecologists has a variety of tools and processes that help them track the impact of the wolves on the elk population.

Similarly, when we look at infographics, we can determine a main idea based on the connection between details as well. In Figure 6.3, check out the infographic "Wolves Keep Yellowstone in Balance" created by Earthjustice (2017), a nonprofit environmental law organization. (This infographic was originally created in color; use the link or QR code below to access the full-color image.)

https://bit.ly/2GOhFFj

6. SYNTHESIS AND MAIN IDEAS

Consider the layout and design of this infographic.

- The image of the wolf is larger than the images of other animals.
- There are arrows drawn from the wolf to several different animals in the center of the infographic. Each of these images has a caption in red print with a description of what happened when the wolves were removed from Yellowstone.
- The arrows continue to another set of animals (closer to the bottom edge). Each of these images has a caption in blue print that describes what happened when the wolves returned.

Notice also that some of the language (in the red captions) describes what happened when the wolf disappeared.

- "Elk populations exploded . . . severe overgrazing."
- "Beavers virtually disappeared . . ."
- "Various scavenger species suffered . . ."
- "Coyote became an apex predator, driving down populations of . . ."

The choice of words like "suffered" and "driving down" can have negative connotations. Red is a color associated with concepts like "stop" and other types of warning signs. As readers of this infographic, we make connections between the carefully chosen details in the graphic as well as connections to what we already know about the world, connections that begin to reveal a main idea.

It is not always easy to determine a main idea. Informational sources come in all shapes and sizes and are frequently more complex than the examples I have chosen here. Many sources have more than one main idea. Our background knowledge also influences which main idea will surface for us. "Noticing connections between details" may be enough with some sources. Other sources require us to think about the author's perspective for writing the piece and even the context of a particular time period when the source was created. In order to figure out the main idea when we are reading, viewing, or listening to a source, we have to continuously ask questions like the following:

- Do I understand what I just read?
- What do I already know about this topic that I can use to help me think about the connections between these details?
- What do I know about how sources are structured that can help me think about the connections between these details?
- What main ideas have I explored in other sources that might be helpful here?

FIGURE 6.3. Infographic "Wolves Keep Yellowstone in Balance" created by the organization Earthjustice.

We also want students to ask questions that help them synthesize information:

- What are the important details? How are they all related, or what do they reveal?
- How is what I've gleaned from this source similar to or different from what I already knew?
- How do I need to revise what I thought I knew?
- How has my thinking changed or been transformed?

DO YOUR STUDENTS NEED TO WORK AT IDENTIFYING MAIN IDEAS?

6. SYNTHESIS AND MAIN IDEAS

Listening to students talk about what they are reading, hearing, and seeing or looking closely at what they have written in response to a source can provide clues as to whether they are synthesizing the information in the source and identifying its main ideas. What follows are questions you can ask to help you determine whether this is an area of instruction some students may need.

During conferences with individuals or small groups:

- Do students share miscellaneous details from the source that may not relate to a main idea, or do they talk about the content in a way that implies real insight?
- Do their responses include vocabulary related to global themes (e.g., *perseverance, determination, courage*) to describe what they are learning?

In evaluating students' written responses:

- Do they write only about the portions of the source they find most interesting?
- Is their writing cohesive, with a clear focus on important ideas they learned?
- Do they elaborate on how their thinking evolved, changed, or was affirmed by what they learned from a source?

Depending on your responses to these questions, your students may need support in identifying and explaining their main ideas and how their thinking has been transformed. If you are unsure of the answers to these questions, try out the lessons described in this chapter and the tools found in Figures 6.9 and 6.10, to assess students' strengths and needs. However, if you notice that your students are not able to recall or identify important details, you might wait to implement the lessons in this chapter. Instead, start by teaching the lessons in Chapter 7, "Monitoring for Meaning."

WHERE TO START?
INTRODUCE THE FRAMED PHOTOGRAPH ANALOGY

Do you have a framed photograph somewhere on your desk at school or at home? What or who is in that photograph? Why did you decide to frame that photograph? Chances are you have lots of pictures of the person, animal, or place shown in that photograph, but there is something special about this particular photograph that made you want to frame it. Maybe the photograph represents a special day in your life that you want to remember, like a wedding or a family trip. Maybe it is the best photograph you have of a beloved dog, cat, or horse. There is something about how the details came together in that picture that made you want to frame it. In other words, the photograph has a main idea or important point.

When you read George's book *The Wolves Are Back* (2008), you will notice that she has arranged familiar facts in such a way as to convey a specific message. The details in this book are similar to details in a photograph; they are connected to each other and to a bigger idea. The message George conveys in this book or her main idea is the frame. Think about what you do when you look at a photograph someone has framed.

- You notice the details in the photograph.

- You make connections between the details.

- You also make connections to what you know about important events or special people in your own life.

- Then you draw conclusions about the importance of that photograph to the person who framed it.

This process is similar to what we do when we synthesize the information in a source. Sharing this analogy might help students. Figure 6.4 on the next page is an example of a framed photograph (of my daughter and her grandfather) that illustrates what I might say to students to introduce this analogy.

This analogy can be introduced to students during Phase 2—Meet the Strategies of the three-phase lesson plan for learning. After a brief discussion of this analogy, students read–view–listen to the selected source or part of that source again and ask themselves these important questions:

- What are details that seem important?
- How are these key details connected?
- How does this information help me figure out the author's main idea?

For tips on how to introduce and apply this analogy when listening to videos, see Figure 6.5 on page 91.

An introduction to the frame analogy might sound like this:

What do you notice in this framed photograph? [Pauses for response.] Yes! It is a picture of my daughter Anna and her grandfather, whom she calls Popsy. What else do you notice? [Pauses for response.] Yes. They are at a playground. She is sitting on his shoulders and her hands are on his head. They are both smiling.

Why do you think I framed this photograph? [Gives students a chance to respond.] These are two special people in my life who are also special to each other. That was during a trip we took to see my dad and I want to remember how they played together.

We call what you just did "synthesis." You looked at all of the details in the photograph and thought about how they are connected. For example, you probably noticed the playground equipment behind them and that Anna and her grandfather are dressed for warmer weather. You used the details you noticed and your background knowledge to infer that they are at a park or playground. Then you thought about why this photograph is important enough to frame and put on my desk. When we read, view, or listen to a source to identify a main idea, we engage in the same process. The key details are the details in a photograph and the main idea is the frame.

Today we will synthesize the information in one source to identify the main idea. While we think about the framed photograph analogy, we will ask ourselves three questions: (1) What are details that seem important?; (2) How are all these key details connected?; and (3) How does this information help me figure out what the author or creator of this source thinks is important to learn?

FIGURE 6.4. Example of a teacher think-aloud with framed photograph analogy.

Answering these questions may require students to consider thematic or "transferable" concepts (Wiggins & McTighe, 2005, p. 74) like *injustice, perseverance,* and *vulnerability.* These are concepts that can be applied across content areas and with all types of sources. Having vocabulary to describe these concepts is a key factor in students' being able to advance their understanding of making connections between important details in order to identify a main idea. Understanding these words includes being able to clearly define them. For example, if a student can define the word *balance* as "having the right amount of something—not too much or too little—which leads to harmony or evenness" (*Vocabulary.com*), then they are more likely to recognize the main idea in *The Wolves Are Back* (George, 2008). In addition, they are more likely to have the language needed to explain their thinking. They can use phrases like "having the right amount of something" or words like *harmony* to explain why wolves are an important part of the ecosystem in Yellowstone National Park. Figure 6.6 lists examples of words and phrases that help students identify main ideas. This vocabulary can be introduced during Phase 1—Meet the Source of the plan for learning, at the beginning of Phase 2, or as part of a larger unit of study in the content areas. (See Chapter 5, Figure 5.4, for tips on introducing these words.)

Video Tips

- Make clear to students that the framed photograph analogy can apply to video as well (see Figure 6.4). The details in the video (like the details in the photograph) come together in a way that conveys the author or creator's main idea (the frame).

- Teach students to notice that *sometimes* the introduction to a video will allude to a main idea. For example, in the video about the wolves (NSF, 2015), the narrator asks the question "How has the park's ecosystem responded to the return of the wolves?" This question becomes the central focus of the video. A main idea in this video is that the wolves influence the number of elk in the park and the movement and behavior of elks.

- Teach the students to notice that *sometimes* the conclusion of a video will allude to a main idea. For example, in the video about wolves, the narrator states, "Fuller understanding of what's happening here could translate to better predator management decisions all over the globe." This is another main idea that can be supported with the numerous details in the video about the work of the scientists and the conclusions they can draw as a result.

- Ask the students to watch a video as a whole while asking the question, "What does the creator of this video want me to know that is important?" After they watch the video, list several "big ideas" they generate on a dry-erase board and then choose one to consider as you watch the video again. Be prepared to think aloud. If needed, model for students noticing a part of the video that supports the main idea the group chose. Think aloud about what you learned from that part and how the details support the main idea.

FIGURE 6.5. Tips for teaching students to identify main ideas in videos.

• perseverance, tenacity	• community	• discovery, curiosity
• humanitarianism	• global citizenship	• change, circle of life, metamorphosis, transformation
• cooperation	• friendship, alliance, harmony, solidarity	
• education		• innovation
• compassion, benevolence, empathy	• courage, endurance, determination	• communication
• destruction, displacement	• hope	• dangers of ignorance, knowledge versus ignorance
• empowerment	• survival	
• rebirth, renewal, restoration	• fear, trepidation, reverence	• progress, breakthrough, momentum
• reunion	• injustice, oppression, tyranny	• essential role of _____ in the system of _____
• collective wisdom, capacity	• peaceful, nonviolent, placid, amicable	
• complexity, diversity	• surmounting obstacles	• similarities and differences between _____ and _____
• adaptation	• vulnerability	
• instigation, agitation, disturbance, perturbation		• unique, distinct

FIGURE 6.6. Examples of language students might use to describe an author's main ideas.

HOW DO WE PLAN AND TEACH
FOR IDENTIFYING A MAIN IDEA?

My first recommendation is to locate a source that has at least one clear main idea and then to read the text (or watch the video) for yourself and write out one or more main idea statements. This source could be a book or article that you would like to read aloud to the students. (For tips on choosing books to read aloud, see Chapter 4, pp. 56–57.) This initial preparation will make planning for instruction easier. It may also help you determine if you need to introduce any vocabulary words, as discussed earlier.

Then you can use the three-phase plan to guide you in planning lessons with this source. To help you picture what this plan might look like in the classroom, there is a sample lesson in Figure 6.7 describing how one teacher implemented this plan with a read-aloud of *The Wolves Are Back* (George, 2008). The teacher chose to read this book aloud because doing so eased the students' cognitive load so that they could focus on how what they are learning reveals a main idea. (The lessons described could easily work with a short text the students read on their own, an infographic they viewed, or a video they watched.) These lessons were part of a content-area unit of study about human impacts on Earth's systems. Using a source that relates to a current unit of study also eases the cognitive load because the students have background knowledge that they have gained during other lessons (as part of this unit) that they can apply to making sense of the source.

Sometimes it is easier to help students begin to identify main ideas *after* they have read or viewed a source for the first time instead of *as* they read–view–listen. Most students finish that first reading, viewing, or listening with some inkling of what the author or creator thought was important. With this initial understanding of a main idea in mind, they can more easily look for key details that support this idea. During Phase 2, in this sample lesson, the teacher does just this, generating with students a list of possible main ideas before discussing how to confirm a main idea.

Another critical aspect of the Phase 2 lesson is the language the teacher uses to describe what readers know about main ideas (e.g., "I know a main idea is . . ."), why readers need to think about the main ideas in a source (e.g., "I am more likely to remember what is important . . ."), and how readers identify main ideas (e.g., "When I am trying to identify a main idea, I . . ."). She has posted similar language on an anchor chart. For some students this type of language opens a window onto what readers need to do to strategically process information in a source. The teacher's think-aloud about how she identified main ideas opens the window even wider. Phrases like "I am going to ask myself," "I am thinking that," and "I actually didn't know" can create clarity for students about the kind of thinking they need to do for themselves.

To help you plan a lesson of your own, Figure 6.8 (pp. 96–97) includes important points to consider as you plan each phase.

TEACHING Phase 1—*Meet the Source*
1. Introduce and preview the source.
The teacher shares the title and cover of the book *The Wolves Are Back* (George, 2008). She asks the students to think about what they have learned so far during a unit of study on the impacts of humans on the Earth's systems and the title of this book to help them predict what the book will be about. The students chat in small groups for a few moments.   Before the teacher begins to read the book aloud, she gives the students a clear purpose for listening: *What do you think the author wants to teach you that is important? What in the book makes you think so?* She posts these questions for all students to view.
2. Read–view–listen and confer.
After she reads several pages aloud, the teacher stops and asks partners to talk about what they have learned so far that they think is important to remember.   She leans in to listen to pairs talk. She notices that one pair of students does not understand why the author thinks that the wolves scaring the elk back up into the mountains was a positive effect of returning the wolves to Yellowstone. The teacher shares the relevant page in the book and coaches the pair in making sense of the information. The elks had overgrazed on the grasses that the Vesper sparrow needed for food and nesting material.   The teacher regroups with all of the students to finish reading the book aloud.
3. Discuss.
She closes by returning to the purpose for listening. She gives the students a few moments to consider the posted question: *What do you think the author wants to teach you that is important? What in the book makes you think so?* In trios, the students discuss their thinking. The teacher leans in to listen to one group talk. She shares highlights from their discussion when the students regroup with her.

TEACHING Phase 2—*Meet the Strategies*
1. Explain and model strategic reading–viewing–listening.
The teacher starts by sharing the framed photograph analogy to make sure the students understand what is meant by "identify a main idea" and "synthesis." She uses an explanation similar to the one in Figure 6.4.   Then the teacher posts an anchor chart with a student-friendly explanation for identifying main ideas like the one in Figure 6.2 for the students to read. She then says: *I know that a main idea is the most important point or thought in a text. If I can identify a main idea, then I am more likely to remember what I read or learned that is important.*   *When I am trying to identify a main idea, I use multiple strategies. I need to ask questions like the three posted here* [refers to chart] *and I need to think about what I already know about the topic or the world and how that background knowledge might help me.*   Next, the teacher asks the students if they think the book *The Wolves Are Back* (George, 2008) has a main idea or a frame. With the students, she generates a few main idea statements and writes them on the board.

(continued)

- When an environment or habitat changes, some animals survive and some do not.
- Wolves were good for the environment at Yellowstone National Park.
- Sometimes humans make decisions that are not good for the environment.

The teacher states that they will return to these ideas a little later. First, she will share what she has been thinking about in terms of a main idea. She begins her think-aloud with a statement such as the following:

> As I read the book The Wolves Are Back, I began to think one of the main ideas is that the wolves are a critical part of the ecosystem in Yellowstone National Park.

She pauses to write this statement near the list on the board for all students to view.

Then she points to the questions on the anchor chart and says:

> I am going to ask myself this first question, "What are the important details in this source?" I am thinking about two details I learned from this book that might be important. One is that when the wolves were gone, the elk had no predators and so there were a lot of them. They ate a lot of the grass that the sparrows needed and those birds disappeared as a result. This was an effect of the wolves being gone, so I think it's important. I actually didn't know this before reading this book. I'm going to write notes with just a few words to help me remember this detail.

The teacher pauses to jot a note under the main idea statement she had written previously. She writes the words *elk ate grass that sparrow needed*.

She continues thinking aloud:

> I also learned that when the wolves were gone, the bison population grew too. They ruined the trees the flycatcher lives in, and so this bird disappeared, too. I'm going to jot down a few more notes.

The teacher writes the words *bison ruined trees that flycatcher needed*. Now her notes look like the following:

Wolves are a critical part of the ecosystem in Yellowstone National Park.
- Elk ate grass that sparrow needed
- Bison ruined trees flycatcher needed

Then she returns to the anchor chart and points to the second and third questions.

> How are these details connected? When I think about what I know about the world or activate my background knowledge, I know that when animals can't eat or don't have a place to live they may die or move someplace else. I'm thinking that both of these details are examples of the bad or negative effects of removing the wolves from Yellowstone.

> [Points to the third question on the anchor chart.] What does this make me think the author's main idea is? [Pauses to reread her notes.] The wolves are a critical part of the ecosystem. If they are not present, then other animals will die or disappear. That's what I was thinking initially, but now I have proved it to myself. Do you agree? [Some students respond in agreement.] And I didn't know these specific details, the actual impact of the wolves being gone. I can add this to what I already know. This whole process of thinking through details that support a main idea and thinking about how that affects my knowledge of the world is called synthesis! Now let's try doing this together.

(continued)

FIGURE 6.7.

2. Practice with sections of the source.
The teacher asks the students to each choose a main idea statement for the book. They can choose one from the list they generated earlier in the lesson, including the one the teacher added and thought aloud about, or they can draft another. (In some cases, a teacher might ask the whole class to choose the same main idea statement, or she might assign a statement to the whole class.)
Students choose and write a main idea statement in their notes. The teacher reads aloud several pages in the book again, pausing every few pages to let the students discuss with a partner key details from that part of the book that might support their main idea statement. They take notes. The teacher leans in to support individuals as needed.
3. Discuss.
One at a time, the teacher presents two discussion prompts for small groups to discuss.
Let's think back to the framed photograph analogy. What was the author's frame or main idea for this book? What were the key details? Use your notes to help you explain what you learned.
The groups discuss how the framed photograph analogy is helpful when thinking about what we mean by "main idea" and "synthesis." Then the teacher closes by referring back to the anchor chart and saying, *I think we also proved that slowing down to think about an author's main ideas can help us not only remember what we read or heard, but it can also help us think about why what we learned is important.*

TEACHING Phase 3—*Meet the Response*
1. Introduce prompt for the response.
The teacher posts and briefly discusses the following prompt for writing: *What is one of the author's main ideas? What in the book made you think so? Be sure to explain your thinking.*
2. Plan and rehearse.
The teacher asks the students to look back at their notes taken during the Phase 2 lesson to think about what they might include in their response; she directs them to circle at least one detail they want to explain in their response. Then she asks them to turn and talk to a partner about what they plan to write.
3. Write and confer.
The teacher leans in to support individual students. She notices that several students need extra support in explaining how the textual evidence supports the main idea. She will follow up on this in later lessons. When the students are done writing, she asks them to find a new partner and share what they have written.

FIGURE 6.7. *(continued)*

PLANNING Phase 1—*Meet the Source*
1. Introduce and preview the source.
• Locate a source that has a clear main idea and supporting key details. • Plan a purpose for reading or viewing the source a first time. A simple example is, *What do you think the author wants to teach you that is important?* Prepare for how you will post this purpose for all students to view. • Plan an introduction to the source. (See Chapter 5 for suggestions.)
2. Read–view–listen and confer.
If you are reading aloud a text or watching a video, determine the point(s) at which you will pause and ask students to turn and talk about what they have learned.
3. Discuss.
• Plan to return to the purpose you gave students for reading or viewing. • Think about a teaching point you might share with the students. This might emerge while you are conferring with students.

PLANNING Phase 2—*Meet the Strategies*
1. Explain and model strategic reading–viewing–listening.

• The purpose for close reading will be to identify a main idea.
• Create an anchor chart with the *what, why,* and *how* related to identifying main ideas. (See Figure 6.2 for guidance.)
• Plan an introduction and think-aloud that includes the following:
  ○ Explaining the framed photograph analogy (see Figure 6.4 for an example of what you might say).
  ○ Stating the *what, why,* and *how* related to identifying main ideas.
  ○ Stating what you think a main idea in the source (read during Phase 1) is.
  ○ Identifying one or two parts of the source that made you think this is the main idea and why.
  ○ Jotting down notes (in front of the students) about those parts.

2. Practice with sections of the source.
• Plan for whether the students will continue identifying details that support the main idea you presented or whether they will generate their own main idea. • If you have chosen to read a book aloud or watch a video, plan for how you will help students access this source again.
3. Discuss.
• Develop a discussion question related to strategic processing. For example, you might ask, "What did you learn today about identifying a main idea? Why is that important?" • Create a prompt related to content learned from the source. For example, you might say, "If you went home and told someone about what you learned from this source today, what would you say? Use your notes to help you explain what you learned."

(continued)

PLANNING Phase 3—*Meet the Response*
1. Introduce prompt for response.
What will be the prompt for writing? You might consider these examples: • *What was one main idea in this source? Why do you think so? Use details from the source to support your thinking.* • *When you go home tonight, who can you tell about what you learned today? Write a paragraph that explains what you learned and why it's important.*
2. Plan and rehearse.
• Decide how students will plan for writing. Possible options include circling key details in their notes that they want to include in their response or talking with a partner about what they want to say in their response. • Plan for how you will help students who need extra support during writing. One option is to write part of a response together and then let the students finish the rest of the response on their own.
3. Write and confer.
What will you try to notice when you lean in to confer with writers? A clearly written main idea statement? Evidence in the form of details from the source?

FIGURE 6.8. *(continued)*

HOW DO WE ASSESS?

We can learn a great deal about students' understanding of the main ideas in a source by leaning in to confer with individuals as they are reading, taking notes, or writing in response to the source. When you listen to a student talk about what she or he is learning during a Phase 2 lesson about how to determine the main idea, try to notice something the student is doing well or attempting to do and then share what you noticed. Your comments might sound like one of the following statements:

- You seem to be tackling the kind of thinking we talked about during my think-aloud.
- It sounds like it helped when you went back to the source to look for key details.
- It seems like you have used the questions on the anchor chart as a guide for helping you determine the main idea.

Then choose one teaching point based on what you noticed. Figure 6.9 on the next page provides suggestions for what to notice and how to respond when you confer with students while they are reading–viewing–listening and taking notes about a source.

Another opportunity to assess students' understanding is during your analysis of their written responses (Cummins & Stallmeyer-Gerard, 2011). Figure 6.10 on page 99 describes the characteristics of students' responses at four stages of development. When you use this continuum to assess a student's written response, you might notice characteristics from more than one stage or level. For example, Maddie's response at the beginning of this chapter has characteristics from both the meeting and exceeding stages. The object is not to decide for certain which stage the student's work fits into, but rather to consider where he or she is on the continuum and how to move the student forward. This

FIGURE 6.9. Synthesis and Main Ideas: Conferring scenarios and suggestions for coaching.

Scenario	Examples of student language	How you can respond
The student is unclear about what a main idea in the source may be.	"I don't know."	Return to the source and engage the student in reading–viewing–listening to a section of the source that reveals the main idea or that is important in gleaning the main idea. Continue with prompts like: • *What did you just learn?* • *Why do you think the author thought this was important to include in this source?* • *What other parts of the source are connected to this part?* If needed, think aloud about what you learned, why you think this section is important, and your own thinking related to a possible main idea in the source.
The student identifies a main idea, but does not share any supporting details from the source.	"It's about when humans removed the wolves, some animals disappeared."	Possible prompts: • *What information in the source made you think this?* • *What are details in the source that support this idea?* If the student is unclear, return to the source and engage the student in rereading–viewing–listening for specific details that support this idea.
The student states the topic instead of a main idea.	"It's about the wolves in Yellowstone."	Possible prompts: • *Tell me more about what you learned.* • *What's important about how this happened?* • *There are lots of sources about this topic. What did this author-creator want to say about this topic that's important for us to think about?* Discuss the difference between a topic and a main idea. Return to your anchor chart with the definition of main idea.
The student shares supporting details from the source, but only in very general terms and with no domain-specific vocabulary.	"It's about how the wolves came back, and so some other animals could come back, too."	Possible prompts: • *When you talk or write about what you learned, you can create a more vivid picture for someone by including specific details.* • *Let's look back at the source and think about specific details you can use to convey or describe what you learned. This will help you remember what you learned as well.*

Stage	Characteristics of Written Responses
Attempting	• Student simply identifies the topic. • Student attempts to identify the topic, but writing is unclear (see Greg's response in Figure 6.11). • Writing appears to be in stream-of-conscious style or lacks a clear focus and organization.
Approaching	• Student identifies a very simple main idea with some general evidence; the main idea stated may not get at the larger ideas in the source (see Juliana's response in Figure 6.12). • Response includes some elaboration but may not make clear the connections between the evidence and the main idea (i.e., the reader of the response may have to infer what the student means). • Some organization or natural flow is evolving in the student's writing.

Meeting	• Student identifies a main idea (that may have a thematic quality to it) with supporting evidence.
	• There is some elaboration on how the main idea and evidence are connected (see Katelyn's response in Figure 6.13).
	• Elaboration on how the evidence cited supports the main idea may include (but is not limited to):
	  ○ Reference to the structure of the source (such as compare–contrast or cause–effect)
	  ○ How the student's thinking changed as he engaged in synthesis
	  ○ Connections to the student's own ideas/experiences or other sources or world events that share similarities with or differences from the ideas in this source
	• Organization is clear; elaboration has a mostly integrated quality or does not appear to be "tacked on."

Exceeding	• Explanation of main ideas moves beyond the source to global themes, including both evidence from the source and from beyond the source. • Elaboration is surprisingly insightful and novel in some way (see Maddie's response in Figure 6.1 at the beginning of this chapter).

FIGURE 6.10. Stages of development in students' written responses focused on "Identifying a Main Idea."

continuum can be a dynamic tool that you can change and revise as you analyze your students' responses and as they grow in their ability to respond thoughtfully to sources. Figures 6.11 (on the next page), 6.12 (page 101), and 6.13 (page 102) are additional examples of student responses at different stages.

WHAT DOES FOLLOW-UP INSTRUCTION LOOK LIKE?

Giving students the time to master identifying main ideas can make a huge difference in achievement. Getting a firm grip on what's involved in identifying a main idea takes time. This is a point for instruction that you may need to return to several times during the course of a school year. With responsive instruction, students can develop their ability to think critically and respond clearly. In the case of the lesson with *The Wolves Are Back*

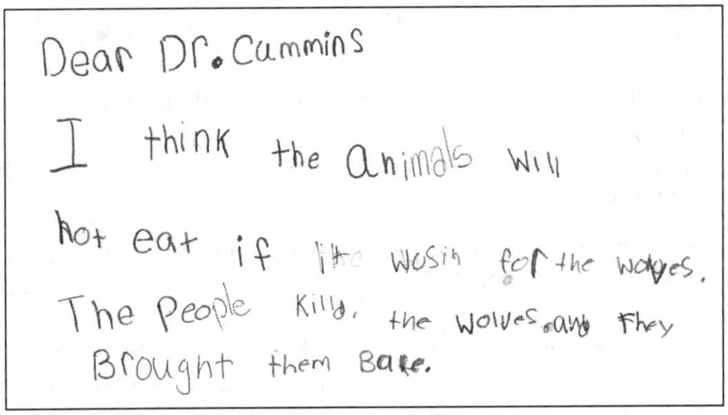

> Dear Dr. Cummins
>
> I think the animals will not eat if it wasin for the wolges. The People Killd. the wolves aand They Brought them Bare.

Greg wrote these words in response to a read-aloud of *The Wolves Are Back* (George, 2008). In the statement "I think the animals will not eat if it [wasn't] for the wolves," Greg reveals some grasp of the author's main ideas. He seems to realize that the wolves are important to the survival of the other animals and appears to understand that there is a cause-and-effect issue at hand.

How could we move Greg forward in his learning during the next lesson?

● To encourage a clearer explanation of the author's central idea, meet with him one-on-one and ask him to share orally what the first sentence of his new written response will be—a sentence that clearly states the author's central idea. Coach Greg in shaping his thinking orally, and then ask him to repeat the sentence a couple of times before writing it down.

● To encourage Greg to include supporting evidence from the text, meet with him one-on-one and write bulleted notes on a scrap piece of paper while Greg shares. Then, give him your notes to refer to when writing his response.

FIGURE 6.11. Example of response at the *attempting* stage.

(George, 2008), when the teacher analyzed the students' written responses, she noticed that they were clearly getting the main idea of the source. However, there were some clear teaching points she needed to integrate into the next lesson, such as:

- Using domain-specific vocabulary or more-detailed terms to describe various animals and plants (e.g., elk, flycatcher, aspen)
- Using specific details from the source
- Using theme-related vocabulary words to identify the author's main ideas

In response, the teacher located another source, a book titled *The Prairie Builders* (Collard, 2005), and planned another set of lessons using the three-phase plan for learning. For Phase 2, her lesson included the following components:

- She reviewed the framed photograph analogy.
- She reread part of the source (placed on the document camera for all students to view).
- Then she thought aloud about what details were important to remember and about specific words she could pull from the source.
- And she modeled writing notes about these details.

FIGURE 6.12. Example of response at the *approaching* stage.

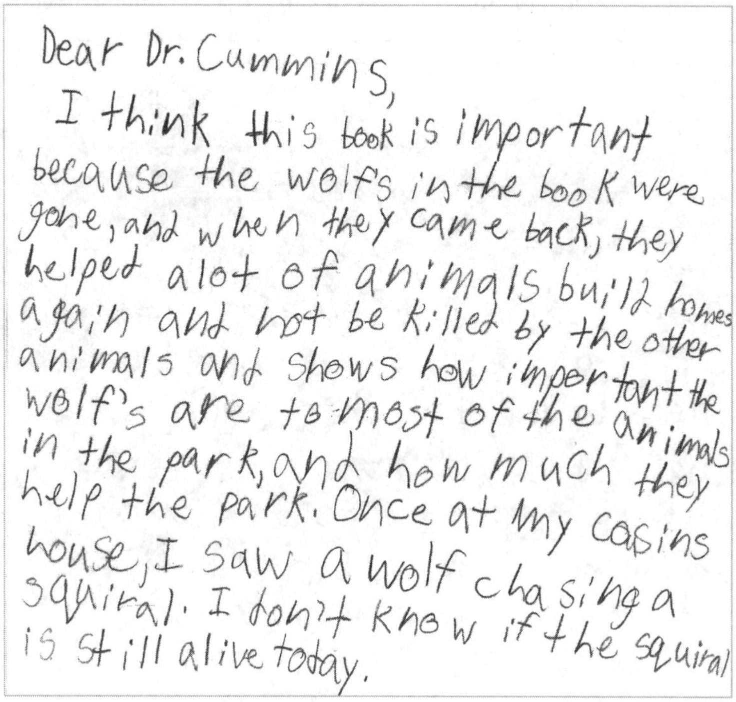

> Dear Dr. Cummins,
> I think this book is important because the wolfs in the book were gone, and when they came back, they helped a lot of animals build homes again and not be killed by the other animals and shows how imporrtant the wolf's are to most of the animals in the park, and how much they help the park. Once at my cosins house, I saw a wolf chasing a squiral. I don't know if the squiral is still alive today.

In Juliana's response to *The Wolves Are Back* (George, 2008), she has made a very literal interpretation of the author's main idea, as revealed in her statement "the [wolves] in the book were gone, and when they came back, they helped." The reader of Juliana's response has to infer to some extent that the return of the wolf population to Yellowstone National Park had a positive impact on the other species inhabiting this area. Juliana includes some supporting evidence from the book, but only in very general terms like "they helped a lot of animals build homes again." Her final statement about the wolf she spotted at her cousin's house was an attempt to connect all of what she had learned to her own experiences. She might not have had the background knowledge to do this successfully, but her attempt nonetheless could be built on in future lessons.

How could we move Juliana and others with similar responses forward?

- To make sure she is grasping enough of the domain-specific (i.e., content-area) terms (like *elks*, *Vesper sparrows,* and *aspen trees*) from the read-aloud to incorporate them into her writing, read the text aloud again, walk back through the text with the whole class or a small group, and then list the key new vocabulary words on the board for them to refer to while writing.

- To enable Juliana to make a clear statement about the author's central idea at the beginning of her response, engage her and a small group of students with similar needs in a *shared writing* of an introductory sentence when they start a new response. Then they can use this sentence to start their own response or write a similar one of their own.

- To encourage Juliana to gather supporting evidence in the text, moving from the general ("animals build homes") to the specific ("Vesper sparrows build nests"), engage her in a one-on-one conference where she shares her thoughts orally (with prompting as needed). Take bulleted notes on a sticky note and leave it with her to use when she writes. Later, with her permission, use her first response and her new response (with more specific details) as a mini-lesson for other students to consider.

FIGURE 6.13. Example of response at the *meeting* to *exceeding* expectations stages.

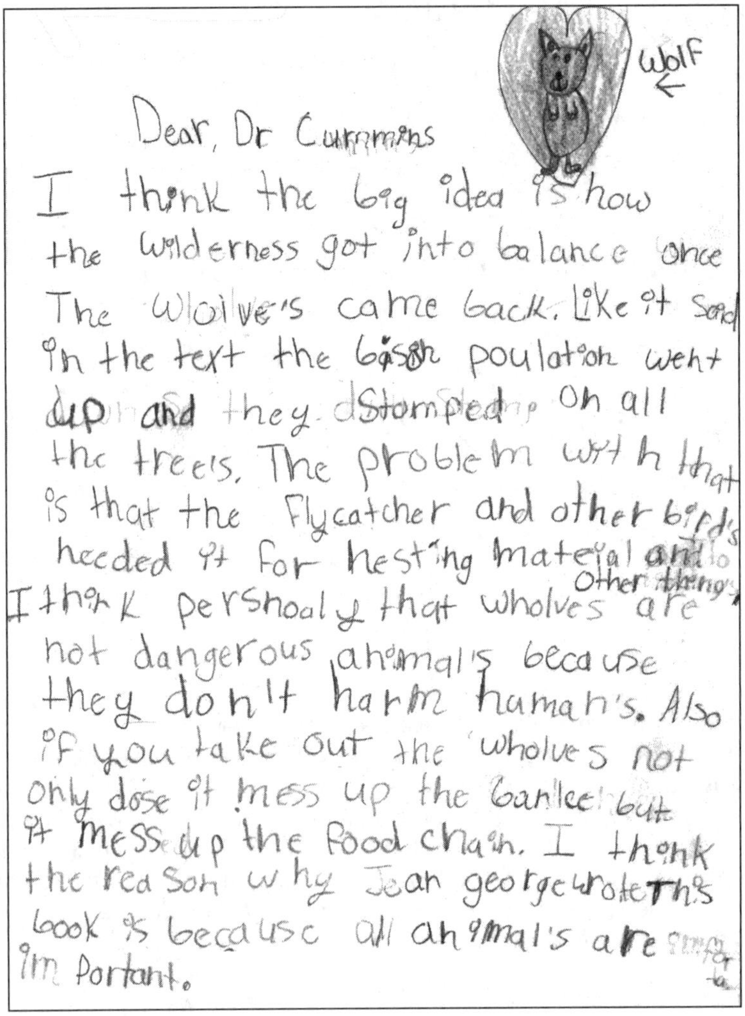

Dear, Dr Cummens

I think the big idea is how the wilderness got into balance once The Wolve's came back. Like it said In the text the bison poulation went up and they stomped on all the trees. The problem with that is that the Flycatcher and other birds needed it for nesting mateal and other things. I think persnoaly that wholves are not dangerous anmal's because they don't harm human's. Also if you take out the wholves not only dose it mess up the Banlee but it mess up the food chain. I think the reason why Jean george wrote This book is because all anmal's are imPortant.

Katelyn's response gets at the main idea in *The Wolves Are Back* (George, 2008) and shares how her thinking changed as she synthesized the content of George's book. She also includes specific supporting details from the book ("Like it said in the text the bison [population] went up and they stomped on all the trees. The problem with that is that the flycatcher and other birds needed it for nesting material and other things.").

How could we move Katelyn and others with similar responses forward?

- Provide opportunities for Katelyn to think about how the main ideas in this source apply to other contexts.
- Introduce vocabulary students can use to explain global themes (see Figure 6.6) and provide opportunities for students to integrate this vocabulary into related discussions.

Then she drew the students into following this approach with her support and then on their own. Figure 6.14 is a response written by Jasmine during the lessons with *The Wolves Are Back* (George, 2008) and my analysis of that response. Figure 6.15 on the next page is a response written by Jasmine during the follow-up series of lessons with *The Prairie Builders* (Collard, 2005). Take a moment to notice the difference as you read my analysis of these two responses. In contrast to Jasmine's first response, her second response reveals a more thoughtful analysis of the author's ideas, and she includes specific details from the source to support her thinking. With just one lesson, by targeting

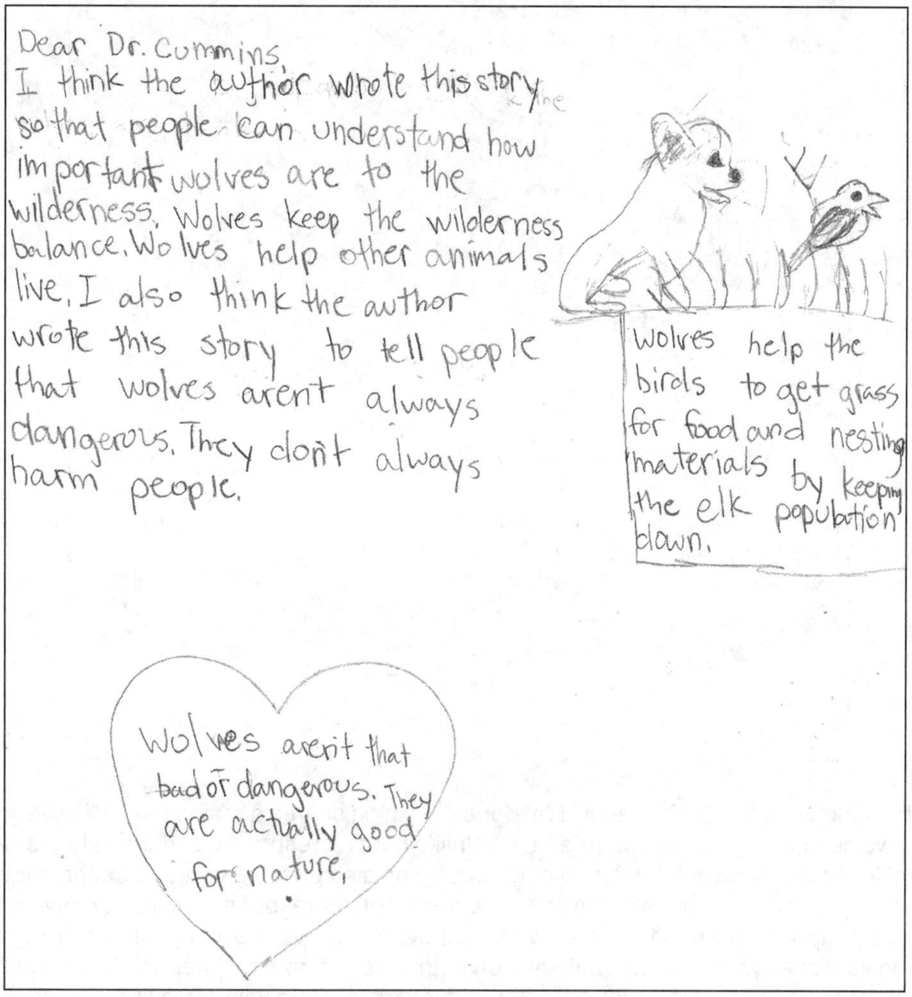

Dear Dr. Cummins,
I think the author wrote this story so that people can understand how important wolves are to the wilderness. Wolves keep the wilderness balance. Wolves help other animals live. I also think the author wrote this story to tell people that wolves arent always dangerous. They dont always harm people.

Wolves help the birds to get grass for food and nesting materials by keeping the elk population down.

Wolves arent that ~~bad or~~ dangerous. They are actually good for nature.

In this first response Jasmine identifies the main idea in very literal terms—"so that people can understand how important wolves are to the wilderness." Her response discusses mostly the main ideas in the text, and the evidence is stated in general terms—"Wolves help other animals live." The caption under the picture of the wolf pup does include more specific details than are shared in the body of the entry ("Wolves help the birds to get grass for food and nesting materials by keeping the elk population down").

FIGURE 6.14. Jasmine's written response during the first lesson.

FIGURE 6.15. Jasmine's written response during the second series of lessons.

> Dear Dr. Cummins,
> I think the big idea of the story is that we need to bring back the praires. We need to bring it back so that children can see what thier land was once. I also think this because animals that was once there are now gone and we need to get them back here. It makes me sad that most of the animals left when the praires were gone. But I was happy when all this people came to bring back the praires. I mean engineers, architects, a biologist, a congressman, scientist, volunteers, and many more helped. I was suprised that all this people came. I also was suprised at what they did. They burned the land. I thought that fire is bad but this made me change my mind a little bit. The fire clears away the Dead vegitation and many larger woody plants. I hope that once more the praires will be back.

> They helped the animals get back to the prairie and live there once more.

As with her first response, in the second response Jasmine shares a main idea (still in very literal terms)—"we need to bring back the [prairies]." Unlike her first response, she then shares why: "so that children can see what their land once was." She also goes on to touch on three ideas in the text. With some inferences required by the reader of her response, Jasmine conveys that the animals disappeared when the prairie was destroyed and "we need to get them [the animals] back." She continues with her personal reaction to this state of affairs. Then she moves on to address the number of people it took to restore the prairie—being very specific in her choice of words—and shares her surprise at this response. She also discusses how her thinking about the burn method shifted. She closes with her hope "that once more the prairies will be back."

There is a natural logical flow, as Jasmine first relates the author's ideas and then integrates her reactions to those ideas. She is now ready to be instructed on how best to break these ideas up into paragraphs and how to develop her thoughts further—particularly with additional evidence from the text to support her own points and the use of domain-specific vocabulary to describe evidence from the source.

her needs (as well those of other students in the classroom), her capacity for responding in a clear, meaningful way has been expanded.

Another example of how targeted opportunities to strategically close read or listen can nurture a student's thinking is revealed in Katelyn's response to the second series of lessons (in Figure 6.16). Her thinking has moved beyond the source. Her response reveals higher-level thinking about the central ideas, and even global thinking, as she considers the information in both books in the context of the world she knows.

Dear Dr. Cummins,

I was a little surprised at the beging [beginning] I tough [thought] they were burning the prairie for a bad reason but torw's [toward] the end I realized they were good people. Especialy [Especially] the coungrass man [Congressman] I thank him so much for helping are [our] earth. He search [searched] 6 years to find a praie [prairie] it took perseverance to so [do] somethink [something] like that it [is] just amazing. I think the government and everyone on earth sould [should] help the environment more. So realy [really] the true meaning of this story is help the earth try try again never give up in what you belive [believe] is right. Like it said in the "The Wolves are back" humans can mess up one large national park imange [imagine] how much they can mess up are [our] earth and how much they can do good to the environment. The congress man [Congressman] is a wonderful example of a human who is help's [helping] are [our] earth. I'm not saying go plant a whole entire praie [prairie] even thoug [though] that would be nice. Recycle, turn the sink off, take sort [short] showers these thing [things] can help animals plants and even humans.
—Katelyn

Unlike her response to *The Wolves Are Back* (in Figure 6.13), Katelyn's written response this time includes thinking that moves beyond the text. She elaborates on the central idea that we all need to help the planet Earth in some way (just as the Congressman did), but she also demonstrates how she has thought this through. She reveals that she has realized that not all of us can "go plant a whole entire prairie." She offers alternative ideas, tapping what she knows about how we can help the Earth. She makes suggestions like "recycle, turn the sink off, take [short] showers." Her drawing of a prairie burning with a ban sign is linked to the beginning of her response; when she first heard about the biologist and her volunteers burning the farmland to begin the restoration project, she thought this was wrong. Her second drawing shows how her thinking changed as she listened more closely and realized the biologist was just using a traditional Native American method for stimulating the growth of prairie plants. Katelyn's response still needs some work, particularly in the areas of spelling and editing, but given the context of writing on demand for 25 minutes, this response reveals higher-level thinking about the central ideas in the text.

FIGURE 6.16. Katelyn's written response during the second series of lessons.

If . . .	Then . . .
Students are identifying source-centered main ideas, but they are not thinking more deeply about global themes.	• During Phase 1—Meet the Source, introduce a vocabulary word like *adaptation* or *vulnerability* that students can use to state a more thematic main idea. Use the four steps described in Chapter 5, Figure 5.4. During Phase 2—Meet the Strategies, integrate this vocabulary into a main idea statement or the discussion about main ideas. • Use sources related to a content-area unit of study that includes vocabulary-laden essential questions like, *What are the positive and negative impacts of humans on the landscape?*
Students' responses reveal some thinking about the main idea but not a firm grasp.	• Provide additional lessons (similar to the one described in Figure 6.7) with multiple sources that have the same main idea. • Share examples of strong student responses as mentors for others. Project on a document camera for students to view. Discuss specific strengths of the responses.
Students' responses lack vocabulary specific to the topic of the source.	• As students read–view–listen to a source, support them by pausing at different points to talk about specific vocabulary the author used that they might also use. List these words on a chart that students can refer to when they write a response. • Share examples of student responses that include vocabulary specific to that topic or source.
Students are not recalling details they read or hear in a source.	• Try out the lessons described in Chapter 7, "Monitoring for Meaning."
Students struggle to identify and explain important supporting details in the source.	• Give students the main idea. Then they can focus cognitive energy on identifying details. • Try out the lessons described in Chapter 8, "Identifying and Explaining Key Details."

FIGURE 6.17. Suggestions for follow-up instruction.

Figure 6.17 above provides suggestions for what follow-up instruction might look like in response to what you have noticed about your students. A key point here is that students need ample time and an abundance of opportunities to begin to grasp what we mean by "synthesis" and "identifying a main idea." In Appendix A, on page 229, you will also find a one-page guide with brief descriptions of what Phase 2 lessons focused on this strategy might look like over time. This guide can be easily used as a reference for planning and teaching.

CLOSING THOUGHTS

Discussions about main, central, or important ideas in a source should be a part of most of our instruction with informational sources—even when such discussions are not the primary objective for a lesson. For example, when we are teaching students to stop and think about whether the information they just heard in a video is new or familiar, there is still room for questions like "What did you learn today that is important to remember?" When we are teaching students to make sense of visual images or graphics, consider asking questions like "How did paying attention to this graphic help us understand the author's big idea better?" We always want to message to students that they are engaged with a source not just to practice strategic close reading, viewing, or listening, but also (and more important) to think critically about what they are learning. One way to accomplish this is to think about the author's main ideas. As you read descriptions of other lessons in this book, you will notice that returning to the bigger ideas in a source is a thread throughout.

One more important point. Synthesis is not a process that is limited to identifying main ideas. Synthesis happens in many contexts for a variety of purposes. For example, we synthesize information whenever we are thinking about a source's structure. As we skim or read or listen to a source for the first time, we begin to notice parts of the source that reveal a structure. For example, we might notice that the author presents a problem and then several possible solutions. When we think about how these parts are connected, we can begin to identify the source's structure. We also synthesize when we are trying to determine an author's point of view. Think about how you notice certain words or phrases that reveal a perspective and then draw a conclusion about what the author thinks about a particular issue or topic. My point here is that the lessons described in this chapter can be used for different purposes for reading–viewing–listening. Synthesis is examined again at various points in the rest of this book because it is a process that is critical to strategic close reading.

CHAPTER SEVEN

Monitoring for Meaning

Consider the image in Figure 7.1 of a teacher thinking aloud in front of her students. What does the teacher reveal about how she is making meaning as she reads and thinks through a tricky sentence in an informational source? You might have noticed the following:

- The teacher is stopping to think about just one sentence in the source.
- She's determining whether this sentence has information she already knew or information that is new or unfamiliar.
- She's wondering what the information in this one sentence has to do with the larger topic of this article.
- She's deciding what to write in her notes and then jotting these notes.

By thinking aloud in front of her students, this teacher is revealing how she monitors for meaning and how she makes sense of the content in a source.

This think-aloud occurred with an article titled "KABOOM!" (Ruane, 2010) about the eruption of a volcano in Iceland and the impact on people living nearby. During Phase 1—Meet the Source, the teacher noticed that the students easily recalled details from the article about how one family and their neighbors escaped the eruption. However, the students were not as clear when the teacher asked them to recall details about what caused the eruption. These details were an important part of the article and included information that would help the students understand key ideas in the article and in their unit of study on changing landscapes. The students may have been unclear about this part of the article because they did not understand the author's explanation of the Earth's structure and the physics of plate tectonics. When the teacher noticed this gap in their comprehension, she realized that she needed to model for them how readers make sense of more complex details in a source.

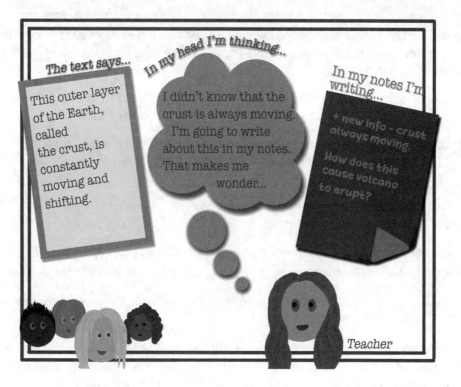

FIGURE 7.1. Example of a teacher thinking aloud.

Do you know students who do not stop to make sense of the tricky parts in a source, but just continue reading? Or students who are aware that something does not make sense, but have no idea what to do in response? These students may need instruction focused on how we monitor for meaning making and what to do when meaning breaks down.

WHAT DO WE MEAN BY "MONITORING FOR MEANING"?

Proficient readers continuously monitor for when they are and are not understanding the information in a source (Almasi & Fullerton, 2012; Cummins, 2013). As described in Figure 7.2 on the next page, there are multiple strategies we use to monitor for meaning, including asking relevant questions and tapping our background knowledge. When we do not understand part of a source, we quickly employ strategies to help us make sense of that part. To comprehend a source fully, we have to make sense of the source or comprehend at the word, sentence, and section or whole-source levels. Examples of how meaning can break down at these levels for a student include:

- Not knowing how to decode a word
- Not knowing the meaning of a word
- Not comprehending a section of the source

What: Readers know that we need to think about our thinking or *monitor for meaning* as we read or view a source. This idea means that we notice when we do and do not understand information in a source.

Why: Monitoring for meaning will help you notice when you need to stop and figure out a tricky part of a source so that you understand the rest of the source better.

How: You can help yourself monitor for meaning by reading a chunk of a source or watching a clip of a video and by asking yourself these questions:

- Is this new information?
- Do I already know this information?
- Do I understand this information?

When you don't understand, you need to use a **fix-up strategy** to help!

FIGURE 7.2. Student-friendly explanation of what we mean by "monitor for meaning."

As stated earlier, with the article "KABOOM!" (Ruane, 2010), the teacher noticed that the students were not understanding sections of the article that explained what causes a volcano to erupt. Here's an example of a paragraph that the students failed to describe in their responses or appeared to not understand during conferences with the teacher.

> The mantle lies under the crust. This layer is really hot. The heat melts rock. This magma flows like molasses in Earth.

There is a lot of information in four short sentences. To process this information our students have to tap prior knowledge about the layers of the Earth or notice and look at a diagram of the layers of the Earth provided on the next page in the text. They have to notice that the author is describing the location of the mantle (i.e., "under the crust"). In the second sentence, they have to understand the concept of "layer" and notice the word *hot* as a descriptor of the mantle. In the third sentence, they have to be able to visualize or understand conceptually how rock can melt. They have to be familiar with "molasses" in order to understand the author's comparison in the last sentence. There are several places in this short paragraph that meaning might break down for some of our students.

As part of their unit of study, the students who read the article "KABOOM!" (Ruane, 2010) about the eruption of the volcano in Iceland might also examine the infographic "Volcanoes Inside Out" created by Kids Discover (n.d.-b) in Figure 7.3. This infographic describes the physical features of a volcano like the crater and the central vent. It also reveals what happens as a volcano erupts. As you look at this infographic, consider where meaning making for our students might break down. Some may have trouble decoding words like *channel, depression,* or *surrounding.* Some may not understand the meaning of phrases like "becomes a thick, flowing substance" or "while still molten." Some may not grasp that to understand the sequence of events involved in an eruption, readers or viewers of this infographic need to start at the bottom and work their way up. If meaning

FIGURE 7.3. Infographic "Volcanoes Inside Out" created by Kids Discover (n.d.-b).

VOLCANOES ┌INSIDE┐ →OUT←

Volcanoes are like sleeping giants. After years — even centuries — of rest, they awake. Some powerful eruptions blow tops off mountains, flatten forests, and dam up rivers. Volcanoes also shape the Earth. They build islands, mountains, plains, lakes, and the ocean floor.

The roots of volcanoes lie 40 to 120 miles inside the Earth in a layer called the mantle. Temperatures there are as hot as 4000° F, so hot that rock melts like a chocolate bar on a summer day. The hot, melted rock becomes a thick, flowing substance called magma. Magma is lighter than the solid rock surrounding it, and it pushes up through cracks in the Earth.

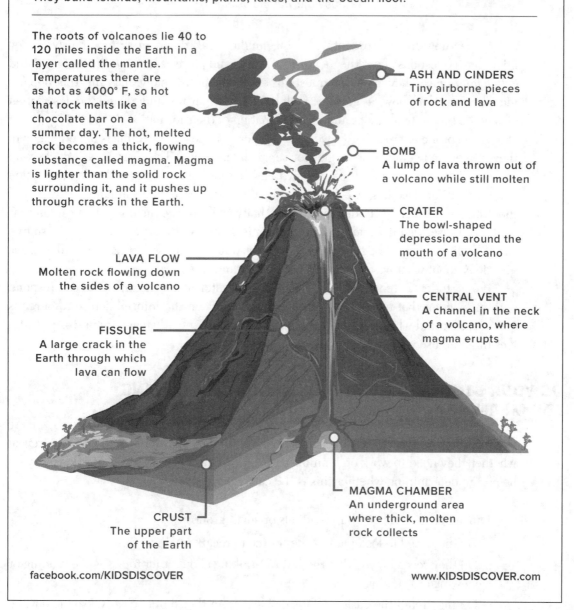

ASH AND CINDERS
Tiny airborne pieces of rock and lava

BOMB
A lump of lava thrown out of a volcano while still molten

CRATER
The bowl-shaped depression around the mouth of a volcano

CENTRAL VENT
A channel in the neck of a volcano, where magma erupts

LAVA FLOW
Molten rock flowing down the sides of a volcano

FISSURE
A large crack in the Earth through which lava can flow

CRUST
The upper part of the Earth

MAGMA CHAMBER
An underground area where thick, molten rock collects

facebook.com/KIDSDISCOVER

www.KIDSDISCOVER.com

breaks down at any of these points, the student's ability to access the bigger ideas in the source may be hindered.

 Meaning could break down in a similar way with a video. Take a few moments to watch the 2-minute National Geographic video titled *Volcanoes 101* using the QR code or link provided below.

https://bit.ly/2mhcODo

Depending on the student, meaning might break down in different ways. They might have questions about the meaning of words and phrases like *volatile, hot spot,* and *active fault lines*. They may have questions about one of the many diagrams that pop up, including one that shows a "geologic fault belt." They may not understand the description of specific types of volcanoes and the explanation of their formation.

When proficient readers, viewers, or listeners realize that meaning is breaking down, they immediately employ strategies for repairing meaning. There are a variety of fix-up strategies that we use almost effortlessly to make sense of a word or a phrase or a section of a source. For decoding, we might chunk and blend parts of an unfamiliar word and then reread to check for understanding of that word. For the meaning of an unfamiliar word or phrase, we might notice a helpful context clue. With a tricky section of a source or video clip, we might begin by rereading it or watching the video again in order to ask questions about what we did and did not understand specifically.

If our students are not actively engaged in monitoring for meaning, we can respond with instruction that helps them become aware of when the information in a source is making sense and when it is not. We may also need to explicitly teach them fix-up strategies they can use when meaning breaks down.

DO YOUR STUDENTS NEED TO WORK ON MONITORING FOR MEANING?

Conversations with our students and analysis of their written responses can reveal whether they need to work on monitoring for meaning. The following questions may be helpful in determining whether this is the case.

During conferences with individuals or small groups:

- Do they need to look back at the source to recall details?
- Do they reveal to you that they were thinking about other topics while reading or viewing or listening?
- Do they retell the easier details or ideas from the source, clearly leaving out the more complex details, ideas, or vocabulary they may not have understood?

In evaluating students' written responses:

- Does the content of their writing reveal a lack of understanding of the content in the source?
- Do they name only the topic and some general details that lack key vocabulary?
- Do they write about what they knew about the topic before reading instead of what they learned while reading?

If you find yourself responding "yes" to any of these questions, your students may benefit from instruction that focuses on helping students become aware of when they are understanding and when they are not and what to do when meaning making breaks down. If you are unsure of the answers to these questions, then I would advise you to find opportunities to talk with students as they are engaged in reading–viewing–listening to complex informational sources. You might start by saying, "Tell me a little bit about what you just learned from this source." The students' responses to these questions may reveal a need to introduce or review the concept of monitoring for meaning.

WHERE TO START? INTRODUCE THE CODING STRATEGY

We know that teaching students to think about their thinking as they read–view–listen to a source can enhance learning (Paris & Winograd, 1990). The coding strategy (adapted from Hoyt, 2008) is an activity that encourages students to stay focused on monitoring for meaning. As a student reads, views, or listens to an informational source, she is asked to consider some of the following questions:

- Is this new information for me?
- Is this information I already knew?
- Does this information contradict what I thought I knew?
- Do I understand this information? Or what are my questions?
- Does this information seem important or interesting to me?

Then the student uses codes to label her thinking. In the text, on a sticky note, or in her notes, she jots down a code and a few words to help her remember her thinking. Below are examples of codes the student might use:

+ This is new information.
* I already knew this information.
X This contradicts what I thought I knew.
? I don't understand . . . or I wonder . . .
! Wow! This is important or interesting.

These codes can be printed on a bookmark (see Figure 7.4 on the next page as an example) or written on piece of chart paper students can view easily. In the photo in

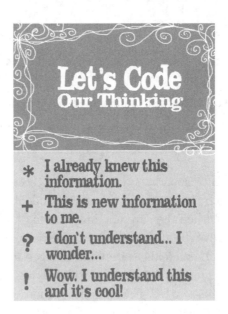

FIGURE 7.4. Sample bookmark for coding strategy.

Figure 7.5, the teacher has posted a chart with the codes (located at the bottom). The codes she has listed vary from the ones in the previous list; the teacher chose these codes to support a particular group of students who were reading a book called *Understanding Biomes* (Sturm, 2012). Notice that the teacher has included a definition for the word *biodiversity*, a theme word the students can use to explain what they are learning. The teacher has also included a very clear purpose for reading, "How do tropical rainforests help people and animals survive?" My point here is that we can use the coding strategy flexibly in a way that meets our students' needs as they learn about the bigger ideas in a source.

Initially, you might introduce only a few codes, saving others for later. As you engage students in this activity, they may also suggest new codes. This is fantastic because it shows that they are using the codes as a tool for thinking critically about what they are reading. The objective is to use codes to help students become aware of their thinking. Eventually, they should not need to "code their thinking"; instead, this kind of thinking will just be a natural part of a student's engagement with the content in a source.

After a student has chosen a code, jotting down notes that explain her thinking is critical. When I first started teaching the coding strategy, the students only wrote the code for their thinking on a small sticky note placed in the text. When I conferred with them later, though, they couldn't recall what they were thinking when they wrote that code. In response, I started asking students to write a few words or sketch an image that would trigger recall of their earlier thoughts. I modeled how to do this with a think-aloud, which seemed to help.

The coding strategy can be used with video clips as well. The video mentioned earlier, *Volcanoes 101* (National Geographic, n.d.-b), features a description of how volcanoes are formed (minute 0:20–1:20). The narrator uses a lot of domain-specific (scientific) vocabulary, and there are animated graphics of what happens when volcanoes form. Even for a more mature viewer, there's a lot of information to grapple with in this 1 minute of video. A close viewing of this 1-minute clip of the video while asking questions like "What is new information?" and "What do I not understand?" can help students understand this source better. These questions can also help them be aware of how they need to be monitoring for meaning. Figure 7.6 on the next page includes tips for teaching the coding strategy with video.

Over the years, I have also noticed that when students start to identify what they do not understand in a source, they also reveal that they do not know what to do next. It is important that we notice where their meaning making is breaking down and teach appropriate fix-up strategies in response. Toward the end of the chapter, I recommend fix-up strategies that can be explicitly taught once students have begun to notice what they do not understand. These strategies can be taught during Phase 2—Meet the Strategies of the three-phase plan for learning. You can teach the strategies as you introduce the coding strategy to students or save this objective for later lessons.

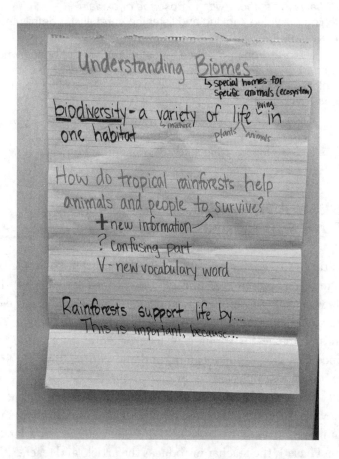

FIGURE 7.5. Example of an anchor chart that includes the vocabulary word *biodiversity* related to the theme of the book, a clear purpose for reading, and codes the students might use for support as they think about their thinking while reading.

Video Tips

- Spend time teaching students how to notice a video's parts or a video's structure. For example, in the video *Volcanoes 101* (National Geographic, n.d.-b) there is an introduction that draws in the viewer's attention (minute 0–0:20). Then the narrative begins to explain how volcanoes are formed (minute 0:20–1:20) before moving on to describing the types of volcanoes (minute 1:20–1:40). Recognizing when the narrator is moving on to a new subtopic will help students intentionally monitor for when they may need to pause the video and think through what they just learned.

- Provide the codes and ask students to give you the thumbs-up when they notice a "part" with information they already knew or new information. Pause the video when you receive the thumbs-up so students can process their thinking and jot down coded notes.

- Encourage students to notice when they do not understand a part of a video, to replay that section, and to look and listen again in a strategic way. If needed, model what this looks like. Start an anchor chart that lists strategies students can use when they do not understand a part of the video. Some of these strategies might include:
  - Play the video clip again and ask yourself, *What specifically do I not understand?*
  - If there's a word you do not understand, look and listen for context clues.
  - Ask yourself, *What is the author trying to describe or explain?*
  - Continue watching the video, looking and listening carefully for details that might help you figure out a tricky part.

- Be prepared to think aloud. You may notice that students are not noting when they do not understand a part of a video. Model how you noticed you did not understand or were unclear about a piece of information and how you made sense of this part when you replayed the video.

FIGURE 7.6. Tips for teaching students to monitor for meaning with a video.

HOW DO WE PLAN AND TEACH FOR MONITORING FOR MEANING?

Start by locating a source that would lend itself to this kind of lesson. I frequently choose sources related to a content-area unit of study. I look for sources that have some parts the students will make sense of easily and some parts that are more complex and would benefit from students "coding" as they think about their thinking.

Then return to the three-phase plan for learning as a guide for planning lessons that introduce monitoring for meaning and the coding strategy. In Figure 7.7, there is a description of a sample lesson similar to the one described earlier for the article "KABOOM!" (Ruane, 2010) that creates a picture of what teaching students to monitor for meaning with the coding strategy might look like initially. The students in this classroom are immersed in a unit of study on land formations and how landscapes change over time. During Phase 1, the teacher introduces the article and teaches the vocabulary word *shift,* which is an important word for students to understand in order to glean some of the bigger ideas in the article. Then the teacher confers with the students as they read the

FIGURE 7.7. Sample three-phase lesson on "Introducing Monitoring for Meaning and the Coding Strategy."

TEACHING Phase 1—*Meet the Source*

1. Introduce and preview the source.

The teacher gives a brief introduction to the article "KABOOM!" (Ruane, 2010) and shares a clear purpose for reading that is posted for all students to view.

- *What happens to cause volcano eruptions?*
- *What are the effects on the land, people, and animals?*

Then she takes a moment to teach the word *shifting,* which is in the article. She shares a kid-friendly definition: "to change or move to a different place." She asks the students to turn and talk with a partner about how they shift when they are sleeping or when they have been sitting for a long time. When they are done, she shares with the students that they will be learning about how parts of the Earth shifting can cause volcano eruptions. Taking a moment to teach this word expands the students' understanding of it and will help them understand the ideas in the text better.

The teacher ends the introduction by briefly reviewing the mnemonic THIEVES and asking the students to preview the article with a partner and make predictions about what they will be learning. She leans in to coach students as needed. When they have made a few predictions, she reminds them of the purpose for reading and then asks them to begin reading the article independently.

2. Read–view–listen and confer.

As the students read, the teacher confers with individuals. She notices that the students do not have a problem understanding parts of the article about the family getting out of harm's way; they can easily retell what they learned. They do, however, have difficulty paraphrasing the author's explanation of how and why a volcano erupts. It is evident that several students have read this part without making sense of it. The teacher tucks this observation away to think about when she plans Phase 2—Meet the Strategies.

3. Discuss.

The teacher closes by returning to the purpose for reading. She gives the students a few moments to consider the posted questions. Then she asks the students to turn in trios and discuss what they learned. She listens to one group talk. She notices that the group is unclear about a part of the source and coaches for problem solving. She encourages them to ask questions like *What do I already know in this part?* and *What is unfamiliar or confusing?* When the students all regroup, she asks members of the smaller group to share how they returned to the source to think through a tricky part together.

TEACHING Phase 2—*Meet the Strategies*

1. Explain and model strategic reading–viewing–listening.

The teacher starts by posting an anchor chart titled "Coding Strategy" with a student-friendly explanation for what it means to monitor for meaning (see Figure 7.2). Then she says:

Readers know that it is important to think about our thinking as we read. Monitoring for meaning means that we notice when the information is familiar or when we already know it and when the information is unfamiliar or new.

(continued)

She hands out a bookmark like the one in Figure 7.4 and explains the coding strategy.

We can help ourselves monitor for meaning by pausing after we read a sentence or section of a source (or watch a short clip of a video) and asking ourselves questions like "Is that new information or information I already knew? Do I understand this information? Do I think this information is important or interesting?" To help us remember what we thought, we can jot down one of these codes and write a few words. Watch while I do this.

Then she places a portion of the "KABOOM!" article (Ruane, 2010) on the document camera and begins to demonstrate what monitoring for meaning looks like while using the coding strategy. She does not start at the beginning of the article, though. Instead, she refers to a part of the article she noticed students were struggling to make sense of during Phase 1—Meet the Source.

 I understood the first part of this article that told me about how Hanna and her family escaped when the volcano started to erupt. I had to slow down, though, when the author started to explain what causes volcanoes to erupt. Let me show you how I did this.

The rest of her think-aloud is similar to the think-aloud revealed in Figure 7.1. She reads aloud one sentence. She stops to think through what she just learned and then thinks aloud about what notes she will write.

2. Practice with sections of the source.

After her think-aloud, the teacher hands a hard copy of the article to each student and then draws the group into a shared think-aloud by saying:

Slowing down and thinking about a word or a phrase or a sentence really helped me think carefully about what I was learning from this tricky part of the source. I think I will remember this information, too. Let's do this together with the next sentence. Take a moment to read this sentence. Give me a "thumbs-up" when you are ready to share what you're thinking.

Together, the group thinks aloud about what was familiar, unfamiliar, and maybe confusing. The students begin to write codes and a few words on a sticky note placed on the hard copy of the text. The teacher asks them to continue rereading the article, pausing at various points to think about their thinking and write coded notes. (In some cases, the teacher will assign more complex sections of a source or, with a video, everyone will tackle the same clip.) Each time she starts a conference with an individual student, the teacher says, "What did you just read? What were you thinking as you read that?"

3. Discuss.

The teacher closes by asking the students to place their sticky notes in the center of a blank piece of paper, leaving room around the edge. She reviews the framed photograph analogy for identifying a main idea. (See Figure 6.4 on p. 90 for an explanation.) She tells them to think about the sticky notes as though they are the details in a photo. Then she asks them to look at all their notes and think about why the author wrote this article. The students finish by writing a main idea statement around the edge of the paper. See Figure 7.8 on page 120 for an example of one student's coded and framed notes.

(continued)

FIGURE 7.7.

TEACHING Phase 3—*Meet the Response*
1. Introduce prompt for the response.
The teacher posts and briefly discusses the following prompt for writing: *If you had a friend who was having trouble staying focused while reading, what could you say to explain how we monitored for meaning with this article? Use the "Coding Strategy" anchor chart and some of your notes to explain your thinking to this friend. Be sure to let your friend know what you learned about volcano eruptions because you monitored for meaning.*
2. Plan and rehearse.
To help students rehearse for writing, the teacher asks them to practice explaining to a partner what it means to monitor for meaning and how to use the coding strategy. Next, the teacher tasks them with looking back at their notes and choosing one coded note they will write about as an example of how they monitored for meaning. This will be a brief response that needs to include a description of what the students learned as a result. To support the students, the teacher shares an example of a response she wrote: When I read the article "KABOOM!," I paid close attention to the meaning I was making. As I was reading, I thought about whether the details were information I already knew or were new information and whether I was understanding this information. When I read a sentence about how the outer layer of the Earth or the crust is "constantly moving and shifting," I realized that this information was new to me. I did not completely understand this until I read a little later about how the crust is broken up into plates that move against each other or away from each other. When the plates split apart, volcanoes form. Noticing that this was new information that I did not completely understand made me pay attention to what the author included next in the text to try to make sense of this new information. The teacher and the students discuss what she included in this response, and then the students begin to write their own.
3. Write and confer.
The teacher leans in to support individual students. She notices that most of the students do not write about what they did not understand or how they made sense of a part they did not understand; instead, they write about what they already knew or new information. She will follow up on this in later lessons. When the students are done writing, she asks them to share in small groups.

FIGURE 7.7. *(continued)*

article for the first time. These conferences are important because they can reveal to a teacher the parts of a source the students are struggling to make sense of and that you can closely read, using the coding strategy during Phase 2. In the sample lesson, the teacher does just this, thinking aloud about a more complex part of the source, demonstrating the use of the coding strategy as a tool for monitoring for meaning during Phase 2.

Sometimes when students engage in "coding their thinking," that objective becomes their primary focus, and they do not think about the bigger ideas in the source that they are learning as they monitor for meaning. They may finish reading with a very fragmented understanding of what they have read (e.g., "I learned this . . . I knew this . . . I didn't understand this . . ."). At the end of the Phase 2 lesson for the article "KABOOM!" (Ruane, 2010), the teacher reminds the students of the point of monitoring for meaning—to make meaning as we read *and* to develop a deeper understanding of the author's message or main ideas. She asks them to think about the framed photograph analogy she introduced in previous lessons (as described in Chapter 6). In a sense the coded notes are the details in a photograph that together (may) reveal an author's bigger idea, which is the frame in this analogy. After the teacher reviews this analogy, the students place their coded notes in the middle of a blank piece of paper and then look at their notes as a whole to help them think about what is important to learn from the source. Then they write a main idea statement around the edge of the paper. Figure 7.8 is an example of one student's framed notes.

During Phase 3—Meet the Response, the teacher shares a prompt for responding and a sample response she wrote. Frequently, students are not sure how to write a response, and a sample response or a response written with the students can launch them forward as they begin to plan for writing a response. When the teacher discusses her response with the students, she might help them notice how she used a coded note to

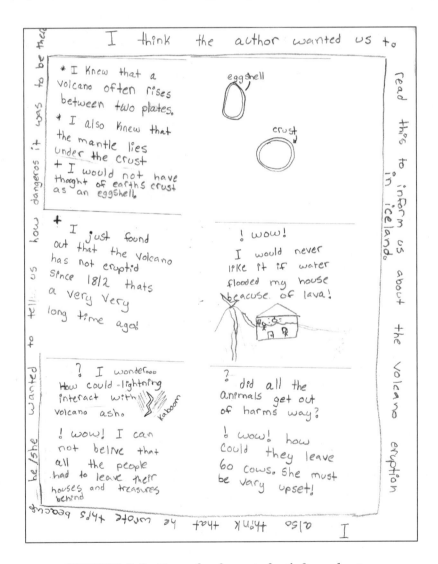

FIGURE 7.8. Example of one student's framed notes.

help her think about her response and how her response refers to how she made sense of the source and what she learned.

To aid you in planning a similar three-phase lesson, Figure 7.9 on the next page includes steps to consider as you plan each phase. While some of the lessons described in this book lend themselves to planning all three phases at once, for this plan I would consider waiting until you have implemented Phase 1 and notice which parts of the source are particularly tricky. These are the parts you will want to incorporate into the think-aloud and guided practice during Phase 2.

HOW DO WE ASSESS?

Assessing students' use of the coding strategy to help them monitor for meaning will help you determine how to move them forward. When you lean in to meet with individual students or small groups during guided practice, start by affirming their attempts at monitoring for meaning. Your comments may sound like one of the following statements:

- I noticed that you are stopping to think about your thinking.
- Your coded notes reveal that you are learning new information as you read.
- It sounds like you are finding this strategy useful and becoming aware of when you are not understanding information in a source.

Then implement a teaching point. Figure 7.10 on page 124 includes suggestions for what you might notice and what you might say and do in response.

The ultimate objective of the coding strategy is to help students make better meaning of a source. Taking some time to look through their coded notes can help us think about whether the students are deepening their understanding of content and can give us clues as to how we can help them progress in their learning. Figure 7.11 on page 125 describes the characteristics of coded notes you might notice in each stage of a continuum. These stages of development can serve as a guide to help you think about what stage students are in.

WHAT DOES FOLLOW-UP INSTRUCTION LOOK LIKE?

Students may need multiple series of three-phase lessons focused on monitoring for meaning to really deepen their understanding of what the activity entails. After the lesson with the article "KABOOM!" (Ruane, 2010), the teacher looked through the students' coded and framed notes. She noticed that many of the students were in the approaching stage, noting what they already knew and what they had just learned. They were not identifying parts of the source they did not comprehend, though, and they were not revealing an analysis of the facts they were learning. Some students had this deeper understanding, however, and she chose five examples of thoughtful notes to share during follow-up instruction as examples of strategic processing. Her purpose was to highlight what each student did well as a model for their peers.

FIGURE 7.9. Planning guide for "Introducing Monitoring for Meaning and the Coding Strategy."

PLANNING Phase 1—*Meet the Source*

1. Introduce and preview the source.

- Locate a source that has some parts the students will understand and some more complex parts the students may need to closely read (and code their thinking) to understand.
- Plan a purpose for reading or viewing the source a first time. An example is *What are you learning that is new or unfamiliar information?* Prepare for how you will post this purpose for all students to view.
- Plan an introduction to the source. (See Chapter 5 for suggestions.)

2. Read–view–listen and confer.

If the students will be watching a video, determine the point(s) at which you will pause and ask students to turn and talk about what they have learned.

3. Discuss.

- Plan to return to the purpose you gave students for reading or viewing.
- Think about a teaching point you might share with the students. This point might emerge while you are conferring with students.

PLANNING Phase 2—*Meet the Strategies*

1. Explain and model strategic reading–viewing–listening.

- The purpose for close reading will be to practice monitoring for meaning.
- Create an anchor chart or bookmark with the codes you want to present to students.
- Plan an introduction and think-aloud that includes the following:
  - Stating the *what, why,* and *how* related to monitoring for meaning (use the language in Figure 7.2 for support).
  - Explaining the coding strategy.
  - Reading a section of the source (for which you will think aloud about how you monitored).
  - Stopping to share what you think about a specific word, phrase, or sentence (in that section) and which code you might use.
  - Writing a code and jotting a few related words in the margins or in your notes.

2. Practice with sections of the source.

Choose particular parts of the source that students should read closely and code. (Another option is to let the students choose a part.)

3. Discuss.

- Develop a discussion question related to strategic processing; for example, *What did you learn today about monitoring for meaning? Why is that important?*
- Create a prompt related to content learned from the source; for example, *What part of this source did you understand better because you focused on making meaning? Tell your partner about what you learned.*

(continued)

PLANNING Phase 3—*Meet the Response*
1. Introduce prompt for the response.
Plan a prompt for a written response. These are some examples you might consider: • *Take a moment to look at your coded notes. Which notes helped you to think more carefully about the information in the source? Choose two to three notes. Describe the notes and your thinking in a short letter to me.* • *What was the author's message to the reader in this source? Which of your notes helped you to understand this message? In your response, state what you think the author's message to the reader is and what you learned through coding and taking notes that supports your position.* • *How was your understanding of this source transformed when you slowed down to closely read–view–listen to a few tricky sections?*
2. Plan and rehearse.
• Decide how students will plan or rehearse for writing. Possible options include choosing coded notes they want to include in their response and/or talking with a partner about what they want to say in their response. • Plan for how you will help students who need extra support during writing. Possible options include shared writing of a sample response and/or pulling together a small group to work with more closely.
3. Write and confer.
What will you try to notice when you lean in to confer? (This will depend on the prompt for writing.)

FIGURE 7.9. *(continued)*

During Phase 1—Meet the Source, in a follow-up series of lessons, the teacher introduced a new article titled "Thirsty Planet" (Geiger, 2010b). As part of the Phase 2—Meet the Strategies lesson, the teacher gave a mini-lesson reviewing the importance of monitoring for meaning. With the permission of the students whose notes she had chosen, the teacher placed each of the chosen student's written notes about the previous article "KABOOM!" (Ruane, 2010), one at a time, on the document camera and thought aloud about what each response revealed to her. Figure 7.12 on page 126 includes images of the students' notes and details about how the teacher thought aloud about two of the responses.

After this short presentation, the teacher asked the students to choose portions of the second article, "Thirsty Planet" (Geiger, 2010b), to practice consciously monitoring for meaning and jotting down coded notes. She conferred first with students whose previous notes revealed they might be in the "attempting" stage. At the end of the lesson, the teacher wrapped up by asking students to share their thinking in small groups.

It is remarkable how much a simple approach to following up—like sharing students' work and describing explicitly what each student did to construct meaning from the text—can do to move students forward. For example, during the lesson with "KABOOM!" (Ruane, 2010), one student, Danuta, wrote sentences on eight sticky notes that started with "I never knew" or "I already knew." She included facts stated almost directly from the text, such as "I already knew that the Earth's mantle lies under the crust." She also asked two questions but did not follow up with answers. In the synthesis frame, she wrote two sentence fragments in response to the question "Why did the author write this?":

123

Scenario	How you can respond
The student has written several "I already knew" notes.	• Move the student toward deeper thinking by asking how she is synthesizing the information in the source. You might say, "I noticed that you have a lot of notes about information in the source that you already knew. What do you think is one of the author's main ideas?" and, if needed, "Tell me more." • Skim the student's notes and notice if there's a more complex part of the source for which there are no notes. Ask the student to return to that part of the source and think aloud with you about what she is learning. This might help her notice details that are new information or details she is not understanding.
The student has not written any notes about what she does not understand.	Prompt the student to consider more complex parts of the source with questions like: • *Was there a tricky part of the source that you didn't understand very well?* • *What could you do to help yourself understand that part better?* • *Let's try to figure this part out together.* The student might identify specific obstacles to understanding, such as encountering unfamiliar vocabulary words or numerous other problems. Be prepared to teach appropriate fix-up strategies at the point of need. See Figure 7.15 (pp. 130–131) for additional fix-up strategies you might introduce.
The student has written responses to facts that do not reveal how this thinking led her to new insights or how she thought beyond the information in the source.	• While conferring, try using one of the following prompts to support the student in thinking beyond the source or in evaluating the source: 　○ *Why is this detail important?* 　○ *What does it make you think?* 　○ *Why do you think the author included this detail?* • Be prepared to think aloud for the student. You might use language like, "When I read this fact, it reminded me of . . ." or "This was new information for me and it made me realize that . . ."
The student has written a variety of notes about several aspects of the source and needs to move toward synthesizing the information written on the notes.	Possible prompts: • *It looks like you are thinking carefully about what you are noticing in this source. When you look across your notes, what are you thinking might be a main idea in this source?* • *When we first looked at this source, we predicted it would be about . . .* [fill in the blank]. *What are you thinking now? Why do you think so?* • *How does what you have learned about this topic resonate with you? How has it transformed your thinking in some way?*

FIGURE 7.11. Stages of development in students' coded notes.

Stage	Characteristics of coded notes
Attempting	• Notes simply restate facts from the source. • They may include low-level responses like "I learned that . . ." with no elaboration. • They rely primarily on one or two codes for responding. Example: > I learned that the platypus has electrical sensors.
Approaching	• Notes reveal the construction of meaning or some level of thinking that reaches beyond the source. • Student uses multiple codes, including "I don't understand" and "I wonder." • Personal responses like "I never knew . . ." and "I'm surprised . . ." reveal engagement with the content of the source. Example: > Wow! That doesn't even look like an animal. It blends in good to get easy food.
Meeting	• Notes reveal thinking that involves the application or analysis of ideas. • Student uses codes flexibly, sometimes adopting new codes or ways of taking notes like sketching. • Coded notes about "I don't understand" or "I wonder" include details about how the student tried to repair meaning. In the example below, a student wrote a question on the first sticky note; then, when he read on and determined the answer, he wrote that answer on the second sticky note. Example: > How is lightning reacting with lava and a volcanic eruption? +Static electricity builds up in the ashes and forms lightning.
Exceeding	• Codes are used flexibly and include notes that elaborate. • Notes reveal an evaluation of the facts or ideas shared in the source. • Notes may tie into an emerging main idea. Example: > I believe Hanna was caring for her cows, but leaving 60? I mean that's 60 lives lost! Wow! It seems like we waste a lot of water and it's very easy to get water compared to other countries.

"To give you information" and "To inform on the volcano that erupted in Iceland." Her responses revealed that she was attempting to think about her thinking but that she still needed further instruction.

Figure 7.13 shows Danuta's notes for the second article, "Thirsty Planet," and includes an analysis of those notes. This article was about the fact that water is a limited resource to which all living things need ready access in order to survive. While Danuta is still responding with "facts" she learned, she is also sharing how she is thinking beyond the

Student example	Teacher think-aloud
Anna's response: *I just found out that the Volcano has not eruptid since 1812 thats a very very long time ago!*	The teacher wants the students to consider how Anna had thought beyond the facts the author had shared. She places Anna's work on the document camera, points to this particular sticky note, and says, *Notice in this student's note that she included not just the specific fact she learned while reading, but also stopped to think about what this fact tells us, namely, it's been a long time since this volcano erupted. I'm thinking she was also considering that this might be why the people living nearby were not worried on a regular basis about the volcano erupting.* The teacher asks Anna to confirm this experience and share additional insights she gained through the experience.
? How is lightning reacting with lava and a volcanic eruption. *+ Static electricity builds up in the ashes and forms lightning*	The teacher wants the students to notice how Luke had written a question and then an answer. She places his work on the document camera and says, *Take a moment to look at the thinking this student has shared in these notes. How did he go about monitoring for meaning? [Pauses and then solicits answers or continues thinking aloud.] I noticed that on the first sticky note he wrote a question. [Removes the student's work and places a page of the article on the camera with an illustration and caption.] I'm guessing that he had read the caption that said, "Lightning sparks in the ash plume of the eruption," and then looked at the picture with all of the ash in the sky and a streak of lightning in the middle of it. [Pauses.] Then he must have continued reading and located the answer in the text, which is what he has written on the second note.* The teacher closes by asking Luke to explain his experience further.

FIGURE 7.12. Using students' notes as models during follow-up instruction.

FIGURE 7.13. Danuta's response completed during the follow-up lesson.

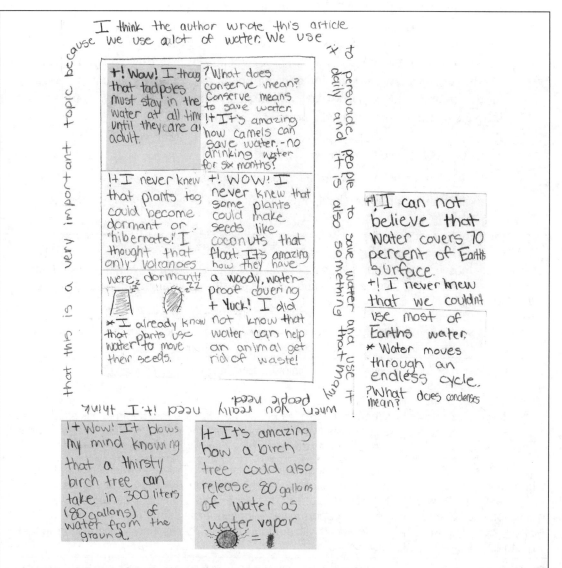

Danuta's coded notes in response to the first lesson on monitoring for meaning with the article "KABOOM!" (Ruane, 2010) included mostly "I already knew" and "This is new information" notes and related facts written almost directly from the article. The notes in this figure were completed after the teacher gave a mini-lesson sharing her peers' notes with a discussion about how to be thoughtful when monitoring for meaning. Notice that the responses are varied and that most of her notes are focused on how animals and plants use or conserve water. She is still stating many facts, but she includes responses that reveal thinking beyond the text (see the comment about "camels"). She also seems to be keeping track of her thinking as she reads (see the two "birch tree" notes). In addition, she seems to be contrasting new information with old beliefs (in her "tadpoles" comment) and asking—and sometimes answering—questions about key vocabulary words (*conserve* and *condense*). The three sentences written around the edge of the notes reveal her thoughtful consideration of the author's central ideas and the implications for the reader.

source. She has clearly moved beyond merely reaching out to monitor for meaning and now is much more in control of her understanding as a result. In Figure 7.14 you will find suggestions for similar lessons you can plan in response to what you have noticed about your students. In Appendix A, on page 227, you will also find a one-page guide with brief suggestions for Phase 2 lessons focused on this strategy. This guide can easily be used as a reference for planning and teaching several lessons over time with multiple sources.

Finally, as students begin to notice and point out what they do not understand, we have to be ready to explicitly teach and model using fix-up strategies. You can start by introducing three areas in which meaning might break down:

- Not being able to read a word (decoding).

- Not knowing what a word means (vocabulary).

- Not understanding what a phrase, sentence, or section of a source means.

If . . .	Then . . .
Students are mostly writing lower-level notes like *I already knew . . .* [fill in the fact directly stated in the source].	• During Phase 2—Meet the Strategies, share examples of students' coded notes and discuss how they reveal deeper thinking about content in a source. • Think aloud in front of students about what you did not understand in a source (or might not understand if you were their age) and write aloud notes that document your thinking.
Students' responses do not include questions about what they do not understand.	• Give a series of mini-lessons in which you share a part of a source that you did not understand (or you might not understand if you were the students' age) and think aloud about how you made sense of that. • When you close the Phase 1 and 2 lessons, begin to ask students to share parts (words, phrases, sentences, and sections) of the source they thought were tricky.
Students are noticing when they do not understand a tricky word or section of a source, but they do not know what to do next.	• Give a series of mini-lessons (during Phase 2—Meet the Strategies) where you explicitly teach and model using fix-up strategies. See Figure 7.15 (pp. 130–131) for examples of these strategies. • Look for opportunities to continue teaching these strategies in conferences with students during Phases 1 and 2 of the three-phase plan for learning.
Students are identifying graphics or visual images that they do not understand, but they are not sure what to do next.	• Try the lessons in Chapter 9 that focus on making meaning of these types of features. • Confer with a student about how to make sense of a particular feature like a diagram and then ask the student to share with the other students what he did to problem-solve.
Students are identifying vocabulary for which they do not know the meaning, but they are not sure what to do next.	• Step away from lessons focused on coding and try the lessons in Chapter 10 that teach students about four types of context clues authors use to clarify the meaning of particular words. • Confer with a student about how to figure out the meaning of a word and then, at the close of a lesson, ask the student to share with the class what he did to problem-solve.

FIGURE 7.14. Suggestions for follow-up instruction.

What's important is that we provide explicit strategies for students to grapple with when they are trying to repair their meaning making and that we model how to use the strategies. Figure 7.15 (pp. 130–131) presents examples of some fix-up strategies you might teach, depending on where the meaning is breaking down, along with examples of how a teacher might model the use of that strategy. This list of strategies is not exhaustive. Keep in mind too that learning the strategies introduced in the following chapters will also help students repair meaning when it breaks down.

CLOSING THOUGHTS

We don't want students to "burn out" as a result of excessive coding. Rather, we just want them to understand conceptually (preferably without having to stop and write codes all the time) what it means to monitor for meaning. We want them to notice what does and does not make sense and to use fix-up strategies whenever meaning starts to break down. Observe and notice when your students are successfully self-monitoring their reading and perhaps don't need to "code" their thinking. Highlight for them how they are doing this and let go of "coding." Be ready, though, to use the coding activity again when needed—perhaps to tackle a more difficult source or even as an occasional reminder of the basics of monitoring for meaning.

FIGURE 7.15. Examples of fix-up strategies for when meaning breaks down.

When students struggle to decode a domain-specific word		
Examples with article "KABOOM!" (Ruane, 2010)	**Strategies students can use**	**Example of teacher think-aloud**
Some students might struggle to decode words like *mantle*, *pressure*, and *kilometer*.	Look for parts of the word you know to help you get started.	*If I was struggling to read this word* [spells aloud] *"m-a-n-t-l-e," I know that one way I can tackle an unfamiliar word is by looking for parts I already know. I recognize the word "man" in that word.*
	Break the word into parts (or syllables) and then blend.	*When I look at the second part* [spells aloud] *"t-l-e," I know that I have seen other words with that ending, like "gentle" and "bottle," so that second part will probably say "-tle."*
	If you blend together the parts of a word, ask yourself the question, *Does that sound like a word I know?*	*Then I put the two parts together—"mantle." I have heard this word before, but I want to make sure I know what it means. Now I need to go back and look at the word in the article and think about what it means.*

Note: If a student is trying to decode a word he has never heard before or that is not part of his vocabulary, he may not figure out the correct pronunciation. Figuring out the meaning is more important; the student should at least reread the sentence or listen to a clip again to identify clues as to the meaning of the word.

When students struggle to understand the meaning of vocabulary		
Examples with article "KABOOM!" (Ruane, 2010)	**Strategies students can use**	**Example of teacher think-aloud**
"An **unpleasant** smell filled the air" (p. 15).	Look for a suffix or prefix that helps you understand the meaning of this word.	*If I was not sure what the word "unpleasant" meant in this article, I might look at the parts of the word to think about the meaning. I notice that this word has the prefix "un", which means not. I also know that the base word "pleasant" means something a person likes. I'm thinking that "unpleasant" means not good or not something a person would like.*
		Let's go back to the source and think about what this word means in this sentence. [Pauses to read aloud the sentence.] *I think what the author is saying is when the volcano began to erupt, there was a bad smell in the air. I'm wondering what that smelled like. I'm going to keep reading to see if I find out.*
"People thought Eyja was **dormant**, or sleeping. It last erupted in 1821" (p. 15).	Look for a context clue to help you determine the meaning of this word. Does the author use a definition, synonym, or example to help you understand the meaning of this word? (See Chapter 10, "Using Context Clues to Make Sense of Unfamiliar Vocabulary," for lessons on types of context clues.)	*If I was not sure what the word "dormant" means, I might reread the sentence again and maybe even the next sentence to look for a clue to the meaning.* [Pauses to read aloud the sentences.]
		I noticed the words "or sleeping" and I know that sometimes authors use the word "or" to signal that they are going to give a synonym for a tricky word. I'm thinking that the word "dormant" also means sleeping.
		I'm going to read the sentence one more time to think about the meaning of the sentence and then paraphrase what I learned. [Pauses to read aloud the sentence.] *I think what the author is trying to say is that people thought this volcano would not erupt again or that it was not active because it hadn't erupted in over a hundred years. This is what the author means by "dormant." People were probably surprised when it did begin to erupt, huh?*

When students struggle to understand a part of the source (e.g., sentence, paragraph, section)		
Examples with article "KABOOM!" (Ruane, 2010)	**Strategies students can use**	**Example of teacher think-aloud**
A student does not understand this sentence or has difficulty explaining what he learned in his own words: "As the **pressure** below a volcano builds, magma starts to rise" (p. 12).	Stop and ask yourself, "Is there any part of this that I do understand or already know about?" and "What is unfamiliar or new to me?" If it's new information, reread or listen again, and identify words that might be important. Think about how you can use those words to explain what the author is saying.	*If I read this sentence and was not sure what it meant, what could I do?* I think I would start by reading it again and asking myself if there are any details that feel familiar or any parts that I already know. [Pauses to read the sentence again.] Okay. I understand the second part of the sentence. I know from the last paragraph that the word "magma" means molten or liquid rock and I understand "starts to rise." That means "go up." So the magma is going up. Let me think about the other part of this sentence that did not seem as familiar. I know "pressure" means pushing on something. So I'm guessing there's some kind of push or force down below the volcano that makes the magma go up and come out of the volcano. I'm still not sure what is causing that "pressure" or what the force is, but I think I know enough to keep going.
The student has difficulty recalling the layers of the Earth and their order as revealed in a short section (six sentences) of the article: "This outer layer of Earth, called the crust, is constantly moving and shifting. . . . The mantle lies under the crust. . . . Below the mantle is Earth's core" (p. 12).	Look for features that might help you understand that phrase, sentence, or section better. (See Chapter 9, "Learning from a Source's Visual Images and Other Features," for lessons that support this strategy.)	*The author provides a lot of information in just these six sentences. When I finished reading this section, I at least understood that the author was trying to introduce me to the three layers of the Earth. I could go back and reread to think about the details he uses to describe each layer, but I also noticed this graphic of the Earth. A section of the Earth is split open, so I can see the layers.* The teacher pauses to examine the graphic. The graphic includes a label for each layer of the Earth with an additional detail like how thick the layer is or how hot. She points to the details as she notices them. *Okay. I have a picture in my mind now that I can think about as I reread this section in the article describing the order of the layers.*
The student is able to recall details related to the family that escaped the erupting volcano, but he is not recalling details from the informational parts of this article or the parts describing how volcanoes erupt.	Think about authors' purposes for writing or creating sources. How can you use what you know about authors' purposes to help you make sense of this part of the source? (See Appendix A, Lesson Idea 9 for more ideas on teaching for understanding of an author's purpose.)	*When I read the introduction to this article that starts with "The night was quiet. In Iceland, Hanna Lara Andrews and her family slept peacefully. . . ." I thought the author's purpose for writing this article was to recount what happened to a family when this volcano erupted. But when I got further into the article, I noticed that the author was not telling me about Hanna in some parts. Instead, I felt like he was trying to teach me about volcanoes or explaining how volcanoes are formed. Examples of these points are the sentences, "Volcanoes often rise between two plates. A volcano is an opening in Earth's surface. It can look like a mountain." So, I noticed that this author has two purposes. He is telling a story. He is also explaining how volcanoes are formed and what happens when they erupt. As I read, then, I'm going to keep in mind two questions:* • *Is the author telling me more about the story of Hanna?* • *Or is he trying to explain something about volcanoes?* *These questions will help me think about what's important.*

CHAPTER EIGHT

Identifying and Explaining Key Details

In the short book *Side by Side* (Pigdon, 2012), readers learn how the impala and the lion coexist on the grasslands of Africa. This book, like many informational sources, is packed with content (see Figure 8.1). The author describes the birth of impala fawns and lion cubs, the first months of their lives, and additional details about their adulthood. Students are usually enthusiastic about reading books like these. (They love lions, right?)

What happens, though, when you ask students to share key details they learned in this book? Or when you ask them to summarize what they learned? In my experience, some students respond with a blank stare. Others share facts they learned during the preview of the source or during a reading conference with me. Some share one detail like "the lions have cubs" or a list of miscellaneous details. Some feel like everything in the book is important and, as a result, try to share every single detail.

Why does this happen?

Consider *Side by Side* (Pigdon, 2012). A student can read this book for a variety of purposes, including:

1. To determine one of the author's main ideas.
2. To answer a question like "What are the physical features that make a lion an effective hunter?"
3. To analyze how the author uses the comparison structure to organize this source.
4. To analyze how the author develops the idea that young impalas are better adapted for survival than young lions.

The key details the student identifies in this book will depend on which of these purposes she chooses for reading. In other words, what we determine is important in a

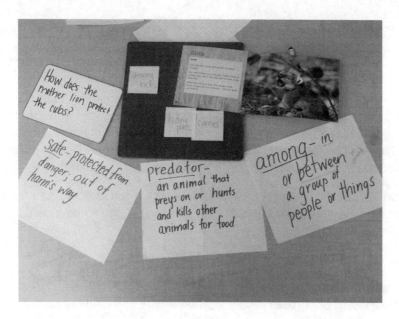

FIGURE 8.1. Identifying key details and vocabulary in the book *Side by Side* (Pigdon, 2012). Reproduced with permission of Eleanor Curtain Publishing Pty. Ltd. (*www.ecpublishing.com.au*) from *Side by Side* author K. Pigdon. © EC Licensing Pty. Ltd. 2002–2018.

source will depend on our purpose. When our students respond vaguely to a prompt like "What are the key details in this source?", they may respond this way because they read without a clear purpose in mind.

Another obstacle for students may be that some of the tasks we give them, such as "summarize what was important" or "summarize what you learned," are too big. There is a lot of information in the book *Side by Side* (Pigdon, 2012). Other types of sources can be just as dense. In a kid-friendly National Geographic video titled *Cobra vs. Mongoose* (n.d.-a), the narrator says all of the following in about 20 seconds:

> At first glance, this curious mammal [mongoose] may not look like much competition for a cobra, but the Indian Gray Mongoose is quite the predator itself, and its lightning fast reflexes and thick hide have enabled it to add snakes like the cobra to its list of favored foods.

There are at least eight facts about the mongoose that we can gather from this sentence—that's if we are *reading* it. Gathering these facts by watching the images and listening to the narration are more difficult. And that's true if we are only required to list the facts we heard. To get at the bigger ideas, an even more complex task, we need to compare these facts to the narrator's description of the cobra earlier in the video. In a short amount of time—less than a minute of the video—there is a lot of information to process before we even begin to think about how to "summarize" what we learned orally or in writing.

So how do we help students? This chapter focuses on how to better clarify for students what we mean by "determine what is important" and "identify key details" and includes suggestions for assessment and instruction.

WHAT DO WE MEAN BY "DETERMINE WHAT IS IMPORTANT" OR "IDENTIFY KEY DETAILS"?

What: Readers know that informational sources have lots of details and that some details are more important than others. We can figure out which details are important by thinking about our purpose for reading (e.g., What is new information that I am learning about this topic?) and then looking for bits of information that help us respond to our purpose. These pieces of information are **key details**.

Why: You can use key details to help you remember what you learned from a source, to compare what you learned to information in other sources, and to think critically about why the author wrote or created this source.

How: You can identify key details by asking questions like these:

- What is my purpose for reading?
- What are words or phrases (or bits of information) that help me respond to my purpose?

You may have to use your knowledge about the world and about how sources work to help you.

FIGURE 8.2. A student-friendly explanation of what we mean by "identify a key detail."

As described in Figure 8.2 above, key details might be defined as pieces of information from the source that can be used to respond to a purpose for reading–viewing–listening. Identifying key details or what is important can help us in numerous ways. We can more easily recall what we read or heard or saw. We can use what we learned to help us summarize and share this information with someone else. As we determine what is important, we can evaluate details and think critically about aspects of the source like the author's purpose or point of view. What does identifying key details for a particular purpose look like in action?

 Let's say the student's purpose for reading *Side by Side* (Pigdon, 2012) is to identify one of the author's main ideas. As the student reads, she might begin to notice that there are several details about how the mother lion protects her young from predators. She realizes that this information could be a main idea. Then the student rereads the book or closely reads a few excerpts with the new purpose of recalling key details that support this idea. On two pages, she notices the following details:

- "the cubs are born in a safe place under a bush or among rocks" (p. 8)
- "the lion cubs stay hidden for the first months of their lives" (p. 12)
- "she [the mother] leaves them in their hiding place while she hunts" (p. 12).

Each of these details could support the idea that the mother lion protects her cubs. What did this student have to do to identify these key details? Keeping a clear purpose in mind, she has to think about what is stated explicitly in the text *and* she has to think about what she already knows about the world. Background knowledge related to how predators stalk their prey, how young animals are vulnerable, and how we stay out of harm's way in dangerous situations is helpful in determining that these are important details. As discussed in Chapter 6, this process of identifying key details and thinking about how they support the main idea is called *synthesis*.

 When a student watches a video like National Geographic's *Cobra vs. Mongoose* (n.d.-a), the process for identifying key details is similar to what a student does with a printed text like a book or article. Take a few moments to use the QR code or link to access and watch this 2-minute video.

https://bit.ly/2IVtcDd

As you watch the video, consider what one of the main ideas presented is. What are details in the narration and visuals that support this idea? What a student might notice when he views this video is that there are numerous details highlighting how these two animals have special features that support them in combating one another. In one part of this video, the narrator describes the cobra as the mongoose approaches it, saying, "The snake tries to warn the mongoose away, making use of that famous hood and raspy hiss." Key words in this statement like *warn, hood,* and *hiss* support the idea that these two animals may oppose one other and that the cobra has special features that help it do so. In addition to listening to the narrator, the student also needs to notice what is happening visually—how the cobra's hood is open and wide, how the cobra pulls itself up from the ground to give it some height, how the cobra's body is built to strike forward and back as it tries to keep the mongoose away. The narrator's description and the visuals are key details that support this main idea.

 With infographics, students need to continue to filter what's important and what's not in response to their purpose. Take a few minutes again to check out PBS Nature's spectacular infographic "All about Snowy Owls" (2015) using the QR code or link.

https://to.pbs.org/2zWkTpC

There are numerous details in this infographic. As you look at it, try to find connections between some of the details that reveal a main idea. You probably noticed that one of the main ideas in this infographic is that the snowy owl has special features that help it catch prey. There are specific or key details that support this idea. For example, down toward the bottom of the graphic, there is a circle drawn around the owl's talons and a caption that states, "Snowy owls use their talons to catch prey." The visual of the talons reveals that they are curved and pointed; they also look to be sharp. We can use our background knowledge about how curved or sharp objects can be used to snag or catch other objects and draw a conclusion that the shape of the owl's talons is helpful in catching prey. The written text in the caption and the visuals discussed serve as key details to support this idea.

The purposes for looking at the three sources I just described can vary beyond identifying a main idea. Our students might have the purpose of just getting to know a little bit about the cobra and the mongoose. Or they might be watching this video to answer a question like, "What are the physical features of the mongoose that make it an effective predator?" They might be looking at the infographic of the snowy owl to draw comparisons between this bird of prey and another or to identify the author's purpose and think about how the structure of this source serves this purpose. Again, the details a student determines are important will depend on the purpose for reading–viewing–listening.

As revealed in the analysis of how we determine what is important with these three sources, it is clear that students have to use a repertoire of skills and strategies to determine importance. They have to keep in mind their purpose for reading, viewing, or listening. They have to tap their background knowledge about the world. They also have to have a grasp of *how* sources are structured. A source's structure is the way that it is organized, or how its components are arranged and how they are interrelated (Cummins, 2015). Commonly taught structures include:

- Enumerative or descriptive
- Sequence/chronology/narrative
- Comparison
- Cause–effect
- Problem–solution

If a student reading *Side by Side* (Pigdon, 2012) recognizes that the source has a comparison structure, then he or she is more likely to begin to notice another set of main ideas emerging—that both the mother lion and mother impala protect their young from predators, that the young impala is more likely to survive than the young lion, and so forth.

The video *Cobra vs. Mongoose* (National Geographic, n.d.-a) also has a comparison structure. Again, if a student recognizes that the narrative and the visuals are revealing similarities and differences in the physical features of these two animals, the student will more likely understand some of the bigger ideas in this source.

The infographic "All about Snowy Owls" (Public Broadcasting Service, 2015) has a descriptive structure. In this source, many different aspects of the snowy owl are described, including its physical features, where it lives, and what it eats. If a student recognizes that this source has a descriptive structure, he can more easily navigate this source—knowing that the author or creator of this source will be addressing many subtopics. Within or across these subtopics, numerous main ideas will emerge. For example, the main part of the infographic is focused on the physical features (a subtopic) of the snowy owl. Recognizing physical features as one of the subtopics and then thinking about how several of the physical features described are connected can help the student glean a main idea; for example, many of the physical features described help the snowy owl catch its prey.

DO YOUR STUDENTS NEED TO WORK ON THIS?

What are you noticing about students' ability to identify key details? The following questions may help you determine whether some students would benefit from instruction in this area.

During conferences with individuals or small groups:

- Do they seem to understand why they are reading, viewing, or listening to a source?
- Do they tend to share just the last fact they read, heard, or noticed in a source?
- Do they talk about the source in a way that lacks insight into important details and the connections between those details?
- Are they recognizing a source's structure and using that structure to help them identify key details?

In evaluating students' written responses:

- Do they write about facts or details from the source in a way that lacks a clear focus on the purpose for reading–viewing–listening to a source?
- Does their writing lack an explanation of key details they have identified?
- Do they simply copy from the source?

Depending on your response to these questions, your students may need support in identifying and explaining key details in a source.

WHERE TO START? IDENTIFY KEY DETAILS

There are three instructional approaches you might consider when contemplating how to help students increase their capacity for identifying key details.

1. Using "making pasta" as an ongoing analogy for conversations about what is important.
2. Providing time for students to learn more from less with the "explode to explain" activity.
3. Creating experiences for students to discover and explore sources' structures.

What follows is an explanation of each approach. Depending on the needs of your students, you may implement all three approaches over time or you may decide that different students would benefit from one or the other. Whichever approach you choose, you will find that students begin to understand sources better (including identifying and explaining key details) if you stick with that approach over the course of several three-phase lessons and with several different sources.

The Pasta Analogy

When I begin a series of lessons focused on identifying key details, I have found it helpful to share an analogy that compares key details to pasta. When you cook pasta by boiling it in water, you drain and discard the water before eating the pasta. You do not eat the pasta until after you have drained the water. We engage in a similar process when we are trying to determine what is important. Some details are pieces of pasta, and some are water. This analogy can be used to help students simply recall and retell what they learned from a part of a source, or it can be used to help students determine what information is important in response to a purpose that requires higher-level thinking.

When I introduce this analogy, I find that most of our students have eaten pasta and have some idea of how it is cooked. I start by asking students to share the steps for making pasta, and they generally list the following:

- Fill a pot with water.
- Bring the water to a boil.
- Put in the pasta.
- Boil for a certain amount of time.
- Drain the water from the pasta.
- Eat the pasta.

During our conversation about these steps, I always emphasize the importance of draining the water from the pasta because we do not want to eat the pasta with the water—we just want to eat the pasta! Students easily agree, and then I compare this concept to determining what is important in a source or what we might call "identifying key details." I tell the students that there are key words, phrases, or sections in a source that we want to remember and to take time to digest. There are other words or phrases or parts of a source that are like the water—we do not need to spend a lot of time thinking about them because they are not as important. I explain to the students that when we are reading–viewing–listening to a source, identifying the pasta or the key details will help us understand the source better and respond to our purpose for reading. Figure 8.3 is a photo I sometimes pull up on my smartphone when I introduce and explain this analogy. Having a conversation about the similarities between pasta and key details can open students' eyes to what they need to pay attention to in a source. This analogy is easily introduced as part of a Phase 2—Meet the Strategies lesson and can be integrated into our conversations with students (e.g., "What's the pasta in this sentence?") as they determine what is important in a source.

To introduce the pasta analogy, I might say the following:

Tell me about making pasta. First you boil water, right? Then you add the pasta and when it is cooked, you drain and eat the pasta, correct? [Pauses for student response.] Oh, yes. *You need to drain the water from the pasta and then you eat the pasta. It is the same way when we read. The author or creator of a source has included both "water" and "pasta" words and phrases. The pasta in a source is the important facts or points the author wants us to remember or that help us think about our purpose for reading–viewing–listening. What the author wants is for us to eat and digest the pasta words; the water words are not as important.*

FIGURE 8.3. Explanation of the pasta analogy.

After I introduce the pasta analogy, I ask students to read a short section of a text with me to identify pasta or key words and phrases with a specific purpose in mind. I model identifying a key word or phrase, and then I begin releasing responsibility to students for identifying key details.

Depending on the needs of the students, I may write the key details they identify on a series of sticky notes. Figure 8.4 on the next page is a photograph of artifacts from a Phase 2 lesson. The sticky notes are key details the students identified when they did a close reading of one paragraph in this book, describing the European fire salamander. These students needed support in remembering or recalling what they had read as well as in determining what was important. Our purpose for closely reading was to identify the physical features that help this salamander survive. During the Phase 1—Meet the Source lesson, I introduced the word *features* with a kid-friendly definition following the four steps outlined in Chapter 5 (see Figure 5.4, p. 68). Then the students read the whole text. During Phase 2, after I introduced the pasta analogy, I eased the cognitive load of determining what is important by writing the details we identified together during the close reading.

Next, the students used the details on the sticky notes to share what they learned with a partner. With some groups like this one, I encourage students to say one sentence or thought per sticky note. This fosters the notion of what a complete thought or sentence includes. For some students who write run-on sentences, this exercise is helpful to do before they write during a Phase 3—Meet the Response lesson. For second language learners or students who do not have strong oral language skills that they can use in this particular context, this exercise is also an opportunity to help them formulate sentences

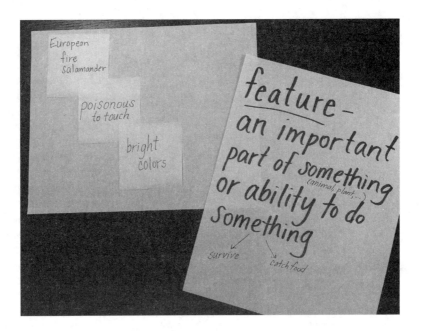

FIGURE 8.4. Artifacts from a close reading lesson focused on identifying key details in one section of the book *Strange Animals* (O'Sullivan, 2004), which describes special features animals have that help them survive.

that "sound right." I gently support students as they attempt to compose their thoughts, coaching them as they do. Then I ask them to repeat the sentence they formulated a few times before they write it. Key words and phrases written on sticky notes can be used as a scaffold at many points during teaching.

With students who have experienced at least a few lessons focused on identifying key details or who are more easily recalling what they have read, I coach them in taking their own notes and then using those notes to write a response. Initially, I guide students in this task and then gradually reduce my support. For example, I was working with a class of students immersed in exploring different careers. I used the three-phase plan to introduce the students to an article about the work of astronauts and then to closely read specific sections of the article. Our purpose for reading was to determine whether we thought the work of astronauts was fascinating, challenging, and/or tedious. I guided them in closely reading and taking notes on one paragraph in this article. Then they worked on another paragraph (that I selected) with a partner and a final paragraph on their own. During a follow-up set of three-phase lessons, the students chose an article they wanted to read (from a list of articles we provided) about another career (e.g., interpreter, stunt performer, app developer). After reading the article once, they thought about their response to what it would be like to work in that particular job. They could choose words from a bank of words we provided or come up with a word on their own. Students used words like *extraordinary, fascinating, intriguing, difficult,* and *exasperating* to explain their thinking. During Phase 2, then, each student chose sections of their article to read closely in order to identify key details that they could use to explain their thinking. Figure 8.5 is one student's bulleted list of key details she chose to support the

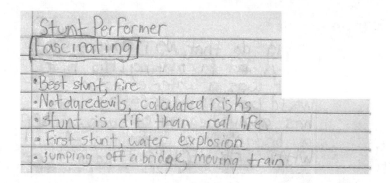

FIGURE 8.5. Example of one student's list of key details she would include in a written response.

idea that being a stunt performer would be a fascinating job. This list was similar to the sticky notes, in that it served as a guide when the students shared with others what they learned, and it became a plan for writing a response.

The pasta analogy can be applied to learning from different types of sources, including video clips. Think about the earlier excerpt from the National Geographic video *Cobra vs. Mongoose* (n.d.-a). One of the main ideas in this clip is that both the mongoose and the cobra have physical features that help protect them from each other. With the pasta strategy in mind, the students could watch the video again, listening for key details that support this idea. When they hear or see details that help them respond to this purpose, they can pause the video and watch that part again before jotting down key words or a few notes describing images they saw. For tips on supporting students as they identify key details in a video, see Figure 8.6.

 **Video Tips**

- Review with students that they need to be clear about their "purpose" for viewing a video and then discuss how the pasta analogy applies to the video.
- Ask students to give you a thumbs-up when they see or hear details that are helpful in responding to their purpose for viewing the video. Pause the video when you see a thumbs-up and engage in a discussion about what they saw or heard. Notice if they can paraphrase what they saw or heard. If needed, replay that part of the video for students to watch again before turning to talk with a partner about what they learned.
- Sometimes students' cognitive energy is consumed by listening, and they do not always "see" key details or vice versa. You might suggest to students that they focus just on the visual images in the video or just on what the narrator is saying, as you replay the clip another time.
- Be prepared to think aloud. You may notice students struggling to identify a key detail, to paraphrase what they learned, or to take notes. If you do, step in and model for them how you listened to or viewed the clip, what you thought in response, and what you decided to write in your notes.

FIGURE 8.6. Tips for teaching students to identify key details in a video.

Explode to Explain

The "explode to explain" strategy requires students to think through the meaning of specific words and phrases in one sentence or in one small portion of a video. This experience serves to deepen students' understanding of what they are learning from a source as well as their ability to *explain* what they have learned.

Take a moment to consider the information in the following excerpt from the book *Side by Side* (Pigdon, 2012). If a student was reading with the purpose of explaining what the author describes in these three sentences, what would you expect her to say?

> The lion cubs stay hidden for the first months of their lives. Their mother picks them up in her mouth and moves them from hiding place to hiding place. She leaves them in their hiding place while she hunts for food. (p. 12)

Frequently when I ask a student to explain what she learned after reading an excerpt like this, she simply restates what was in the source without any elaboration. She might say, "The mother lion hides her cubs" or "The lion carries the cubs from hiding place to hiding place." Some students like this one may need support in explaining what these details mean. When I notice this, I introduce the activity "explode to explain." When we explode to explain, we look at the key details in a few sentences and annotate our thinking as a way to help us go beyond simply regurgitating the facts. We ask questions like, "What does this word or phrase mean in this sentence?" and "Why is this important?" Our responses to these questions are our annotations. Figure 8.7 is an example of what this type of annotation might look like with the excerpt you just read from *Side by Side* (Pigdon, 2012).

The first time I introduce the explode-to-explain strategy, the students and I share the experience of thinking through and annotating a sentence with key details. Figure 8.8 is a photograph from a lesson with a group of students who were reading about the problem of sewage and waste in Guanabara Bay where Olympic athletes sailed during the summer games of 2016 (Associated Press, 2014). During a Phase 1—Meet the Source lesson, I introduced the article and kid-friendly definitions for the words *sewage* and

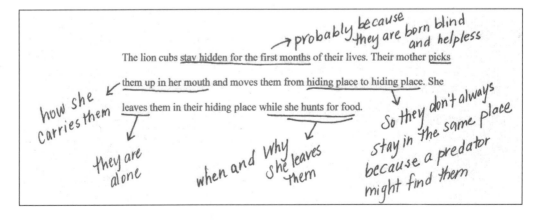

FIGURE 8.7. Example of an "explode-to-explain" exercise completed as a shared experience. For more information about this lesson, visit a blog entry I wrote at *https://bit.ly/2EKTRQJ*.

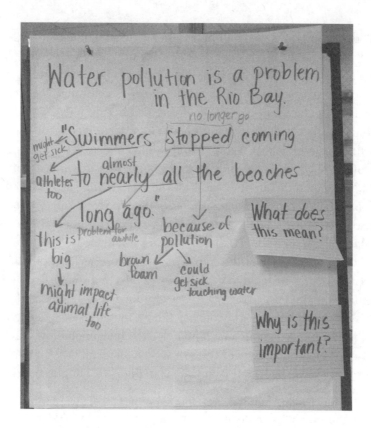

FIGURE 8.8. Example of "explode to explain" with a sentence from an article on the problem of pollution in Guanabara Bay (Associated Press, 2014).

waste. Then the students read and discussed the article as a whole. When we met for a Phase 2—Meet the Strategies lesson, I provided a main idea statement for them to discuss, that water pollution is a problem in the Rio de Janeiro bay. They agreed that this was definitely a main idea in the article. Then we chose one sentence from the source that we thought was important to support this idea; I wrote the sentence on a piece of chart paper and together we annotated our thinking and orally explained what we had learned. Next, they chose a second sentence in the article to write out in their notebooks and to practice "exploding to explain" on their own.

What would this explode-to-explain strategy look like with video? What seems to work with traditional text is a close reading of a short amount of text, just a sentence or two. The strategy would work the same with a video as a source. Students listen to 10–20 seconds of a video multiple times. In my experience with students, the first time they listen, they are only beginning to grasp what the narrator is saying. It takes watching a clip two or three times for the students to be able to paraphrase (or even just repeat verbatim) what they heard and jot down their thinking as notes. If they are exploding to explain, I ask them to jot down the specific words in the narration they hear and then jot down what those words mean or make them think. Then we watch again and think about the visuals. They take notes about what they saw and then what they are thinking in response. The result, though, is a deeper understanding and the ability to explain their thinking and learning.

Explode to explain is also an opportunity to teach students how to recognize types of details (Cummins, 2015; Mesmer & Rose-McCully, 2017). Students have to distinguish between phrases that tell *how* and *why*. They have to notice when an author is using words that describe the *physical features* or the *function* of something. They have to notice when an author is giving an *example* of something or offering a *definition* or *synonym*. As I engage students in explode to explain, I begin to observe when students are not recognizing particular types of details. I step in and think aloud as needed. For example, with the excerpt from *Side by Side,* the students I taught knew that "while she hunts for food" was important, but they didn't understand that the word *while* signals *when*. I used this as a teachable moment. Figure 8.9 includes some of the types of details authors of informational sources use or language you and your students can use for annotations and for explaining one's thinking. For more support, there is a quick guide focused on teaching students how to identify types of details over the course of several lessons in Appendix A, page 232.

For students who struggle to explain key details in a source, explode to explain provides language they can use to describe their thinking or elaborate on their learning. A key step in this process is helping students use their annotated notes to explain their learning orally and in writing. I demonstrate how to look at my annotations, how to choose which ones I'll use to help me, and what I'll say or write as a result. My think-aloud for the annotated excerpt from *Side by Side* (Pigdon, 2012) in Figure 8.7 might sound like the following:

> When I explain what I learned from this excerpt, I think I want to talk about some of the ideas in the words I've underlined, like how the cubs are "hidden for the first months" [I point to these words in the annotated excerpt of text] of their lives and how the mother moves them around by carrying them. [I point to my written annotation "how she carries them."] On a previous page, I learned that the cubs are born blind and helpless, so when I read that the mother hides them for the first few months, I understood why she does

• Name of topic (e.g., simple machines)	• Function, purpose
• Name of subtopic (e.g., wedge)	• Parts of something
• Where or location	• Statistic (fact or data stated in numbers)
• When or duration	• Definitions
• Why or cause–effect	• Synonyms
• How something behaves	• Real-life examples
• How something works or is done (may include cause–effect, sequence of details, and variables)	• Comparisons (including similes, metaphors)
• Physical attributes (movement or action, color, size, shape, number, texture, composition, construction, organization)	• Other types of figurative language
	• Quotes from experts (for the purpose of sharing relevant knowledge or an opinion)

For more discussion on teaching students to notice "types of details," check out the following blog entries I have written:
- Teach *example* as a type of detail information text authors use (*https://bit.ly/2HoaHdv*).
- Do our students understand what we mean when we use the words *definition* and *example* (*https://bit.ly/2m2Cnsr*)?
- Teach students to recognize the comparisons authors use (*https://bit.ly/2HDVGSk*).

FIGURE 8.9. General types of details students might notice and name (in primarily non-narrative or expository sources).

this. [Again, I point to a specific annotation.] They cannot fight off a predator, so they need to be in a safe or secure spot.

So this is what I think I will say to a friend: I learned that for the first few months of their lives, the mother lion hides her cubs from predators because they are still helpless or cannot protect themselves without her. She does not hide them in the same place every time, though. Instead, she carries them from one place to the next and leaves them there alone while she goes to find food.

When I finish this think-aloud, the group and I discuss how I used my annotated text to help me explain what I learned from the source. Then I coach partners as they practice explaining to each other what they learned using their "explode-to-explain" notes. This process can begin to prepare students for writing a response. For more details about integrating this strategy into your instruction, please see Appendix A, page 233.

"Aha!": Noticing a Source's Structure

I am not a big fan of giving students a list of text structures and a handful of graphic organizers to tackle as they read sources with different structures. I think that this approach can easily become a fill-in-the-blank, sometimes mindless exercise for students. This approach also becomes problematic when authors use multiple structures in a source or, as discussed in Chapter 2, when a source has a macro- or overarching structure, but also includes microstructures or sections of a source with a structure that is different from the source as a whole. What we want students to do is think about structures *conceptually* as well as *flexibly*. When they read a book like *Side by Side* (Pigdon, 2012), we want them to think and say something like the following:

Hey, I noticed that this book has *two* structures. One is a comparison structure. The author compares the lives of the lion and the impala. For example, first he describes the birth of the impala. Then he describes the birth of the lion. The second structure the author uses is the sequence or chronological structure. He describes different points in the lives of these animals in order. For example, first he describes their birth, then the first few months of their lives, then the first year, and so forth. So, basically the author blends these two structures. Since I noticed these structures during the preview of the source, I was able to anticipate what I would be reading about next.

This response would be a pretty sophisticated one from a student, but my point is that we do not want students to try to "fit" a structure onto a text or a text into a structure. Instead, I would suggest engaging students in "aha" moments where they discover a source's structure(s) and, as a result, gain a deeper understanding of the source.

What does this deeper understanding look like? After the students have read, viewed, or listened to a source during Phase 1, engage them in closely reading a source with the purpose of noticing its structure and identifying related details during Phase 2. When I teach these Phase 2 lessons, I introduce one or more of the traditional structures with a kid-friendly definition written on an anchor chart. (See Figure 8.10 on the next page for kid-friendly definitions.) Then I ask the students, "Do you think the author has employed this structure (or one of these structures)?" We look back at the source

Structure	Student-friendly explanation	Sentence stems for students
Descriptive/ Enumerative	After introducing the topic or issue, the author includes information about subtopics or different aspects of the main topic or issue. The content for each subtopic may build on the previous subtopic or content in the source.	• *The author discusses several subtopics, including . . .* • *In this section, the author explains . . .* • *The author describes . . .* • *I noticed that the author builds on this idea (or topic) in the next section by . . .*
Sequence/ Chronology/ Narrative	The author describes a series of steps in a process or episodes related to an event. Authors may use a sequence as a structure for most of the source or just for part of the source. A chronology is a sequence of events during a specific time period. A narrative tells the story of a person, a group, or an event. The author usually tells this story in the order that the events occurred.	• *I noticed that this source included a series of steps . . .* • *In this section of the source, the author explains the process of . . .* • *As I was reading this, I noticed that the author is describing the events in chronological order . . .* • *In this source, the author tells the story of . . .*
Comparison	An author examines how two or more people, places, things, or ideas are alike and different. Many authors use the comparison structure in short parts of their source instead of as a structure for the whole source.	• *In this source, the author compares . . .* • *The author contrasts . . .* • *As I was reading this, I noticed that the author shares the similarities and differences between _____ and _____.* • *In this section of the source, the author compares the _____ to the _____.*
Causal	An author uses a causal structure to explain why something happens or occurs. There may be more than one cause and more than one effect in a source with this structure.	• *The author shares several causes of . . .* • *The author describes the effects of . . .* • *There were several effects caused by . . .*
Problem– Solution	The author identifies a problem and then explains how the problem was solved or could be solved.	• *I noticed that the author identifies a problem . . .* • *The author offers several solutions to . . .* • *The author describes how one group is trying to solve . . .*

FIGURE 8.10. Explanation of structures.

carefully to confirm or disconfirm their responses. We look for key details that we can use to make our case that a source has a particular structure.

When we are having this conversation, it is helpful if students can use some of the language listed in the last column of Figure 8.10. This language describes what "authors do" in a sense. Authors *compare, explain, describe,* or *tell the story of* and, in so doing, they reveal the structure of a source. If students can recognize and explain (orally and in writing) what authors do, then they are more likely to recognize a source's structure. In preparation for teaching, I would recommend creating an anchor chart like the one in Figure 8.11, with a kid-friendly description of a particular structure as well as some of the sentence stems provided. When I teach, I find myself pointing to specific words or phrases or language on the chart to help students when they hesitate or need support in explaining their thinking.

During a Phase 2 lesson, you could also ask the students to take notes about the source's structure or create a graphic of their own that includes key details from the source. For one lesson I gave, during Phase 1, a small group read the article "Active Earth" (Geiger, 2010a). This article has an enumerative or descriptive text structure. The author introduces the topic of the active Earth and then addresses subtopics related to this concept—the Earth has layers, the crust is made up of tectonic plates that move back and forth, the movement of these plates led to the formation of continents, and so forth. During Phase 2, I introduced the descriptive text structure. Through conversation and close reading, the students determined that this article did indeed have a descriptive text structure; the author addressed several subtopics related to a bigger topic. As part of this lesson, I asked the students to reread the article again and create a graphic that included key details to illustrate this structure. Figure 8.12 on the next page illustrates one student's attempt. Notice how he describes the content in each section. The arrows show the flow of the content. As the students decide what to include in the graphic, they have to reread the source (or watch short clips again) to determine which key details they will include or summarize in the graphic. (By the way, the students *loved* the challenge of creating a graphic that illustrated the source's structure.)

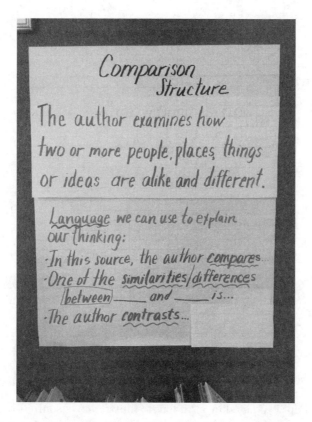

FIGURE 8.11. Example of an anchor chart for the comparison structure.

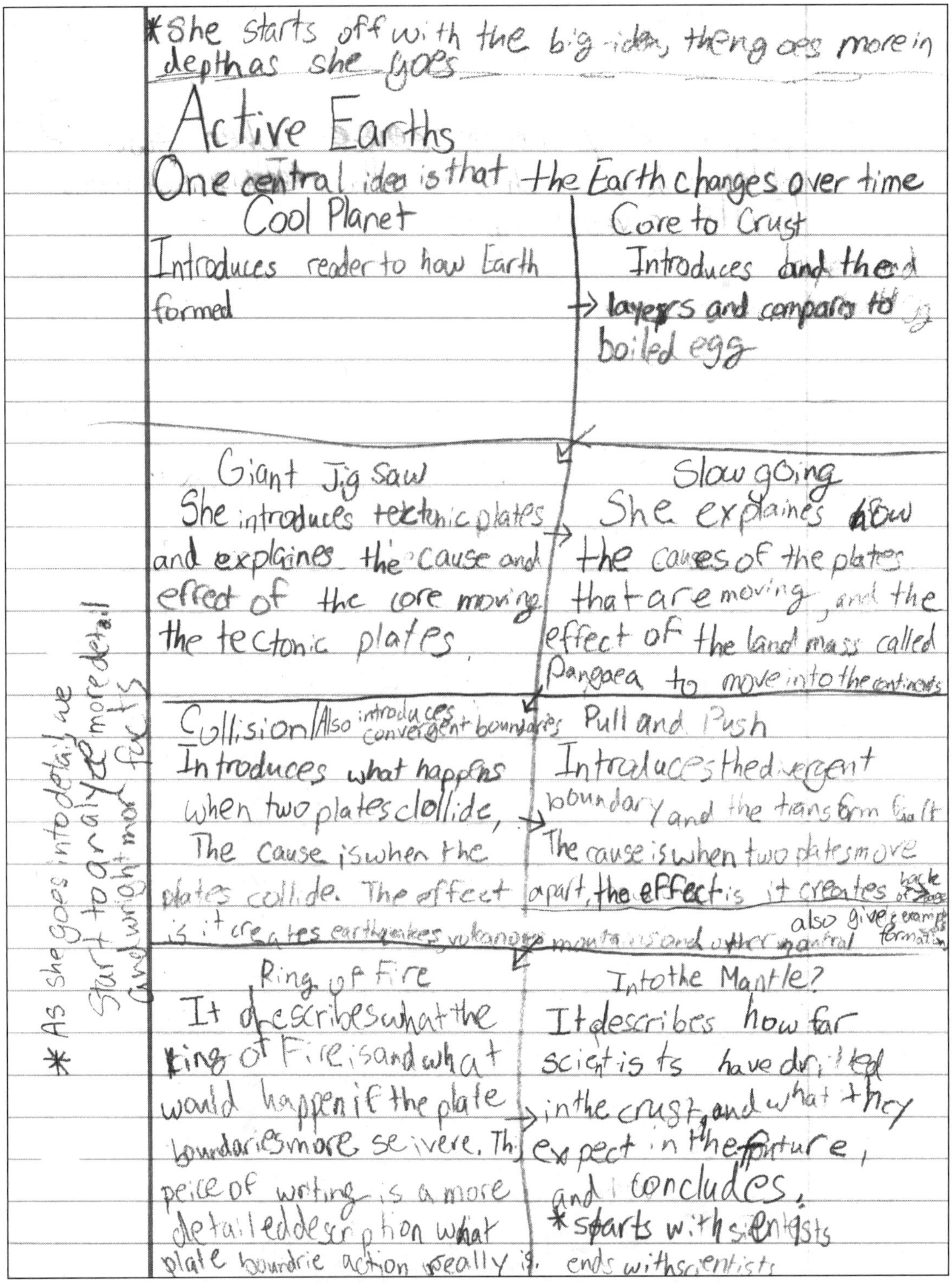

*She starts off with the big idea, then goes more in depth as she goes

Active Earths

One central idea is that the Earth changes over time

Cool Planet	Core to Crust
Introduces reader to how Earth formed	Introduces and then → layers and compares to boiled egg

Giant Jig Saw	Slow going
She introduces tectonic plates and explaines the cause and effect of the core moving the tectonic plates.	She explaines how the causes of the plates that are moving, and the effect of the land mass called Pangaea to move into the continents

Collision/Also introduces convergent boundaries	Pull and Push
Introduces what happens when two plates collide, The cause is when the plates collide. The effect is it creates earthquakes volcanos mountains and other natural	Introduces the divergent boundary and the transform fault The cause is when two plates more apart, the effect is it creates back or page also gives example formation

Ring of Fire	Into the Mantle?
It describes what the King of Fire is and what would happen if the plate boundaries more se ivere. This peice of writing is a more detailed description what plate boundrie action really is.	It describes how far scientists have drilled in the crust, and what they expect in the future, and concludes. * starts with scientists ends with scientists

* As she goes into detail we start to analyze more detail (and write more facts)

FIGURE 8.12. Graphic created by a student to illustrate one source's descriptive structure.

Through this exercise the students who analyzed "Active Earth" (Geiger, 2010a) also began to notice how each section in the article added to the previous section. For example, in one section the author introduces the layers of the Earth—the core, the mantle, and the crust. Then in the next section she explains how the movement of the tectonic plates, which make up the crust, is affected by dynamics in the core and the mantle. So, the author introduces information in the first section that describes what the reader needs to know in order to understand the next section. This was a big "aha" for these students. When I met with them during Phase 1, I noticed that they were able to recall details from the source easily, but when I asked them to talk to me about how the author developed her ideas, they had no response. Engaging in an analysis of the author's structure (which included thinking about key details in each section) revealed to them how the author developed the ideas in the source—pushing them to think more deeply about this source. The student who created the graphic in Figure 8.12 attempts to reveal a deeper connection in the sentence he wrote at the top of the graphic, "She starts off with the big idea, then goes more in depth as she goes."

These conversations and learning experiences can occur with different types of sources, including video and infographics. Have you ever watched a video about a problem and what a group or organization is doing to solve this problem? Have you ever seen an infographic that lists the steps for how to make or do something? Noticing these sources' structures can help the students determine what details are important to pay attention to in the source.

In the real world, we do not read, view, or listen to a source to identify its structure. Instead, as we are reading a source, we may notice the structure, and noticing helps us continue making meaning as we continue reading. In the case of the students reading "Active Earth" (Geiger, 2010a), if they notice the source's descriptive structure, then they can anticipate that each section will address a subtopic and that each section may add to the ideas in the previous section. If they begin to see how the author is developing an idea or deepening their understanding of a topic, they can more easily glean the author's bigger ideas. If you are watching a video in which a problem is posed (e.g., whales frequently get caught in fishing nets), then you are more likely to look for and identify key details that describe how the problem is being solved (e.g., the fishing industry is designing nets that dissolve, releasing creatures entangled in the nets).

For more information on teaching students how to notice a source's structure, visit a blog entry I wrote at *https://bit.ly/2Axxnk9*. In this entry, I explain in detail a Phase 2 lesson I gave in which I introduced the problem–solution and descriptive text structures. In Appendix A, page 234, you will also find a quick guide for teaching students to identify a source's structure.

HOW DO WE PLAN AND TEACH FOR IDENTIFYING KEY DETAILS?

The approaches just described can all be introduced as part of a Phase 2—Meet the Strategies lesson in the three-phase plan for learning. A key consideration before planning is what purpose your students will have for reading, listening to, or viewing a source. Will you provide the purpose or will the students identify one? This is where we have to consider the cognitive load or the energy students bring to the task of identifying and explaining key details. With some students, a lot of effort is spent on identifying an author's main idea or point of view or a source's structure. The students can become worn out and have little energy for close reading. If this is the case, then I ease the cognitive load by providing a main idea statement or a statement that names the text's structure or author's point of view. Or I make sure that we draft a similar statement during the closing discussion of the Phase 1—Meet the Source lesson. Then, during the Phase 2 lesson, we can focus our energy on closely reading the source or parts of the source to identify relevant supporting details.

Whether you are introducing the pasta analogy or the explode-to-explain strategy, both will work better if you use a short source or just part of a source that the students read–viewed–listened to during Phase 1. With a printed text, you might choose just one or two key sentences. With an infographic like PBS Nature's "All about Snowy Owls" (2015), you might choose just the image of the talon and the caption. With the National Geographic video *Cobra vs. Mongoose* (n.d.-a), you might use just the 20 seconds the narrator spends describing the cobra.

As discussed in Chapter 4, when I consider a source, I make sure that it has three or four parts (e.g., sentences, paragraphs, graphics, and clips) that are worthy of having students closely read, view, or listen to in order to identify key details. There has to be enough information in the source or a part of the source for you to model for students, for you to guide them, and for students to practice on their own. In the case of the lesson described earlier with *Side by Side* (Pigdon, 2012), we only read three sentences. With another group, we might have closely read paragraphs on three separate pages in this book that all provide details about how the mother lion protects her cubs. What's "enough" text to be worthy of close reading depends on your students' strengths and needs and their purpose for close reading, viewing, or listening. This is the case with any purpose for which students are reading to identify and explain close details. For example, if you are going to teach students to identify key details that reveal an author's point of view, then the source needs to have several parts that serve this purpose. This way you will have a part you can model with and other parts for students to work through together and on their own.

In Figure 8.13, I have described a three-phase lesson that introduces the pasta analogy and provides an opportunity for students to closely read a small section of a source. This lesson is geared for a small group of students who are at an introductory level of identifying key words. Some are even struggling to recall specific details they read or learned from a source. During Phase 1—Meet the Source, the teacher introduces the short book *Side by Side* (Pigdon, 2012), and the students have an opportunity to read the book as a whole.

During Phase 2—Meet the Strategies, the teacher introduces the pasta analogy and a clear purpose for close reading to identify key details in one page of text. Then she thinks aloud about how she identifies a key detail in the first sentence. As you read what the teacher says during this think-aloud, notice how she thinks aloud about how some of the information in the excerpt *does not* help her respond to her purpose. This is important for students to see us do—they need to know that there may not be a key detail in every sentence or part of a source. After she thinks aloud, the teacher guides the students in closely reading the rest of the excerpt to identify key details and take notes as they do.

FIGURE 8.13. Sample three-phase lesson on "Introducing the Pasta Analogy and Close Reading to Identify Key Details." *Note:* This small-group lesson occurs over the course of several 20-minute sessions.

TEACHING Phase 1—*Meet the Source*

1. Introduce and preview the source.

The teacher briefly introduces the book *Side by Side* (Pigdon, 2012). Before previewing the book with the students, she shares a kid-friendly definition for the word *predator*—"an animal that preys on or hunts and kills other animals for food." She asks the students to consider whether a cat who lives outside is a predator and then to turn and discuss this idea with a peer. She leans in and coaches one pair of students on how to use the word *predator* in their explanation.

Then the teacher leads the students in previewing and predicting what they will be learning about the impala and lions in the book. As they preview the book, the teacher nudges the students to notice the comparison structure.

When they finish previewing the first several pages, the teacher provides a purpose for reading by saying, "As you read, ask yourself, 'What am I learning about the impala and the lion that is new information?'"

2. Read–view–listen and confer.

As the students read, the teacher begins conferences with individuals by saying, "Tell me a little bit about what you learned on this page." She notices that their responses are very general, like "I read about the cubs." The students do not elaborate without prompting. She coaches individuals on how to stop at the end of a sentence and ask themselves, "What did I just learn?" and how to reread to identify important words they might want to remember.

3. Discuss.

The teacher asks the students for a "thumbs-up" if they learned something new. She encourages them to turn and share with a partner. She leans in to listen to one pair talk. She notices that one of the partners is speaking about what he learned in very general terms. She directs him to return to the book and reread a specific section. She coaches him and his partner to think about important words in that section that can help them remember in greater detail what they read. When she closes with the larger group, she asks this pair to share how rereading this section to identify important words helped them remember the details in the text better.

TEACHING Phase 2—*Meet the Strategies*

1. Explain and model strategic reading–viewing–listening.

The teacher starts by introducing the concept of "key details."

> *Remember when we read a text or watch a video, we always have a purpose in mind. Yesterday your purpose was to look for new information. So, as you read, you probably noticed facts or details about the lion and impala that were new to you, right? Those would be key details. Those details help you respond to your purpose for reading. Key details are a lot like pasta.*

Then the teacher introduces the pasta analogy with an explanation similar to the one in Figure 8.3.

(continued)

She follows by stating to the students:

> *Today we are going to closely read a few parts of this book to identify key details that support one of the author's main ideas. I've written this main idea as a question to help guide us as we look for key details or pasta words and phrases. How does the mother lion protect her cubs?* [Points to a piece of paper with the question clearly written in large print for all students to view.]

> How does the mother lion protect her cubs?

The teacher hands each child a 2″ × 2″ sticky note, asks them to turn to page 8, and says:

> *When I read this page, I noticed some pasta words that will help me answer my question. Will you read this again and show me a thumbs-up if you agree?*

The students read the following excerpt silently:

> Lion cubs grow inside their mother for about 110 days.

> The cubs are born in a safe place under a bush or among rocks. Up to four cubs may be born at the same time.

> When they are born, lion cubs usually weigh about two pounds (one kilogram). They are blind and helpless. (Pigdon, 2012, p. 8)

They agree that there are relevant details by giving a thumbs-up.

Then the teacher says:

> *Watch as I show you how I identify key details or pasta words. I'm going to start by reading this first sentence.* [Reads aloud the first sentence and pauses.] *In this sentence, I learned that the mother is pregnant for about 110 days. If I think about my purpose, I don't think this detail helps me explain how she protects the cubs, so I'm going to keep reading.* [Reads aloud the next sentence and looks up.] *I think there might be pasta in this sentence or a key detail. I learned that the cubs are born "in a safe place under a bush or among rocks."* [Points to the words in the text as she reads.] *The word* safe *makes me think the cubs must be in danger. Maybe there's a predator hunting them for food. I know that you can hide under a bush or shrub or in between rocks. I'm thinking that this is one way the mother lion protects her cubs. I'm going to write down a few pasta words that will help me remember what I learned. I think that the words "safe" and "under a bush or among rocks" will be enough for me to remember what I was thinking.*

The teacher writes a bullet on the sticky note and jots down these words. Then she encourages students to copy her notes or write words of their own on sticky notes she gave each one.

> • Safe under a bush or among rocks

2. Practice with sections of the source.

Together the teacher and students think through the next three sentences on that page. Through discussion, they decide to write down the words *blind* and *helpless*. The students each write these details on their own sticky note. The students think that these details can be used to explain why the cubs need the mother to protect them and how she does so.

Next, the teacher asks the students to locate another page with a key detail and to try to locate pasta or key words and phrases on their own. (In some cases, the students will need to do this task as a group.) She leans in to coach individuals. By the time the students finish, they have written

(continued)

FIGURE 8.13.

three or four bulleted notes with words or phrases that will help them remember the key details. One student's notes look like the following:

> - Safe under a bush or among rocks
> - Blind, helpless
> - Hidden for first few months
> - Moves from hiding place to hiding place
> - Alone while mother eats and hunts

3. Discuss.

The teacher asks the students to use their sticky notes to turn and tell a partner how they would answer the question, *How do mother lions protect their cubs*? She closes by asking them to share how the pasta analogy helps them think about what is important in a source.

TEACHING Phase 3—*Meet the Response*

1. Introduce prompt for the response.

The teacher says the following:

> *If you were going to tell someone about what you learned, who would you tell? What would you say to explain how the mother lion protects the cubs? Let's use your notes to help you write what you would say to someone.*

2. Plan and rehearse.

The teacher and students write the beginning of a response together on a piece of chart paper. Then she asks the students to look at the first set of bulleted words in their notes: *safe under a bush and among rocks*. She poses this question, *How can we use these words to write about how the mother lion protects her cubs*? She coaches one student as he orally composes a sentence. Once he has done this, she writes his sentence on the chart paper. Then she encourages another student to add to what the first student said; as needed, she helps this student orally compose. The teacher writes this sentence as well.

> Today I learned about how the mother lion protects her cubs. She gives birth to the cubs in a place that a predator will not find them like under a bush or among rocks. The cubs cannot see and they are helpless so it's important that they are in a safe place.

She moves on by asking the students to look back at their notes to think about what they can write next. She asks them to each begin a response of his or her own that starts where the shared writing stops.

3. Write and confer.

The teacher continues providing support to individual students. She encourages students to use their notes as a guide or plan for what to write. When the students are done writing, she asks them to read and comment on a partner's response. She closes by asking them to give a thumbs-up if they know someone with whom they can share what they learned.

FIGURE 8.13. *(continued)*

During Phase 3—Meet the Response, the students have an opportunity to look back at their notes from the previous phase and consider how they would explain what they learned to someone else. The teacher acts as a coach while they write this explanation.

Students should not be limited to writing summary-like responses. They can use their key-detail notes as a support for writing a variety of responses. A group of students and I engaged in close reading of a source about how scientists and engineers designed, built, and launched a Mars rover. The students identified key details in the source that revealed how this group of professionals collaborated to accomplish this project. A few days before this three-phase lesson, the students had worked in teams to build bridges as part of a STEM experience. During Phase 3, I asked the students to write a thank-you note to a team member who had made it easy to collaborate on this project. The students integrated what they had learned about the Mars rover team collaboration into their thank-you notes to a peer.

Up to this point, I have described several variations of what an introduction to the pasta analogy and identifying key details might look like. What you plan will depend on the needs of the students. Figure 8.14 provides guidance for planning a series of lessons focused on identifying key details that support a main idea. This type of learning experience, though, can work with different purposes. If your students are reading an essay to identify the author's point of view, they can hunt for pasta words or phrases that reveal this view. If your students are reading to identify a source's structure, they can hunt for key details that reveal the structure or structures. As you use the lesson plan guide, make appropriate adjustments based on the needs of the students and their purpose for reading–viewing–listening.

HOW DO WE ASSESS?

After students have had an opportunity to see us model, and then practice, identifying key details with our guidance, we need to observe them closely as they tackle doing this type of strategic processing with less support. During Phase 2 lessons, when you lean in to confer with individuals, start by looking for strategic thinking the student is attempting in some way and sharing this observation with the student. Your affirmation might sound like one of the following statements:

- You clearly understand what our purpose for watching the video is.
- It looks like you have found an important part of the source to reread.
- It seems as though you are asking yourself some questions about what is important.
- Your notes reveal that you are trying to identify key details in this source.

Determine a teaching point, too. What small step does this student need to take to increase his ability to engage in strategic processing? Figure 8.15 on page 157 provides suggestions for what you might notice when you confer with a student and suggestions for what you can say in response.

Analyzing students' written responses can also reveal whether they are able to identify and explain key details. Figure 8.16 on page 158 is a continuum showing the stages of development for students, with descriptors of what you might notice in their responses

FIGURE 8.14. Planning guide for "Introducing the Pasta Analogy and Close Reading to Identify Key Details."

PLANNING Phase 1—*Meet the Source*

1. Introduce and preview the source.

- As you determine which source you will use, keep in mind the purpose for reading during Phase 2. The purpose may be to answer a question related to a main idea in the source (e.g., *How does the mother lion protect her cubs?*), or it might be to identify a main idea and key details. The source needs to have key details that clearly support that purpose. You might use this purpose for Phase 1, or you can ask a more general question like, "What are you learning that is new or unfamiliar?" Plan accordingly.
- Plan an introduction to the source. (See Chapter 5 for suggestions.)

2. Read–view–listen and confer.

If you are watching a video, determine the point(s) at which you will pause and ask students to turn and talk about what they have learned.

3. Discuss.

- Plan to return to the purpose you gave students for reading or viewing.
- Think about a teaching point you might share with the students. This point might emerge while you are conferring with them.

PLANNING Phase 2—*Meet the Strategies*

1. Explain and model strategic reading–viewing–listening.

- Create an anchor chart with the *what, why,* and *how* related to identifying key details. (See Figure 8.2 for student-friendly language.)
- Plan an introduction and think-aloud that may include the following:
  - Explaining the pasta analogy.
  - Stating the *what, why,* and *how* related to identifying key details.
  - Sharing the purpose for close reading.
  - Closely reading a sentence or section of the source and identifying key words or phrases that help you respond to the purpose for reading.
  - Underlining or copying that detail into your notes to help you remember.

2. Practice with sections of the source.

Choose particular parts of the source that students should read (or watch) closely to identify key details. (Another option is to let the students locate a relevant part.)

3. Discuss.

- Develop a question related to strategic processing. For example, you might ask, "What did you learn today about identifying key details? Why is that important?" or "What is the role of 'purpose' in helping you identify key details?"
- Create a prompt related to content learned from the source. For example, you might say, "What did you learn today that you can explain in detail to a friend?"

(continued)

PLANNING Phase 3—*Meet the Response*
1. Introduce prompt for the response.
What will be the prompt for writing? These are examples of prompts for writing: • *One of the main ideas in this source is that the mother lion protects her cubs. What are key details in the source that support this idea?* • *What was the author's main idea in this source? Use textual evidence to explain and support your thinking.* • *Pretend you are a mother lion. Write a response from the point of view of the mother lion about how you protect your cubs from predators.*
2. Plan and rehearse.
• Decide how students will plan or rehearse for writing. Possible options include choosing key details from their notes that the students want to include in their response and/or talking with a partner about what they want to say in their response. • Plan for how you will help students who need extra support during writing. Possible options include writing together the first part of a response or asking individuals to orally compose the first sentence they will write.
3. Write and confer.
What will you try to notice when you lean in to confer? You might want to observe how students use their notes to help them write.

FIGURE 8.14. *(continued)*

at particular stages. This continuum is only a guide; as you think about your students' strengths and needs or observe growth in their understanding and use of strategic processing, you might revise or add descriptors.

With the continuum in mind, take a look at Leti's written response and my analysis in Figure 8.17 on page 159. Leti, an English learner, struggles to recall details and determine what is important in sources. She participated in a three-phase lesson similar to the one described earlier in Figure 8.13. While her writing is very listlike, she is attempting to take control of sharing what she learned by adding details that were not discussed in detail during the lessons, like sharing how the mother lion and the mother impala are similar and sharing her interpretation of why the mother lion would have to carry the cub—"because the cub can't run so fast." Figure 8.18 on page 160 shows Karley's response and my analysis. While Karley is clearly using her key details as a plan or guide for what to write in the response, she includes a lot of her own thinking or personal responses to what she read in the article about a stunt performer. She reveals a sense of engagement and thoughtful evaluation of the key details she has chosen.

WHAT DOES FOLLOW-UP INSTRUCTION LOOK LIKE?

With the small group reading *Side by Side* (Pigdon, 2012), the teacher noticed that the students did not have a firm control of identifying key words after the first three-phase

Scenario	How you can respond
The student is looking to see what others are writing and seems unclear about which pieces of information in the source might be key details.	• Prompt: *Tell me a little about what you are planning to do to identify a key detail.* • Think aloud about a portion of the source, modeling how you would determine which words, phrase, or visual image you think are important. • Ask the student to read–view–listen to a portion of a source and then think aloud with you about "pasta" words or phrases. Have a conversation that explores why these particular words or phrases are important.
The student is writing too much information from the source in his or her notes or is copying directly from the source.	Prompt the student as follows, and be prepared to step in and think aloud as needed: • *Tell me why you have chosen these words or phrases.* • *Remember we want to write down just enough to help us remember. Which of these words that you've written down would be just enough?* • *How can you say this in your own words? What does the author mean in this sentence?*
The student is writing words and phrases from the source that seem clearly tied to a central idea.	• Prompt: *Tell me how you chose these particular words.* • If appropriate, prompt the student to think about how he will combine the ideas into a written summary or another type of response. • Prompt: *What are you going to do to figure out how to start a written summary?*

FIGURE 8.15. Key Details: Conferring scenarios and suggestions for coaching.

lesson. She led a second three-phase lesson focused on identifying key details for another main idea in the source. During Phase 1—Meet the Source, a lesson that went quickly, the students read the book again. (There's always more learning that can be done in a second read of a dense information source.) During Phase 2—Meet the Strategies, the teacher stated a different main idea: the mother impala protects her fawn. The teacher reviewed the pasta analogy and then posed the purpose for reading: to find key details that support this idea. By focusing on the same task using the same source, the teacher eased the cognitive demands on the students. The students found this task easier to tackle because they had engaged in a similar learning experience with the same source. They could begin to take control of their learning and could move toward higher-level thinking, as they would be able to compare the lion and the impala.

Figure 8.19 on page 161 provides suggestions for follow-up instruction you might consider based on your observations of students; Appendix A, page 227, includes suggestions for how to, over the course of several lessons, gradually release responsibility to the students for this type of strategic processing and note-taking.

Stage	Characteristics of oral and written responses
Attempting	• The written response includes language copied directly from the source. • The oral or written response includes some key details from the source. • The reader of the response can infer the purpose for reading (e.g., reading to identify details that support a main idea, reading to identify the author's purpose, reading to support a personal response like "this career is fascinating").
Approaching	• Notes or summary reveals some insight into a main idea or other critical aspect of the source. • The student's summary is "listlike," in that it appears that the student worked his or her way down the list of key details, writing a sentence for each in a rote fashion. • The student integrates all of the details from his notes into one very long sentence.
Meeting	• The student is easily identifying words and phrases or ideas in the source that are clearly tied to a main idea. The student is able to share aloud why he or she chose particular details. • The student recognizes when key words or phrases in notes are related to each other and successfully combines them to make a point in the response. • The student integrates into the summary relevant ideas, responses, or facts not directly stated in the source that reveal insights gained as a result of thinking thoughtfully about the key details.
Exceeding	• The student extends the ideas in the source by sharing relevant background knowledge, ideas, or facts not found in the source. • If assigned to do so, the student evaluates how the author's organization of facts and ideas works to convey the central ideas in the source.

FIGURE 8.16. Stages of development in identifying key details that support a main idea.

CLOSING THOUGHTS

Being able to identify key details that help a reader–viewer–listener respond to their purpose is a critical skill that takes time to learn. I find that students need to continually practice this skill with and without our guidance. Students may start to struggle again when we switch to a new genre of text, a different type of source, or a different purpose for reading–viewing–listening. That is okay. Step in and take more control of the learning and then gradually release responsibility. Releasing control to the students may begin to happen more quickly as they notice how strategic processing related to identifying and explaining key details looks similar in a variety of contexts.

FIGURE 8.17. Example of response at the *approaching* stage.

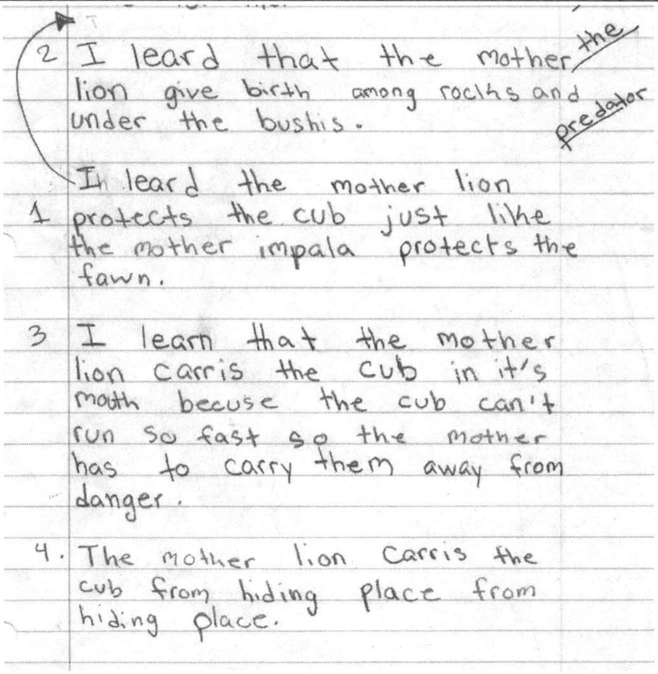

> 2 I leard that the mother the
> lion give birth among rochs and
> under the bushis. predator
>
> I leard the mother lion
> 1 protects the cub just like
> the mother impala protects the
> fawn.
>
> 3 I learn that the mother
> lion carris the cub in it's
> mouth becuse the cub can't
> run so fast so the mother
> has to carry them away from
> danger.
>
> 4. The mother lion carris the
> cub from hiding place from
> hiding place.

For this lesson, the students' purpose for close reading an excerpt from *Side by Side* (Pigdon, 2012) was to answer the question, How does the mother lion protect her cubs? As the students closely read two pages that provided an answer to this question, the teacher coached them in identifying key words or phrases they could use to respond. As they did, the teacher recorded the details on sticky notes. (Figure 8.1 is a photograph of artifacts from this lesson.) When they finished identifying key details together, the teacher asked the students to practice orally summarizing their learning. Then the students used the key words as their plan for writing.

Above is an example of one student's response. Notice that Leti, an English learner, attempts to use each key word to help her formulate an idea for each sentence. Her response is very listlike, but she appears to understand one of the main ideas as well as the details that support this main idea. She takes a risk in the third sentence and tries to elaborate on her thinking by explaining why the mother lion carries the cub—"because the cub can't run so fast." While the author did not state that the cub could not run quickly, earlier in the book he did share that the cubs are born "blind and helpless" (p. 8). Leti is grappling with how to convey her thinking in writing using standard English or the kind of English we use at school and would benefit from orally rehearsing sentences before writing.

FIGURE 8.18. Example of response at the *meeting* stage.

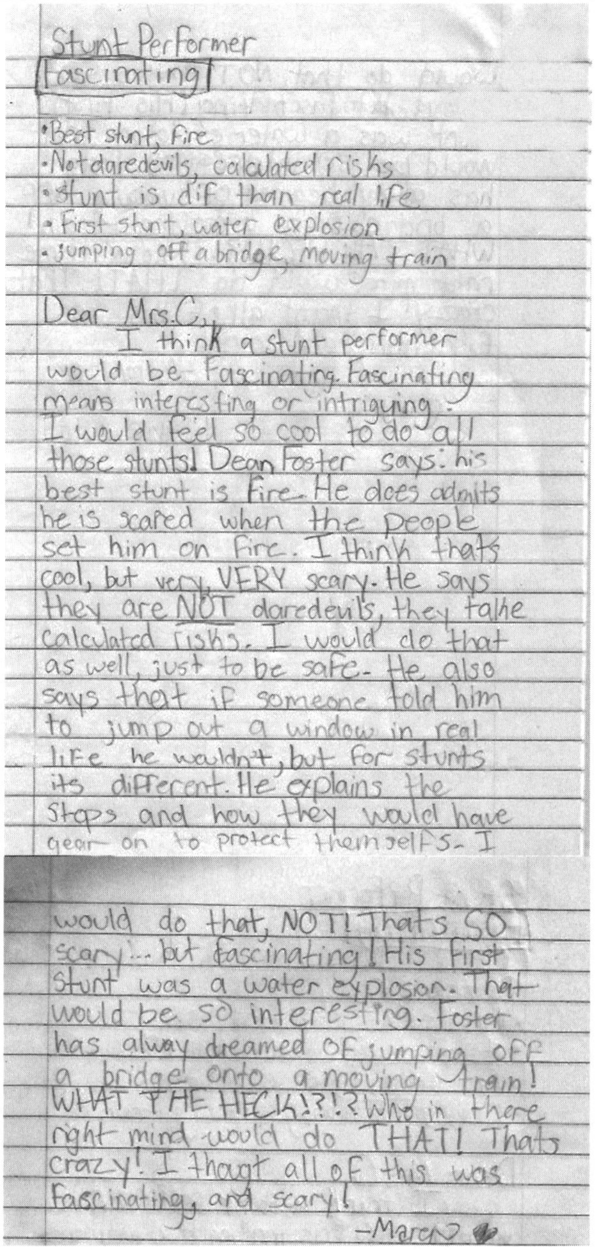

Stunt Performer
[fascinating]

• Best stunt, fire
• Not daredevils, calculated risks
• Stunt is dif than real life
• First stunt, water explosion
• jumping off a bridge, moving train

Dear Mrs. C.,
   I think a stunt performer would be fascinating. Fascinating means interesting or intriguing. I would feel so cool to do all those stunts! Dean Foster says: his best stunt is fire. He does admits he is scared when the people set him on fire. I think thats cool, but very, VERY scary. He says they are NOT daredevils, they take calculated risks. I would do that as well, just to be safe. He also says that if someone told him to jump out a window in real life he wouldn't, but for stunts its different. He explains the steps and how they would have gear on to protect themselfs. I would do that, NOT! Thats SO scary... but fascinating! His first stunt was a water explosion. That would be so interesting. Foster has alway dreamed of jumping off a bridge onto a moving train! WHAT THE HECK!?!? Who in there right mind would do THAT! Thats crazy! I thaugt all of this was fascinating, and scary!
                              —Marena

As described earlier in this chapter, this student, Karley, wrote this essay in response to an article she had read about stunt performers. When she read the article the first time, she decided that being a stunt performer would be a fascinating experience. Then she did a close reading of this article to identify key details that supported her response. The details are noted in her bulleted list at the top of the response. Her response meets expectations. The key details are clearly tied to her response that this career would be fascinating, and she makes this clear throughout her essay. She integrates her personal response to particular details. She also reveals her personal response to details in a variety of ways—with words written in all capital letters, by underlining a word, by including exclamation marks, and so forth.

FIGURE 8.19. Suggestions for follow-up instruction.

If . . .	Then . . .
Students are struggling or are just beginning to get a grip on identifying key details on their own.	• Implement several lessons over time focused on identifying key details with a similar purpose for reading–viewing–listening (e.g., to find supporting evidence for a main idea, to find key details that reveal an author's point of view). • Be prepared to step in and think aloud about how you determined what was important (in response to a specific purpose) with a section of a source. • At the end of Phase 2—Meet the Strategies lessons, share examples of strong student notes and/or ask students to discuss how they determined what was important while reading–viewing–listening. Begin an anchor chart with "tips for identifying key details" that students can refer to later.
Students struggle to use their key ideas to explain their thinking orally or in writing.	• Extend the amount of time you spend in Phase 3—Meet the Response, so that students can orally compose or practice saying aloud exactly what they will write (one sentence at a time). • With a list of key words or phrases, think aloud about how you go about combining certain words and ideas from the list into a sentence when you are planning to write. • Try using the "explode-to-explain" strategy during Phase 2. Allow students the time to think through the meaning of one or two sentences.
Students rely on key details in the main part of a source and ignore key details in graphics and other visual images.	• During Phase 2, demonstrate how you noticed key details in a particular graphic and how you decided what to write in your notes. • Implement the lessons in Chapter 9, "Learning from a Source's Visual Images and Other Features."
Students are beginning to identify key details more easily.	• Release responsibility to partners during Phase 2. Ask partners to locate key details, think through them together, and decide collaboratively what they will write in their notes. • If you have been providing the main idea (or the source's structure or the author's point of view), release responsibility for doing this task to the students.
Students have a grasp on identifying key details that help them respond to a purpose for reading–viewing–listening.	• If you have mainly been using texts in a particular genre, shift to other types of sources or more complex genres. • Implement the lessons in Chapter 11, "Synthesis of Information from Multiple Sources."

CHAPTER NINE

Learning from a Source's Visual Images and Other Features

Take a moment to consider the page from the short book *How Do We Measure Matter?* (Peppas, 2013, p. 14) in Figure 9.1. There are four sources of information on this page— the heading, the printed text, the caption, and the photographs. Each of these sources plays a critical role in helping the reader understand the concept of measuring volume.

- The **heading** "Measuring volume" explicitly states what will be addressed on this page.
- The **running text** introduces this subtopic and includes the following information:
  - A definition for volume ("the measurement of how much space matter takes up")
  - A list of examples of tools that measure volume ("measuring cups," "graduated cylinders and beakers")
  - The purpose of the lines of measurement ("number values . . .").
- The **caption** contains the following information:
  - A description of the physical characteristics of tools for measuring volume ("see-through," "numbers on the outside of it")
  - An explanation of how to measure volume ("read the number at the very top").
- The **photographs** of the cylinders and measuring cup extend the information in the caption by providing examples of what these tools with "numbers on the outside" look like.

To fully understand the information on this page, a reader needs to make meaning from the running text *and* the features. As is the case with many informational sources our students tackle, nearly every page in this source has features that contribute important information to the student's learning experience. Videos and infographics are also dense with features; some infographics are made up entirely of features. Each feature contributes in some way to the meaning being conveyed by that source. In other words, the features and the rest of the source work together to create the content in that source. So, it is essential that students pay attention to the features in a source. If a student skips or disregards the value of the caption and photographs on this page, he will miss out on important learning.

While many students can practically close their eyes and locate the table of contents or photographs with captions, they cannot always clearly articulate what they have just learned after examining a particular feature closely. Many students tend to treat the features as purely supplemental to the source, perusing them quickly and often solely for their aesthetic appeal. They might say to you that the pictures in a text are "really cool," but they cannot necessarily explain how a feature helped them understand other parts of the source better. What is lacking is the students' full realization that a source's features contribute a great deal to its meaning and support the reader–viewer–listener in many ways as he or she makes meaning.

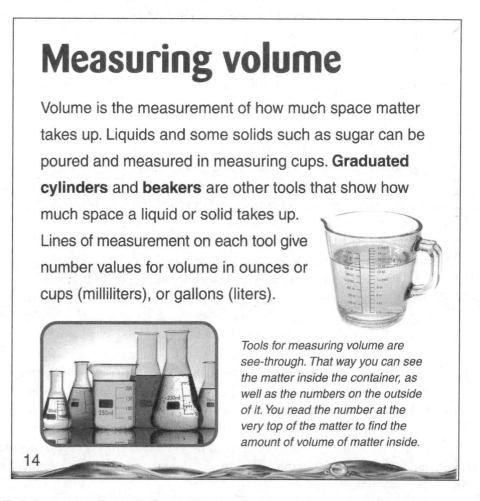

Measuring volume

Volume is the measurement of how much space matter takes up. Liquids and some solids such as sugar can be poured and measured in measuring cups. **Graduated cylinders** and **beakers** are other tools that show how much space a liquid or solid takes up. Lines of measurement on each tool give number values for volume in ounces or cups (milliliters), or gallons (liters).

Tools for measuring volume are see-through. That way you can see the matter inside the container, as well as the numbers on the outside of it. You read the number at the very top of the matter to find the amount of volume of matter inside.

14

FIGURE 9.1. Excerpt from *How Do We Measure Matter?* (Peppas, 2013, p. 14). Reprinted with permission from Crabtree Publishing Company.

WHAT DO WE MEAN BY
"LEARNING FROM A SOURCE'S FEATURES"?

What: Readers know that informational sources have lots of features that we need to pay attention to and learn from as we read, view, or listen to them. Examples of *features* are titles, headings, maps, photographs, diagrams, charts, and graphs.

Why: Paying attention to some features like titles and headings can help us locate particular information in a source or make predictions about what we will be learning about. Carefully reading or looking at features, like photographs, maps, and diagrams, can help us learn more about the topic of that source and understand the rest of the source better.

How: You can make sense of a feature by asking questions like these:

- What is the purpose of this feature?
- What am I learning from this feature?
- How does this feature help me understand other parts of the source?

You may have to use your knowledge about the world and what you already know about features to help you.

FIGURE 9.2. Student-friendly explanation of what we mean by "learning from a source's features."

Nowadays students are bombarded with features that they need to pay attention to in sources. A source's features are the printed text or visual images that stand out or are distinct from the rest of the source. As described in Figure 9.2 above, paying attention to features can help a reader in many ways. Some features, like titles and headings, help us predict what we will be learning about next in a source. Some may also help us locate specific information that we are looking for. Other features, like maps, diagrams, and other visual images, provide information the author could not convey as easily in words or serve to support or extend the information in the main part of a source.

There are multiple features on every page in the book *How Do We Measure Matter?* (Peppas, 2013). Photographs throughout the book serve as *examples* of concepts the author is trying to *describe* or *explain*. For example, on one page that has a discussion of "displacement," there is a photograph, similar to the one in Figure 9.3, of an orange being dropped into a clear bowl of water. This picture is used as an example of how water is displaced by another object. In this visual, water is clearly splashing out of the bowl. The water that is pushed out of the way by the orange illustrates the concept of liquid displacement that the author explains in the text. Taking a moment to consider this visual makes it much easier for a student to understand this concept, especially if he understands that the photograph's purpose is to serve as a real-life example of what the author is explaining.

Features like titles and diagrams that we commonly find in traditional texts can also be found in video clips and infographics. Students who read *How Do We Measure Matter?*

(Peppas, 2013) might also watch the video *3 States of Matter* (Free School, 2015). Using the QR code or link below, take a moment to watch this video. Similar to the book, this video includes features like photographs of different liquids, gases, and solids. There are also static diagrams that reveal how closely the molecules are placed together in solids, liquids, and gases. Other videos on the same topic include animated diagrams in which the viewer can see the molecules in liquids moving close together and the molecules in gases moving freely about. Through close examination of these diagrams (and the differences between them), a student can begin to understand how and why the molecules move differently.

https://www.youtube.com/watch?v=wclY8F-UoTE

 Some sources are almost entirely made of up features. Check out the infographic by Kids Discover in Figure 9.4 on the next page. What are features that students might notice and name? There is a title and a deck (a caption of sorts that follows or sits under the title and provides additional information about the source). These two features give the reader clues as to the topic of the infographic. Three headings help the reader notice that there are three main parts to the infographic, one for each state of matter. Each of the main

FIGURE 9.3. In informational sources, some photographs like this one serve as *real-life examples* of concepts like liquid displacement.

165

FIGURE 9.4. "States of Matter" infographic created by Kids Discover (n.d.-a).

States of Matter

Water freezes. Ice melts. Steam condenses. These are ways that water—and all matter—can change. Scientists refer to these changes as "changes of state." However, the molecules that make up the matter do not change.

Gases

If it fills the entire space of the container it's in, it's a gas. Unlike liquids and solids, the molecules in a gas are spread far apart and full of energy. They bounce around, spreading out to fill the volume and shape of the container they're in—a balloon, for example.

Gas molecules move around freely.

Liquids

If it flows, it's a liquid. Think of water coming out of a hose. Like all liquids, the water changes shape. If it flows into a container, such as a bucket or a pool, it takes the shape of the container. The molecules that make up liquids are close together but are free to move around. This is what makes the shape of a liquid changeable.

Water molecules are close together but can move around.

Sublimation

Deposition

Condensation

Evaporation

H_2O

Melting

Solidification

Solids

If matter is a solid object, it maintains its own shape. Take rocks, for example. A rock is a solid object. It keeps its shape unless it is crushed or something else happens to it. This is because the molecules in solids are so tightly packed that they are not free to move around.

Solid molecules are tightly packed and stay in a fixed position.

parts has a graphic illustrating the movement of molecules in that particular state of matter and a caption that describes this movement (e.g., "move around freely," "close together but can move around," and "stay in a fixed position"). The illustrations and photographs are part of a larger diagram that has arrows with titles naming the processes (e.g., sublimation and deposition) that occur when matter changes from one state to another.

It is one thing to be able to name these features. It is another to be able to explain what you are learning from them. Think about the academic vocabulary I've used to describe the information a student might learn from these three sources. I used words like *title, diagram,* and *deck* to name features, but I also used language that reveals the purpose of the feature or what the author is trying to do with that feature—words like *explains, describes,* and *provides examples.* My language also included the types of details or information that a student could learn that reveal *how, why, when, where,* and more. So then ideally, we want students to go beyond simply identifying features. We want them to use these features to deepen their understanding of the topic or idea being addressed in a source. In order to do this, students need to demonstrate independence in carrying out the following tasks:

- Identifying various types of features.
- Thinking about the types of details the author is using in the feature—*description, example,* and *explanation.*
- Reading and then paraphrasing the content they learned in a feature.
- Making connections between the content in the feature and the content in the primary part of the source (e.g., running text in an article or narration in a video).
- Assessing the author's or creator's use of features to clearly communicate an idea.
- Evaluating the choice of features and how that choice may reveal the author's or creator's perspectives.

DO YOUR STUDENTS NEED TO WORK ON THIS?

Do some of your students need support in making meaning from features in informational sources? Asking ourselves the following questions may help us determine if our students need instruction in this area of comprehension.

During conferences with individuals or small groups:
- Do the students talk about content in a source that is not drawn from any of the features?
- Do they talk about the appeal of a feature ("That's a cool photo!") but not what they learned from that feature?
- Do they share what they learned from a feature, but not necessarily how that helped them understand the main part of the source or the author's main ideas?

In evaluating students' written responses:

- Do they write solely about content learned in the main part of the source (versus the features)?

- Do they write about the content in a feature that reveals a misunderstanding of the information in that feature?

- Does their writing lack insight they would have developed if they had used the features to help them think more deeply about the main part of the source or the source as a whole?

There are several types of lessons that we can implement in response to what we notice about our students. We might give lessons that introduce the names and purposes of specific features, that use features to make predictions, or that teach students how to learn from visual images like maps, diagrams, and charts. In Chapter 5, there are recommendations for teaching students how to use features to make predictions using the mnemonic THIEVES; the sample lesson described lends itself to introducing the names of features and purposes as well. The rest of this chapter offers suggestions for the last type of lesson—learning from visual images (e.g. photographs, diagrams, and maps) and their related print features (e.g., captions and labels).

WHERE TO START? INTRODUCE KEY QUESTIONS AND RELEVANT LANGUAGE

Visual images like photographs, diagrams, graphs, and maps have become a dominant presence in many informational sources. These features usually include some combination of pictures, words, numbers, and/or graphics. Frequently they are supported by print features, like the caption that accompanies a photograph or the labels that name the parts of an animal or object portrayed in a diagram. Figure 9.5 (pp. 170–173) includes descriptions of several types of visual images and supporting print features that might be used in anchor charts or as part of your work with students.

We can make strategic processing of visual images (and supporting print features) clear for students by teaching them to ask three important questions:

- *What is the purpose of this feature?*
- *What am I learning from this feature?*
- *How does this feature help me understand other parts of the source?*

To answer these questions, the students need to realize that they will need to use information in the source *and* relevant background knowledge. They need to think about what they already know about the topic as well as what they know about particular types of features.

One way to teach for this kind of strategic processing is through close reading (or viewing) and discussion of one visual image and its supporting print features. During this learning experience, we also need to highlight for students the language we use to describe what we are learning. As discussed in Chapter 8, when we engage students in thinking carefully about the details in a source—whether in a printed text or in a visual image—we need to be aware of the language we can use to describe our learning. This means that students can name the features *and* explain what the author is doing or what the information in the feature represents. What do I mean by this statement? Take a moment to look back at Figure 9.1 and then consider the following explanation of what can be learned from the features on this page in *How Do We Measure Matter?* (Peppas, 2013).

> In the caption, the author *describes the physical characteristics* of tools I can use to measure volume—"see-through" and "numbers on the outside." She also *explains how* I can use these tools to measure volume—by looking at "the number at the very top of the matter." The photograph shows me *examples* of these tools. I notice the numbers on these tools and understand better *how* I can use the number at the top of each to measure matter.

This explanation includes not only reference to the specific features, but also the language that describes what the author is doing or the type of information being learned.

With some students, we have to be intentional in teaching them how to use this type of language. The following are examples of stems you might provide students when they are trying to explain what they are thinking and learning (about a feature):

With traditional texts, infographics, and video

- In this feature, the author *explains* [how to do something] . . .
- In this feature, the author *describes* [the physical characteristics of something] . . .
- In this feature, the author *shows* me an *example* of . . .
- In this feature, the author *defines* . . .
- When I looked at (or saw) the [name a feature], I *learned* that . . .
- When I looked closely at the [name a feature], I *noticed* that . . .
- This feature helped me notice the *differences and similarities between* . . .
- In this feature, I learned *where/how/why/when/what* . . .

With animated diagrams in video

- I noticed that this part of the animated diagram is moving in order to show me how . . .
- I think the creator of this video chose an animated diagram because . . .
- Now I understand what the narrator said about . . . because the diagram shows . . .

Figure 9.6 on page 174 includes images of two anchor charts I created with a group of students as we engaged in this type of learning experience. At the beginning of the Phase 2—Meet the Strategies lesson with these students, I posted these two charts with just the titles, "Words I can use to share my thinking" and "Notes about Features." As we closely read features in the source, we paused periodically to discuss what we had done

FIGURE 9.5. Examples of visual images and supporting print features.

	Visual images		
Feature	**Student-friendly purpose**	**Description**	**Important for students to note . . .**
Photograph	Shows an example of what the author (or narrator) is describing in the source.	Photographs are pictures of real-life people, places, or things. They can be used to represent the real world or to symbolize an idea. They are frequently used in sources as examples of what the author is describing. 	A photograph may have been taken in a certain time period. The student's background knowledge about that period should influence the meaning they make from the photograph. Photographs or still images are also frequently seen in videos. In *3 States of Matter* (Free School, 2015), the creator includes photographs of *examples* of different states of matter. When students notice a photograph in a video, it may be helpful to ask, "What is the author's purpose for including this photo?"
Illustration	Shows what something the author (or narrator) is describing looks like.	Illustrations may be sketches, drawings, or paintings that represent in some way people, places, things, or ideas. Illustrations also include animations created for videos. Illustrations can be part of another type of visual image like diagrams. 	Some students may not realize that drawings are depicting the distant past or that the drawings were created during historical times that predated cameras. With video, there is frequently a narrator speaking during the animations. Similar to how traditional texts are structured, the narration and the animations in a video work together or support each other to convey an idea, so students need to pay attention to both. A good question to ask is, "What are the similarities and differences between the content in the animation and the content in the narration?"

170

| Diagrams | A drawing that helps the reader visualize what is being described in the source. Authors may include labels to show the parts or steps in a process. | Diagrams are simplified drawings of a construct (e.g., a cell) or concept (e.g., solid state of matter) or process (e.g., evaporation). Frequently arrows or lines are incorporated to show change over time or the direction or movement from one state or place to another. The parts of a diagram may also have labels and/or words that act as supporting features. Some videos include animated diagrams that show how or in what way something occurs.

Solid Liquid Gas
Heating
Cooling | Diagrams are abundant in infographics and are also used in video sources. In the video *3 States of Matter* (Free School, 2015), there are diagrams of atoms in different states. When viewing a video, students may need to pause on the frame with the diagram so they can look closely. If there is accompanying audio, the student may need to also listen to that section of the audio several times to understand what is in the diagram.

There are several different types of diagrams students might learn to name, including cycle diagrams, flow charts, tree diagrams, and cutaways or cross-sections. |
| Graphs | An organization of data or information that shows how two or more things are related. | Graphs convey some type of organized data or statistical information. They may incorporate pictures, bars, numbers, lines, or dots. Common examples are bar graphs and line graphs.

Solid to Liquid to Gas (Ice to Water to Steam)
— Solid   − − Liquid   ⋯ Gas
Degrees in C
120 100 80 60 40 20 0
Liquid to Gas
Solid to Liquid
Time in Minutes 0 2 4 6 8 10 12 | Noticing the differences between diagrams and graphs can be helpful. However, a reader does not need to spend a lot of energy labeling a graphic as one of these. Instead, the reader needs to focus on what the author's purpose for this graphic is and how this graphic helps the reader visualize or understand what the author is describing in the main part of the source.

There are several different types of graphs students might learn to name, including line, pie, and bar graphs. |

(continued)

Feature	Student-friendly purpose	Description	Important for students to note . . .
Insets or Close-Ups	A picture that gives the reader an up-close view of a small part of a bigger picture.	Smaller visual images set within or near a larger visual image. The smaller image, usually a close-up of something, highlights some aspect of the larger picture.	Students need to understand that the smaller image is frequently a magnification of something important (but not as easily noticed) in the larger picture.
Maps	A drawing of a location or place that gives the reader more information about that place.	Maps are a visual depiction of a small or large area. A map usually represents particular features of that area like the climate or certain boundaries, locations of certain places, or a particular route. Some maps represent cultural aspects of the people that live in that area. A map has its own features, which may include a title, compass rose, scale, key, and symbols that represent certain pieces of information.	Readers can easily identify maps, but the greater difficulty is in identifying the purpose of a map and/or when the map was created. Both of these factors influence the meaning that can be made from this map. Introducing language to describe maps like *political, road, world, boundaries, demographics,* and *symbols* can help students describe what they are noticing.

172

Feature	Purpose	Description	Important for students to note . . .
Tables	An organization of data or information in rows and columns that provides the reader with an easy way to look at the information.	Tables display data or information and are usually constructed in matrices with rows and columns. _State of matter table:_ | State of Matter	Shape and Volume	Motion of Particles | |---|---|---|
Solid	Definite shape and volume	Locked in position; vibrate
Liquid	Takes shape of container; definite volume	Limited movement as they are very close together
Gas	Does not have definite shape or volume	Move freely		Readers and viewers need to be conscious of how tables are organized, reading from top to bottom and left to right, as needed.
Timelines	A graphic that shows the reader the order of a series of events.	Timelines represent a series of events that happened within a particular time frame or how objects or inventions have changed over time. The major points on the timeline may be marked with photographs or illustrations and dates. They may include other supporting print features like labels or short descriptions of major events or points on the timeline.	Students need to be aware that not all timelines are organized from left to right or vertically. Some are horizontal and some curve back and forth as though following a path. Others may include a map or some other type of background that is important to consider when noticing the specific points on the timeline.

Print features that support visual images

Features	Purpose	Description	Important for students to note . . .
Captions	Give the reader more information about what is in a picture.	Captions provide readers with more information than they could have assimilated from the visual image alone. Captions typically describe a visual image like a photograph or drawing. Sometimes the caption provides information that is not provided in the main part of the source.	The caption and its accompanying visual image support each other. To learn the most from these partner features, readers need to move back and forth between each, reading and looking, rereading and looking again.
Labels	Words that name the parts of something in a picture or an illustration.	Labels typically name the parts of something represented in the image (like the parts of a cell). Similar to captions, labels also provide readers with more information than they could have drawn from the image by itself.	Labels may be taken for granted or, if there are numerous labels for one image, may seem overwhelming to students. Students need to keep the purpose of a label—to name the parts of something—in mind as they make sense of the visual image.

FIGURE 9.5. (*continued*)

173

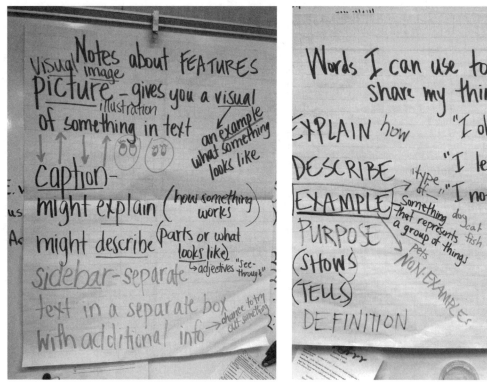

FIGURE 9.6. Anchor charts created with students during a lesson focused on learning from features.

to make sense of the features and to write notes on the chart about any aspects of the features we wanted to remember or the language we used that was helpful. Providing time for students to analyze the language they needed to use to explain their thinking is critical.

What does this instruction look like with videos and infographics? There are *a lot* of features in videos. As stated earlier, many of these features are similar to those in traditional printed texts. The video *3 States of Matter* (Free School, 2015) includes a title, headings, and visual images. Videos also include special effects that might be considered features, such as audio and visual backgrounds, different types of transitions, and so forth. Similarly, the layout, color, and size of the fonts in infographics are also features to be considered. In Figure 9.7 I have included some tips for teaching students to make sense of print features and visual images in video.

HOW DO WE PLAN AND TEACH FOR LEARNING FROM VISUAL IMAGES?

Take a moment to read the sample three-phase lesson described in Figure 9.8 (pp. 176–178). Notice that the teacher introduces the source during Phase 1—Meet the Source and then, while she confers with students as they read the source, she takes notes about what they are doing to make sense of the visual images in the source. Taking notes is helpful in that you can get an idea of how particular students are strategically processing and which visual images in a source seem harder than others for students to understand. You can use this information to plan for Phase 2—Meet the Strategies when you make decisions about which visual images in the source you will ask students to consider as you think aloud and as they practice with a partner or independently.

During the Phase 2 lesson, the teacher follows through by thinking aloud about a visual image, using the three questions posed earlier in this chapter. Depending on your students, when you introduce the concept of learning from visual images, you may only want to pose the first two questions: "What is the purpose of this feature?" and "What am I learning from this feature?" This eases the load of a cognitively demanding task. You can save the last question for later lessons.

The Phase 3—Meet the Response lesson described in Figure 9.8 on the next page might be very short. (Remember that each of the "phases" in the three-phase plan for learning can vary in length, depending on the source and the tasks.) The teacher's objective is to nurture a hyperawareness of the important learning that can happen when students pay attention to or closely read visual images and supporting print features. The example of a response the teacher shares creates clarity for the students regarding what this awareness looks like. The teacher weaves in what she learned from the photographs and the caption, what the author does in those features, and her personal connections to the content. At this point, she does not try to tackle the connections between the information in the features and the information in the main part of the text. She plans to integrate this task into later lessons.

Video Tips

- Encourage students to *notice and name* visual images like charts, diagrams, and tables that appear in videos. (Sometimes they take these images for granted.)
- Pause a video when a visual image like a chart or table appears and then demonstrate how you make sense of that feature. Think aloud in front of students about the purpose of this feature, why it is important to consider, and the questions you ask as you make sense of the feature.
- If there is a narration occurring when a visual image like a table is presented, demonstrate for students how a person has to look at the visual image closely *and* also listen to the narration (if present) carefully. Model jotting down notes that you learned from both the image and the narration.
- With an animated diagram, think aloud about what you notice as the clip plays. You might use language like the following:
  ○ "I noticed that this part of the diagram is moving in order to show me how . . ."
  ○ "I think the creator of this video chose an animated diagram because . . ."
  ○ "Now I understand what the narrator said about . . . because the diagram shows . . ."
- Start an anchor chart similar to the charts in Figure 9.6. You might title this chart "Tips for Making Sense of Visual Images in Video." Encourage students to create the tips with you.

FIGURE 9.7. Tips for teaching students to learn from a video's features.

FIGURE 9.8. Sample three-phase lesson for "Learning from Visual Images."
Note: The short book *How Do We Measure Matter?* (Peppas, 2012) is available for classroom use at *www.getepic.com.* For the Phase 1—Meet the Source lesson, the students read the book on individual laptops. For the Phase 2—Meet the Strategies lesson, the students wrote directly on a copy of one page from this book and then returned to the online version to closely read and take notes about additional visual images.

TEACHING Phase 1—*Meet the Source*
1. Introduce and preview the source.

The teacher briefly introduces the short book *How Do We Measure Matter?* (Peppas, 2012).
 	
She shares a kid-friendly definition for the word *example*—"some person, place, thing, or idea that is representative or similar to others in a group." (This word is not in the book, but the author shares examples of particular concepts in both the printed text and visual images.) The teacher illustrates what the word *example* means by giving examples of fruits and pets. Then she asks the students to collaborate with a partner in listing examples of sports. Before moving on, the teacher states that in *How Do We Measure Matter?,* the author provides lots of examples of the concepts or topics she is explaining in the book.
 	
Next, the teacher states a clear purpose for reading that is posted for all students to view.
 	
   • *What are you learning about the properties of matter?*
   • *What is important to think about when we measure matter?*
 	
The students work with a partner to make predictions about what they will be learning before they read independently.

2. Read–view–listen and confer.
The teacher begins conferring with individual students by saying, "Tell me a little bit about what you have learned on this page." As each student shares, the teacher notes whether she or he reveals information learned from the features on that page. Many do not. When this occurs, the teacher prompts the student to consider the image and engages him or her in a short discussion about what she can learn from that image. She also takes notes about the images that seem hardest for the students to talk about in a meaningful way to consult later when she plans for the Phase 2 lesson.
3. Discuss.
The teacher closes by returning to the purpose for reading. She gives the students a few moments to consider the posted questions. Then she asks them to turn in trios and discuss their thinking. She leans in to listen to one group talk. One of the students discusses a visual image she noticed in the book. The teacher nudges the students in the group to discuss this visual image further by asking them, "Why is this visual image important to pay attention to in this book?" When she regroups with all of the students, she shares highlights from the smaller-group conversation.

TEACHING Phase 2—*Meet the Strategies*
1. Explain and model strategic reading–viewing–listening.

The teacher starts by sharing what readers know about visual images in informational sources and why it is important to consider these features. Her comments sound like the following:
 	
   Authors and creators of informational sources like books, videos, and infographics use
   visual images to help readers learn about the topic of that source. A visual image can be a

(continued)

photograph or illustration, but it can also be a graphic like a diagram or a map. Sometimes there is print or text like a caption or labels that support this image. Carefully reading or looking at visual images can help us learn more about the topic of that source and understand the rest of the source better. Let's look through this source and notice the visual images.

The students notice many visual images—specifically, photographs and captions. With the teacher, they define the terms *photograph* and *caption* and discuss the purpose of these features. The teacher writes notes on a piece of chart paper titled "Notes about Features." (See Figure 9.6 for examples of what these notes might look like.)

Then the teacher posts three questions that students can use to guide them as they closely read visual images:

- *What is the purpose of this feature?*
- *What am I learning from this feature?*
- *How does this feature help me understand other parts of the source?*

The teacher thinks aloud about what she does to glean meaning from the visual image on page 14 in *How Do We Measure Matter?*. (See Figure 9.1.) She starts by placing a hard copy of this page on the document camera for all students to view. Her think-aloud sounds like the following:

When I look carefully at this photograph, I notice that the author is giving me examples of tools that can be used to measure volume. That's the purpose of this image. This makes me think about what I read in the text. [Points to words in the text.] I notice the words "graduated cylinders and beakers." This is probably what I'm looking at in this photograph. The other photograph is of a measuring cup. I recognize this because I have one at home, and I know this is another example of a tool I can use to measure volume. Now I am going to read the caption and think about what the author is trying to teach me.

She closes the think-aloud by jotting down what she has learned in the margins of the hard copy of this page. She writes the word *example* and draws an arrow to the photographs. In the margin near the caption, she jots down the phrase "how to measure volume—look at top line on."

The teacher begins to draw students into thinking with her about another visual image in the source. She hands out copies of the image and asks the students to view the image independently first. Then she says, "What did you notice?" She encourages them to consider the three posted questions. She also guides them in discussing the types of details revealed in the image. As needed, she provides language they can use or highlights language they use to describe what the author communicates through the visual image or supporting print features, such as *she gives examples, she explains the cause and effect, she describes the physical characteristics,* and *she compares.* The students annotate their copy of the text. With the teacher, the group returns to the anchor chart and adds additional notes.

2. Practice with sections of the source.

The teacher asks the students to find and closely read a few additional visual images in the format of the book available online. She coaches pairs of students as they think through the posted questions, examine a particular feature, and jot a few notes on lined paper about their thinking.

3. Discuss.

To close the lesson the teacher prompts small groups to discuss the following questions:

- *What did you learn from a visual image today?*
- *Why is paying attention to this visual image important to understanding the rest of the book?*

(continued)

FIGURE 9.8.

TEACHING Phase 3—*Meet the Response*
1. Introduce prompt for the response.
The teacher posts and briefly discusses the following prompt for a short, written response: *Take a moment to look at your annotations or notes on what you learned from visual images in this source. Which image helped you understand the topic of the source better? Describe what you learned and why you think it is important in a short letter to me.*
2. Plan and rehearse.
The teacher places an example of a response on the document camera. > The visual image and caption on page 14 helped me understand how to measure volume better. I already knew a little bit about this, but it was good to review. The pictures showed me examples of different tools I can use to measure volume. These pictures reminded me of all the different ways you can measure volume. I have a measuring cup at home that I use to measure oil when I am making a cake. In the caption, the author reminded me of how we measure volume—by looking at the number at the top of the liquid. I do this when I measure the oil for the cake batter. After a brief discussion of the different details the teacher included in her response, she asks the students to look back at the notes they took during the Phase 2 lesson; she directs them to circle at least one detail they want to refer to in their response. Then she asks them to turn and talk to a partner about what they plan to write.
3. Write and confer.
The teacher leans in to support individual students. She encourages the students to look at the anchor chart as well as the posted questions they created during Phase 2. When the students are done writing, she asks them to find a partner and share what they have written.

FIGURE 9.8. *(continued)*

When you are planning similar lessons, start by looking for a source that has plenty of visual images for your students to think through. Figure 9.9 provides additional guidance in planning lessons for students. Make adjustments as needed according to what you have learned through informal assessments.

HOW DO WE ASSESS?

Conversations with individuals and small groups can reveal a great deal about the meaning they are making from visual images and other types of features during a Phase 2 lesson. Start by noticing what the students are attempting and provide positive feedback. Some examples of what you might say include the following:

- You seem to be stopping to notice or look carefully at the features in this source.
- When I was listening to you, I heard you share information from this feature.
- When you were talking about what you learned from this feature, you revealed to me

FIGURE 9.9. Planning guide for a lesson on "Learning from Visual Images and Supporting Print Features."

PLANNING Phase 1—*Meet the Source*
1. Introduce and preview the source.
• Locate a source that has several visual images (e.g., photographs, charts, diagrams) that your students may find challenging. • Plan a purpose for reading the source a first time. The purpose might be answering a question related to the topic of the source like, "What do we need to think about when measuring matter?" • Plan an introduction to the source. (See Chapter 5 for suggestions.)
2. Read–view–listen and confer.
If the students will be watching a video, determine the point(s) at which you will pause and ask students to turn and talk about what they have learned.
3. Discuss.
• Plan to return to the purpose you gave students for reading or viewing. • Think about a teaching point you might share with the students. This point might emerge while you are conferring with students.

PLANNING Phase 2—*Meet the Strategies*
1. Explain and model strategic reading–viewing–listening.

• The students' purpose for closely reading or viewing will be to learn from a visual image and supporting print features.
• Create an anchor chart with the *what, why,* and *how.* (See Figure 9.2 for student-friendly language you can use.) Another option would be to prepare charts similar to those in Figure 9.6.
• Your think-aloud might include:
  ○ The *what, how,* and *why* of learning from visual images.
  ○ Describing how you looked closely at an image (including, if appropriate, how you navigate that image, looking left to right or top to bottom, and so forth).
  ○ Saying aloud what you are learning from the image and related print features,
  ○ Stating how you decided to use words like *definition, example, explain,* and *describe* to help you explain what the author is doing or teaching in this feature.
  ○ Jotting what you learned in the margins or in your notes.

2. Practice with sections of the source.
Choose additional visual images and supporting print features for students to closely read, or plan to ask students to self-select a visual image for close reading.
3. Discuss.
• Plan a discussion question you can pose at the end of the lesson related to strategic processing. For example, you might ask, "What did you learn today about studying visual images and their related print features? Why is that important?" • Create a prompt related to the content learned from the source. For example, you might say, "What did you learn today that you can explain to someone else studying the same topic?"

(continued)

PLANNING Phase 3—*Meet the Response*
1. Introduce prompt for the response.
Plan a prompt for a written response. You might simply ask the students to look at their annotations in the source or their notes and write about what they learned from one feature and why that information is important to the source as a whole. Or you might ask them to write in response to bigger ideas in the source that were discussed during Phases 1 and 2. For example, the students examining the features in *How Do We Measure Matter?* (Peppas, 2012) might write about how what they learned from a feature is connected to understanding the properties of matter. This response may be very short—just a few paragraphs. Here are examples of other prompts for writing: • *Take a moment to look at your annotations or notes on what you learned from visual images in this source. Which image helped you understand the topic of the source better?* • *Describe what you learned and why you think it is important in a short letter to me. How was your understanding of this source transformed when you slowed down to closely read or view the visual images in this source?*
2. Plan and rehearse.
• Decide how students will plan or rehearse for writing. You might ask them to circle one set of annotations on their copy of the text that they would like to explain. • Plan for how you will help students who need extra support during writing. This support might include sharing a model response like one shared by the teacher in the sample lesson.
3. Write and confer.
What will you try to notice when you lean in to confer?

FIGURE 9.9. *(continued)*

that you understand the purpose of this feature or why an author would include it in this source.

After you provide this feedback, take a moment to teach in a way that pushes at the edge of what the students can already do. Are they thinking deeply about the information in that feature? Are they using that feature to help them understand the topic of the source better? Figure 9.10 provides suggestions for what you might notice as you work with students and how you might respond. Consider jotting notes about these conferences in your anecdotal records to reference as you plan follow-up instruction.

Reading students' written responses to visual images can also be helpful in determining whether they are beginning to use these features in a helpful way. Figure 9.11 on page 182 is a continuum that shows the stages of development in student responses that is similar to the continuums you have seen in the last three chapters. You can use this continuum as a guide for noticing and describing the kind of thinking students are doing. As an example of how you might analyze a student's response, take a moment to look carefully at the feature and caption from *How Do We Measure Matter?* (Peppas, 2013) and one student's response to them in Figure 9.12 on page 183. Lisa, a student, completed this response during a series of lessons I gave that were similar to the ones described earlier in this chapter. The first entry in Lisa's response was completed with support. Lisa's second entry was written independently in response to a visual image in the book that she selected on her own. Notice how she is paraphrasing the content presented in the features, putting this information in her own words. She also integrates language that explains what the author is doing or what she is noticing about the purpose of the feature ("shows examples," "tells/explains"). She is meeting expectations but would benefit from additional lessons with a similar focus on comprehending the content in visual images and supporting print features.

Scenario	How you can respond
The student has not written anything in his notes (after being given adequate time to do so), or the student shrugs his shoulders when you ask what he has learned from a visual image.	• Suggest to the student, "Why don't we look at this together? Think aloud about what you notice and learn from the image." • As the student shares what he has noticed, if needed, provide language stems like: ○ *"I noticed that . . ."* ○ *"This feature shows me what . . ."* ○ *"This is an example of . . ."* • If the student does share information, say, "So, I hear you saying that you learned [revert to what he or she said], right? Please write that in your notes to share with others."
The student orally restates or copies information presented explicitly in the visual image or supporting print feature.	• Gently cover the feature and what the student has written. Then say, "Tell me about what you just learned. Try to use your own words." • If the student does not respond, be prepared to think aloud about what you noticed in the feature or to say, "Let's look at this together." • After some conversation, say, "Share with me what you have learned from this feature now that we have thought about it together."
The student has clearly thought about the information revealed explicitly in the feature and may need support in thinking beyond this.	• Encourage the student to look at the visual image again and then ask one of the following questions: ○ *"What else do you notice?"* ○ *"Why do you think this feature is important for the author to include in this source?"* • Coach the student in making connections between the information in the main part of the source and the information in the feature. Be prepared to demonstrate what this looks like for the student. • If the student reveals thinking beyond the source, pose the question, "How can you reveal this thinking in your notes?"

FIGURE 9.10. Visual Images: Conferring scenarios and suggestions for coaching.

Stage	Characteristics of written responses
Attempting	• The student has some awareness of the feature. However, she writes information that is not conveyed in the feature. • The student copies directly from the source. • The student may be resorting to prior knowledge or may actually misunderstand the strategic processing being taught.
Approaching	• The student is making some sense of the content of the feature(s) but may not yet be synthesizing the key ideas or useful information being imparted. • She has attempted to paraphrase content that is conveyed explicitly in the feature. • She may be using language she has appropriated from the source (or from language stems provided by the teacher) that she does not have complete control of or that she does not completely understand.
Meeting	• The student has paraphrased content that is explicitly conveyed in the feature and is beginning to include additional meaning. • The student is beginning to make connections to useful prior knowledge related to the content of the feature and to draw valid conclusions about the author's purpose in using this feature. • The student's response reveals some connections between the feature and information in the main part of the source.
Exceeding	• The student writes and speaks with ease about the implicit ideas (including how features communicate someone else's perspective) and explicit information conveyed in the feature. • The student's response reveals an understanding of the connection between the information in the feature and information or bigger ideas in the main part of the source. • The student is drawing conclusions about the value of using features in informational sources, and there has been some transfer of this understanding to work completed at other times of the school day.

FIGURE 9.11. Stages of development in learning from features like visual images.

WHAT DOES FOLLOW-UP INSTRUCTION LOOK LIKE?

With a class of students studying global warming, the teacher engaged the students in several lessons focused on making sense of the features in the texts they were reading. During these lessons, she noticed that the students were not making connections between the features and the information in the running text. As revealed in the continuum for learning, we knew that this is where we needed to head next and designed a series of lessons in response. During Phase 1—Meet the Source, we presented the students with a set of books on global warming and gave them time to browse and read. During conferences we asked the students to share what they were learning from particular features, and when we closed, we had small groups meet to discuss features they found helpful.

I began the Phase 2—Meet the Strategies lesson by reviewing the work we had done during the first lesson. Then I stated the following:

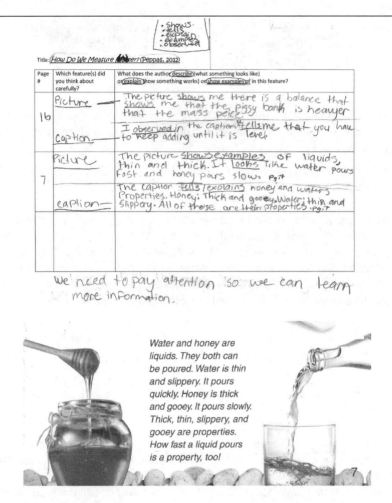

These responses were written during a Phase 3—Meet the Response lesson. The first entry was written with support. I engaged the students in a shared writing of an entry on a similar handout placed on a document camera so that all students could see what we had composed together; Lisa did not copy exactly what I had written about the picture with the balance, but her language was very similar to mine. The second entry was written independently in response to a photograph and caption Lisa self-selected from *How We Measure Matter?* (Peppas, 2013; see the image above).

In the first part of this second entry (in response to the photograph), notice how Lisa has written what the author is doing ("shows examples") and what she is noticing ("looks like"). She has borrowed language from the whole-group discussions about words and phrases you can use to explain your thinking (which she underlined at the end of the lesson), and she has also borrowed language from the caption ("thin and thick"). She paraphrases her learning, smoothly integrating this language. In the second part of this entry (regarding the caption), she shares what the author is doing or her purpose ("tells/explains"), paraphrases what she has learned ("honey: thick and gooey"), and sums up what the author is saying ("all of these are their properties").

Lisa would benefit from additional opportunities to explain what she is learning from different types of features orally and in writing as well as from lessons focused on making connections between the content in the features and the content in the main part of a source.

FIGURE 9.12. Example of a response *meeting* expectations. Image an accompanying text reprinted with permission from Crabtree Publishing Company.

When we read informational texts, we need to pay attention to more than just the features in order to determine what is important and how to synthesize the information. What we have to do is think about how the information in the features and the main text *work together* to help us understand the author's central ideas.

Next, I shared a cake-baking analogy to help the students better understand. I asked them to list the ingredients for a cake, and as they did I drew a rough sketch of each listed ingredient on the board and put a plus sign between each ingredient. I finished the equation by drawing an equal sign at the end of the list and then sketched the completed cake. I said the following:

What we have to do to read strategically is to think about all of the ingredients or elements the author has included, like the headings and subheadings, the captions and photographs, and the main text. As we think about the ingredients, we can begin to determine the author's central idea. When we do that, it's like stirring together and baking the ingredients for a cake. The finished cake then represents our understanding of the author's central idea. Let me show you what I mean.

I then projected the image of the text on global warming (Johnson, 2002). (See Figure 9.13.) I started my think-aloud by drawing separate circles around the heading "How Well Are We Doing?" and the subheadings "Good News" and "Bad News." I read these headings aloud as I drew the circles and then thought aloud by saying the following:

Well, I know this book is about global warming. So, I'm thinking the author is going to tell me about what we know is happening. Because he has written "Good News" and "Bad News," I'm thinking there must be some positive effects of global warming as well as negative effects. I have never thought of there being positive effects, so I definitely want to read more.

At this point, the students were eager to contribute, so I followed their lead and we engaged in a shared think-aloud with me stepping in and stepping back as needed. I started by saying, "If I am going to take in all of the information on these two pages, what do I need to do now?" One of the students responded, "Read the captions and look at the pictures." As we read and discussed each of these features, I drew arrows directed at the feature. Doing this helps the students keep track of what we are discussing and how we are being strategic. Through our conversation the students revealed to themselves how a picture and caption on an earlier page showed a positive effect of global warming—two people in Colorado farming during a longer growing season—while the picture and caption in Figure 9.13 showed a negative effect—sea lions possibly having to struggle to survive in Alaska if there are warmer temperatures.

When we started to read the two columns of bulleted text, I stepped in and thought aloud by saying the following:

When I look at these lists, I am thinking that there is a lot of information. So, as I read each bullet, I am going to think carefully about what content I want to remember.

FIGURE 9.13. A page from *Global Warming* (Johnson, 2002) visually projected for a think-aloud. Text of figure from National Geographic Learning. *Reading Expeditions (Science: Science Issues Today): Global Warning, 1E.* © 2004 South-Western, a part of Cengage, Inc. Reprinted by permission. Photo © Joel Sartore/*www.joelsartore.com.*

How Well Are We Doing?

Good News

- Global warming may lead to shorter, warmer winters.

- Longer summers mean a longer growing season. Farmers may be able to grow more food.

- Plants need carbon dioxide to live and grow. More carbon dioxide in the air could be good for some kinds of plants.

- Reducing the amount of carbon dioxide in the air could slow the warming trend.

Bad News

- Warmer temperatures could melt glaciers and polar ice sheets.

- Melting glaciers and ice sheets add water to the sea. As sea levels rise, coastlines and some islands could disappear underwater.

- Global warming may change the weather in ways that lead to more severe storms, floods, and droughts.

- Getting everyone in the world to work together to reduce carbon dioxide is not easy.

Warmer temperatures could make it difficult for sea lions like these in Alaska to survive.

7

185

I read aloud the text by the first bullet.

Global warming may lead to shorter, warmer winters.

And then I said:

As I read this sentence, I was also thinking about the heading above it, "Good News." I'm thinking that shorter, warmer winters sound good to me. Since we live in Illinois, that may mean less snow to shovel. Maybe that's what the author means by "good news." I'm wondering, though, if that really is good news or if the author will bring this back up again when I read the "bad news" part of this page. See how is thinking about the two headings helping me make sense of this sentence?

The students and I continued by thinking aloud together about the content in the rest of the bulleted statements under "Good News." During this discussion, I helped the students notice the connections we were making between the features and the information in those statements.

Before releasing responsibility for tackling the second column of bulleted text, I wanted to make sure the students understood the steps we had already taken together. So, I asked them to share aloud with me what we had just done as strategic readers to "tackle" the text. On a piece of chart paper, I wrote the following instructions as we generated a list of steps for strategic reading:

- **Read the title and subheadings. Make a prediction about what I will be reading.**
- **Read the pictures and captions, and take notes about what I learned.**
- **Read the text and think about what is important to remember. Take notes.**
- **Compare what I learned in the text to what I learned in the features, and think about the author's central idea.**

Then I asked the students to strategically read this same two-page section of text again, but on their own. They read the material and jotted down notes. In the example shown in Figure 9.14, you can see how one student placed the sticky notes (as I directed the students to do) in a way intended to convey what she understood about strategic reading. Her notes include identification of the central idea in the main text, two supporting examples, and a summary of the content in each of the pictures and captions. Her final note, written inside a drawn image of a decorated cake, states the author's central idea.

The next day, I met with these students again for an additional Phase 2 lesson. I projected examples of their responses from the previous lesson, and together we identified what the students had done well. Then I asked the students to write their own strategic plans for reading on a large sticky note. See Figure 9.15 for an example of one student's plan.

I then instructed the students to tackle another two-page section in the same book on global warming. As in the previous lesson, they jotted down their thoughts on sticky notes. As the students finished, I moved into Phase 3—Meet the Response by asking

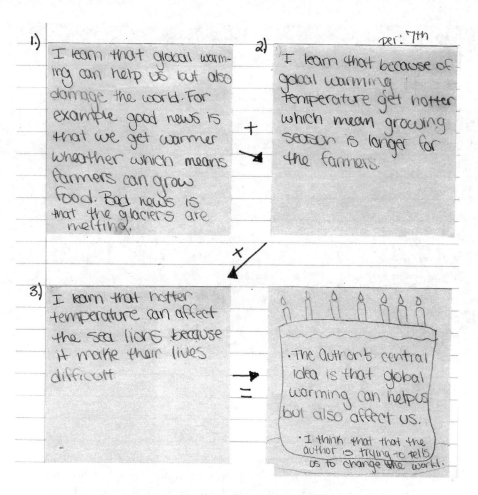

FIGURE 9.14. Example of a student's notes.

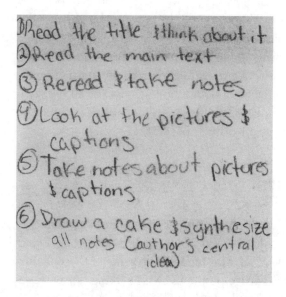

FIGURE 9.15. Example of a student's strategic reading plan.

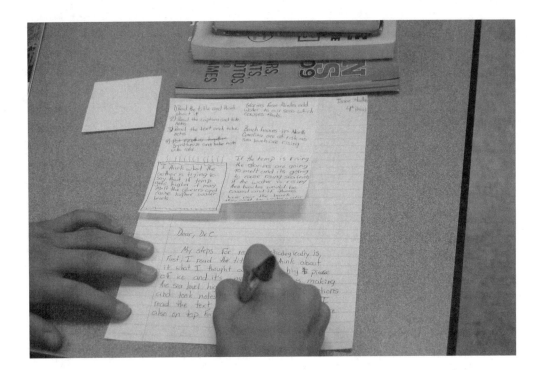

FIGURE 9.16. A student using his notes from close reading to write a response.

them to write a longer response using their notes. I made clear the steps in this process (which I had posted on a piece of chart paper at the front of the room) and then asked them to "give it a try." Figure 9.16 above presents a photograph of how one student used his notes from close reading to write an extended response during Phase 3.

With this class, the teacher and I used the continuum to think about where to take them next. Then we followed up with instruction that, pedagogically, looked very similar to previous lessons. We just upped the ante, pushing the students to think more critically about the information in the features by thinking about how this information is connected to the information in other parts of the source.

Figure 9.17 provides recommendations for instructional moves you might make as you work with students, noticing their strengths and needs. For suggestions about how to plan lessons similar to those described in this chapter, over time and with several sources, please see Appendix A, page 235.

CLOSING THOUGHTS

Visual images (and other features) come in many shapes and sizes. They pop up in lots of different types of sources. We cannot teach students how to tackle every single one. What we can do is nurture an awareness of the value of these features and provide opportunities for students to engage productively in making sense of these features as they synthesize information and evaluate the bigger ideas in the source.

FIGURE 9.17. Suggestions for follow-up instruction.

If . . .	Then . . .
Students are restating verbatim information that is in the source or are not revealing thoughtful analysis of the feature.	• Post sentence stems for students to consider using as they respond. (See p. 169 for examples.) • Invite students who fall into this category to meet in a small group with you. Engage the students in a shared think-aloud about a particular feature. Write the first part of a response with them (on chart paper for all to view) and then task them with finishing the response. This task might include asking them to orally rehearse what they will write first.
Students' responses reveal some thinking about the content in a feature but not a firm grasp of the content or what they are doing to strategically process the content.	• Before students engage in writing a response to a feature, share examples of model student entries or responses. Visually project the examples so that all students can view them, and mark on the examples where the students specifically used language that reinforced the lesson's objectives. • After students write a response, ask them to underline words or phrases they used to help them describe the author's purpose for that feature or the language they used to help them explain their thinking. (See the student's example of underlined language in Figure 9.12.) • Provide an opportunity for students to teach what they have learned about "what readers do," "why," and "how" to younger students or students from another class.
Students have a firm grasp on making meaning from one particular type of feature but are not transferring this learning to other features in a variety of sources.	• Introduce an anchor chart to students with a series of features listed and described. (See Figures 9.5 and 9.6 for support.) Review the three questions students can ask themselves as they closely read a feature. (See Figure 9.2.) Ask students to choose a feature they are less familiar with and can locate in a source; coach them as they work with a partner to fully understand the content and value of that feature. • Meet with a small group and focus instruction on a less-familiar feature. Review the questions readers ask themselves and engage in trying this out with the new feature. Then ask that group to teach other students what they learned. • Engage the students in making a "Features of Informational Sources" handbook with written entries that include the following: purpose of the feature, example of the feature (cut and paste or sketch the feature), and responses about what they learned.
Students are tackling making meaning from features more easily, but they are not making connections between the information in the main part of the source and in the features.	• Move the discussion toward connections between the information in the features and the information in the rest of the source. Introduce the cake-baking analogy. (See p. 184 and Figure 9.14.) Model for students how you made sense of the feature by thinking about specific details in the main part of the source or how you made sense of the details in the source by thinking about the details in the feature. In front of students, jot notes about what you learned by thinking about both sources of information—the main part and the feature. • During nonfiction writing instruction, encourage students to add visual images and supporting print features to their compositions. • Develop an opportunity for students to add features to an already published source that may not employ particular features, such as books by Seymour Simon.

CHAPTER TEN

Using Context Clues to Make Sense of Unfamiliar Vocabulary

Authors of informational sources rely heavily on domain-specific vocabulary to develop ideas. These are content-area words that students may see only when they are studying a particular topic or issue. Notice the domain-specific vocabulary in this excerpt from a *Science News for Students* article titled "Males and Females Respond to Head Hits Differently" (Brookshire, 2015).

> Large numbers of kids play sports that can result in an accidental bump to the head. If the blow is hard enough, a *concussion*—brain injury—may occur. But symptoms and the time it takes to recover can differ depending on whether the patient is male or female, a new study in mice shows.

What are the words or phrases in this excerpt that students might not see on a regular basis in their everyday reading? Some examples include *concussion, brain injury, symptoms,* and *new study.*

It is always helpful if students already have some knowledge of these words when they read or hear them in a source. If they do not, though, there are frequently context clues provided by the author that indicate the meaning of these words. For example, in the excerpt above, the word *concussion* is followed by the phrase *brain injury,* which serves as a synonym for this word. The author signals that she is providing a context clue for this word by placing the phrase *brain injury* just after *concussion* and setting it off with dashes. Many students, though, do not notice these context clues and continue reading without understanding the meaning of a word or term. Not knowing the meaning of unfamiliar words may impair their comprehension of the bigger ideas in this source and their ability to explain what they learned (Wright & Cervetti, 2016). This chapter explores how to help students recognize and use context clues to help them figure out the meaning of unfamiliar words.

WHAT DO WE MEAN BY "USE CONTEXT CLUES TO MAKE SENSE OF UNFAMILIAR VOCABULARY"?

What: Readers know that sometimes there are words in a source for which we do not know the meaning. We also know that authors sometimes provide context clues to help us figure out the meaning of a word. There are certain types of clues authors use like definitions, synonyms or antonyms, examples, general clues, and visual images.

Why: Figuring out what a new word means can help you recall details in the source. This may also help you understand a part of the source better or the big ideas in the source.

How: You can figure out the meaning of a word by asking yourself these questions:

- What type of clue do I notice?
- What does this make me think the word means?

FIGURE 10.1. Student-friendly explanation of what we mean by "using context clues to figure out unfamiliar vocabulary."

As shown in Figure 10.1 above, a context clue is any detail in a source that gives the reader–viewer–listener an idea of what a particular word or phrase means. There is a process that proficient readers engage in when they use context clues to figure out the meaning of unfamiliar words.

1. The first step is noticing when we do not know the meaning of a word—a word that may be important.

2. Once we notice this word, we begin to look for clues, either as we continue reading or viewing or by going back to reread or re-view.

3. Then, if there is a clue present, we proceed to think through the information in this clue to make sense of the unfamiliar word.

 Some clues provide explicit or direct information about the meaning of the word (Beck, McKeown, & Kucan, 2013). What is the explicit clue as to the meaning of the word *neuroscientist* in the following sentence from the article previously discussed?

As a *neuroscientist*, he studies how the brain functions. (Brookshire, 2015)

The phrase "he studies how the brain functions" is an explicit clue about what a neuroscientist does. The author has basically defined the word in this clue.

Some clues are less direct or more general (Beck et al., 2013). They give the reader some idea of the word's meaning, but not an exact one. In the next excerpt, notice the clues the author gives as to the meaning of the word *symptoms*.

When a person gets a hard blow to the head, she might experience dizziness, nausea and memory problems. But even after these *symptoms* fade, headaches and a persistent feeling of sadness, known as depression, might continue. (Brookshire, 2015)

The author does not provide an explicit definition of this word. Instead, she lists examples of symptoms: dizziness, nausea, and memory problems. These examples and the idea that people experience these symptoms when they get a hard blow to the head give the reader the sense that "symptoms" are an effect or evidence of something else.

Sometimes there is no clue as to the meaning of a word. In the following sentence (and the sentences before and after in the actual text), there is no clue as to the meaning of the word *fibers:*

The scientists used fibers to measure the amount of dopamine in the animals' brains. (Brookshire, 2015)

As proficient readers who have a general idea of what this word means, we can get the gist of what the author is saying and move forward. For a reader who does not know what a fiber is, it may be difficult to comprehend what the author is discussing here, that is, the way in which the scientists measured the chemical dopamine in animals' brains. He has to decide whether not knowing this word will get in the way of understanding most of the content in the article. This decision will determine whether he consults outside sources for a definition or if he continues to read the source and make do with what he does understand about the researcher's methods.

The authors or creators of infographics also include clues as to the meaning of words. Pause for a few moments to look at the infographic titled "Traumatic Brain Injury (TBI) in Kids: Causes and Prevention Strategies" (National Institutes of Health, 2017) in Figure 10.2. Notice how the term *traumatic brain injury* is clearly defined in the following sentence (located in the top left-hand corner of the figure).

TBI is an injury caused by a blow, jolt, or penetrating object that disrupts normal functioning of the brain.

The word *is* serves as an indicator that the narrator is going to provide a clue as to the meaning of the word. While authors of infographics use clues that are similar to those used by authors of traditional print texts, they also use visual clues to support the reader in making sense of a word. In the section titled "Causes," check out the visual that accompanies the term *unintentional blunt trauma*. If a student does not know what this term means, he can see in the image a ball hitting a girl in the head; it looks as though the girl may have been kicking the ball or is at least playing in some way. This visual serves as an example of how unintentional blunt trauma can occur. Most people can relate to this visual, having been in or seen a similar situation. So, if a reader is unfamiliar with this term, he can gather a general idea of what it means from the visual.

FIGURE 10.2. Infographic "Traumatic Brain Injury (TBI) in Kids: Causes and Prevention Strategies" (National Institutes of Health, 2017). Available at *www.nichd.nih.gov/newsroom/digital-media/infographics/TBIinKids.*

Traumatic Brain Injury (TBI) in Kids: Causes and Prevention Strategies

 TBI is an injury caused by a blow, jolt, or penetrating object that disrupts normal functioning of the brain.

 TBI can be mild to severe.

1.7 million people in the United States sustain a TBI each year; of those, **50,000 die** and more than **250,000 are hospitalized.**

Severe TBI can lead to permanent disability and even death.

75% of brain injuries are mild (not life-threatening). Concussion is a type of mild TBI.

All types of TBI can seriously affect a child's daily life.

Brain injury can cause problems with speaking or understanding, movement or mobility, thinking or memory, and personality or mood.

Causes

The **leading causes** of TBI in the United States are

| Falls | Unintentional blunt trauma | Motor vehicle crashes | Assault |

55% of brain injuries in children are caused by falls from objects like stairs and bicycles.

24% of brain injuries in children are caused by being hit in the head with an object, like a baseball or soccer ball.

Car accidents are the #1 cause of TBI-related death in children older than age 5.

Assault (e.g., physical abuse) is the #1 cause of TBI-related death in children age 4 and younger.

Prevention Strategies

Take the following actions to **reduce the risk of TBI in children.**

Use a child safety seat or a seat belt when the child is in a motor vehicle.

Make sure the child wears a helmet when riding a bicycle, skateboarding, and playing sports like hockey and football.

Install window guards and stair safety gates at home.

Avoid shaking your baby. Learn how to prevent <u>shaken baby syndrome.</u>

NICHD supports research to better understand and find safe and effective treatment options for TBI. To learn more, visit: http://www.nichd.nih.gov/health/topics/tbi.

Eunice Kennedy Shriver National Institute of Child Health and Human Development

193

Visual images provide clues as to the meaning of words spoken by narrators in videos as well. Pause again to watch the video *Injury Prevention in Youth and Teen Sports* (Cincinnati Children's Hospital, 2016) using the link or QR code.

https://www.cincinnatichildrens.org/service/s/sports-medicine/research

At minute 0:35 the expert being interviewed, Dr. Greg Myer, explains how the Division of Sports Medicine at Cincinnati's Children's Hospital has worked to reduce the frequency of anterior cruciate ligament (ACL) injuries. In the video, Dr. Myer only uses the term *ACL injury*. He does not describe what this injury is or what happens to cause the problem. Instead, he talks about training programs that are being used to teach athletes how to play more safely. The viewer of this video can infer what an ACL injury is, however, through the images presented—an up-close view of some type of monitor attached to an athlete's legs, then a clip of an athlete running on a treadmill, and another one doing squats. These images provide general clues that an ACL injury is some type of injury to the legs.

As proficient readers, our vast experience with making meaning allows us to locate a clue and determine the meaning of an unfamiliar word without much thought. If there is no clue immediately present, we also know whether the word is important enough to look for or notice clues in other parts of the source. For our students who have much less experience, clarifying the process we engage in when using context clues may be critical in moving them toward a better understanding of the content in sources.

DO YOUR STUDENTS NEED TO WORK ON THIS?

Would your students benefit from conversations about how to make meaning of unfamiliar vocabulary using context clues? The following questions can serve as a guide in helping you make this decision:

During conferences with individuals or small groups:

- Do they continue reading after they have come across unfamiliar words or phrases without pausing to figure out the meaning of those words or phrases?

- Do their conversations about what they learned from a source lack key vocabulary?

- Do they recognize and use some types of clues but not others?

In evaluating students' written responses:

- Do their written responses include domain-specific vocabulary from the source?
- Do their written responses include an explanation or some insight into the meaning of less familiar words?

Depending on your students' responses, some of them may need instruction in this area.

WHERE TO START?
EXPLICITLY TEACH TYPES OF CLUES

We know that children and young adolescents benefit when we explicitly teach them word-learning strategies, and they have an opportunity to practice these strategies in contexts like reading (Ash & Baumann, 2017). This is the case for native English speakers as well as English learners (Manyak & Bauer, 2009). Teaching students to recognize and use context clues to learn an unfamiliar word is one approach to teaching for word learning. Authors or creators of informational sources employ several types of clues to help their audience unpack the meaning of unfamiliar words or phrases that are important to understanding the topic. Figure 10.3 on the next page is a list of types of clues you might introduce to students. Notice that the examples of clues are drawn from a variety of sources. Similar to authors of traditional printed texts, creators of infographics and videos include clues as to the meaning of words. When I teach students to use these clues, I give them a simple bookmark like the one in Figure 10.4 on page 197 for each student to refer to as they become aware of these clues.

A context clue may belong to more than one category of clues, or it might not fit perfectly into a category of clues. In the article about the research study on concussions, the term *brain injury* might be considered a synonym or a definition for the word *concussion*. If, in the end, the student is able to figure out the meaning of the word or phrase, an exact or correct identification of the type of clue is not important. Thinking about the types of clues is simply a strategy for making sense of the information in a source. And sometimes there is just *no* clue. This is another point that is worthy of discussion with students, including having a conversation about what to do in response.

What does this type of instruction look like with video? In many videos, there is a lot happening at once. The student has to make sense of the visual images as well as any messages conveyed via the spoken word. As discussed in Chapter 7, it is important to help students notice what they do not understand and then to use fix-up strategies to repair the meaning. In the case of unfamiliar words, they would need to listen and look for clues. Figure 10.5 on page 198 provides additional tips for helping students problem-solve when they notice a word they do not understand in a video.

FIGURE 10.3. Types of context clues.

Context clue type	Example [*Note:* The vocabulary word is in **bold *italics***. The context clue(s) is in **bold.**]
1. **Definition:** Words that explain the meaning	As a **neuroscientist, he studies how the brain functions.** (Brookshire, 2015)
2. **Synonym:** Word(s) that are similar in meaning	Large numbers of kids play sports that can result in an accidental bump to the head. If the blow is hard enough, a ***concussion—*** **brain injury—**may occur. (Brookshire, 2015)
3. **Comparison:** Word or phrase that represents something similar	So that layer of fluid helps protect the brain. But the water changes shape easily. And when the head rotates, the fluid can ***rotate*** too—**like a whirlpool.** (Stevens, 2015)
4. **Contrast:** Word(s) that go against the meaning	The concussions that Raghupathi's group gave to the mice were designed to be very ***mild***. **But males still showed effects** suggestive of depression as much as two months after their injuries. (Brookshire, 2015)
5. **Example:** One or more words that illustrate a concept or idea.	When a person gets a hard blow to the head, she might experience **dizziness, nausea and memory problems.** But even after these ***symptoms*** fade, headaches and a persistent feeling of sadness, known as depression, might continue. (Brookshire, 2015)
6. **General:** Several words or statements, including comparisons, that give clues to the word's meaning.	We're a rather unique organization in our focus on ***prevention***. What we're doing is **creating programs and techniques so that our athletes don't have to come to the hospital.** They can stay out and play. (Cincinnati Children's Hospital, 2016)
7. **Visual:** Visual images or graphics that gives an explicit or implicit clue to the meaning of a word or phrase in a source.	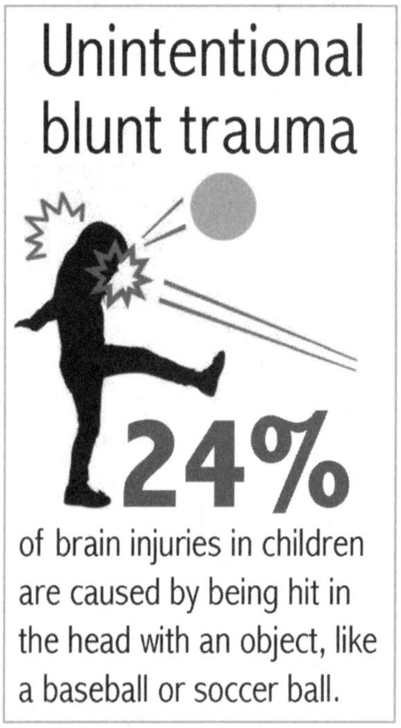 Unintentional blunt trauma **24%** of brain injuries in children are caused by being hit in the head with an object, like a baseball or soccer ball.

5 Types of Context Clues
Readers Can Use To
Figure Out Tricky Words

1. Definition: the author explains the meaning of the word right in the sentence or in that part of the source.

2. Synonym: the author uses a word similar in meaning.

3. Example: the author provides one or more example words or ideas.

4. General: the author provides several words or statements that give clues to the word's meaning.

5. Visual Cues: the author provides a visual image or graphic that gives an explicit or implicit clue to the meaning of a word or phrase in a source.

FIGURE 10.4. Bookmark for using context clues.

HOW DO WE PLAN AND TEACH FOR IDENTIFYING CONTEXT CLUES?

The three-phase plan can be used to teach students the types of context clues. During Phase 1—Meet the Source, the students read–view–listen to the source as a whole. (For an infographic or video, this phase may be a short one.) During Phase 2—Meet the Strategies, the process of noticing unfamiliar words and then looking for and using context clues can be demonstrated for students.

In preparation for this Phase 2 lesson, it is important to choose a source with several potentially unfamiliar words and context clues that the students can look for and analyze. Knowing which words might be tricky for students and what types of clues the author uses will help you plan the demonstration and guided practice portion of the lesson. Figure 10.6 (pp. 199–201) describes a lesson that introduces types of clues. During Phase 2, the teacher thinks aloud first about how she "noticed" an unfamiliar word. Her modeling is helpful for students who are not monitoring or realizing that they need to think about whether they know the meanings of words they are reading. Then the teacher begins thinking aloud about clues, drawing the students into thinking with her. Her think-aloud

Video Tips

- Demonstrate for students noticing an unfamiliar word during the video. Stop the video and share aloud the word you don't know (or might know if you were the students' age). Show the students how you skip back to the clip with the word (or just continue viewing) to look and listen for clues. When you notice a clue, think through how you use that clue to help you figure out the meaning of the word.
- Ask students to give you the thumbs-up when they notice a word they do not entirely understand. Skip back to the clip with that word. Play the clip again and, if needed, continue viewing the video. Ask the students to give you the thumbs-up when they notice a clue that supports them in making sense of that word. Together talk through the clue and how it helps them (or maybe does not help them).
- Prior to asking students to watch a video, list three to four words you want students to notice during the video. As you watch the video with the students, pause it when one of these words and the respective clue for the word is presented. Ask partners to think aloud together about the clues and then, if appropriate, share with the class what they think the word means and why.
- Students need to understand that they do not have to know the meaning of every unfamiliar word in a video. Some words are more important than others. Engage the students in conversations about this point. You might pose the question, "When is it important to know the meaning of a particular word?"

FIGURE 10.5. Tips for teaching students how to use context clues to figure out the meaning of unfamiliar vocabulary in a video.

is an auditory scaffold. She provides a visual scaffold for what this strategic processing looks like by pointing to relevant spots in the text, which is projected for all students to view, and by placing the bookmark with the types of clues on the document camera momentarily as she refers to it. She also jots annotations on the text as the students watch, and then finishes by summing up what she has learned.

This type of lesson requires a lot of thought on the part of the teacher in locating and analyzing sources to make sure there are unfamiliar words and helpful clues. The think-aloud that occurred at the beginning of Phase 2 may also need to be repeated during conferences with individual students and small groups who are struggling to identify or explain clues. Knowing the source well is critical. Figure 10.7 (pp. 202–203) provides suggestions for planning a similar lesson.

HOW DO WE ASSESS?

When we lean in to confer with readers, we can check their understanding of the vocabulary words in a source. This conversation can occur during instruction or during other parts of the day when students are engaged in reading, viewing, or listening to informational sources. Generally, when I lean in to confer with a student, during Phase 1,

FIGURE 10.6. Sample three-phase lesson for "Teaching Students How to Use Context Clues to Figure Out the Meaning of Unfamiliar Vocabulary."

TEACHING Phase 1—*Meet the Source*
1. Introduce and preview the source.

The teacher gives a brief introduction to the article "Males and Females Respond to Head Hits Differently" (Brookshire, 2015).
 	
She takes a moment to teach the term *research study*—"when a group of scientists or others takes time to learn about a problem or topic in a systematic way." Taking a moment to teach this term expands the students' understanding of this word and will help them understand the ideas in the source better.
 	
The teacher cues them to think about what they might be learning about a research study as they preview the source with a partner to make predictions.
 	
Then the teacher shares a clear purpose for reading that is posted for all students to view.
 	
   • *What is this article mostly about?*
   • *What did you learn that was new?*

2. Read–view–listen and confer.
As the students read, the teacher confers with individuals. She starts by saying, "Tell me a little bit about what you are learning." If the student seems to comprehend the content, then she checks on their understanding of vocabulary. For example, she asks, "What does the word 'mild' mean in that sentence?" She takes notes about whether the students are noticing context clues or not. Several of them have a basic idea of what a word means, but struggle to deepen that understanding using context clues. As needed, she thinks aloud about the clues she notices and how she uses those clues to figure out the meaning of a word.
3. Discuss.
The teacher closes by returning to the purpose for reading. She gives the students a few moments to consider the posted questions. Then she asks them to turn in trios and discuss what they learned. She listens to one group talk. She notices that a few of the students are using vocabulary like *concussion* from the source. When the students regroup, she closes with a teaching point by talking with them about how using specific words from the source can help others better understand what they are sharing. For example, the words *concussion* or *brain injury* are more specific than a phrase like *hurt your head*.

TEACHING Phase 2—*Meet the Strategies*
1. Explain and model strategic reading–viewing–listening.
The teacher starts by reviewing the concept of monitoring for meaning. *Remember when we are reading or watching a video, we are always thinking about what makes sense and what does not. When part of a source does not make sense, then we need to figure that part out. This will help us understand the rest of the source better. Today we're going to talk about what to do when you notice that you do not know the meaning of a word.*

(continued)

She hands out a bookmark like the one in Figure 10.4 and then explains the strategy.

When we notice that we do not fully understand an important word in a source, we can think about the types of context clues that authors use. Thinking about the types of clues an author uses can help us find and make sense of those clues.

The teacher and students spend a few minutes discussing each of the types of clues listed on the bookmark. They also discuss the idea that sometimes when there are no clues and we have to just continue reading–viewing–listening.

Then she places a copy of the article "Males and Females Respond to Head Hits Differently" (Brookshire, 2015) on the document camera and begins to demonstrate what looking for and using context clues looks like. She reads aloud the following excerpt:

Large numbers of kids play sports that can result in an accidental bump to the head. If the blow is hard enough, a concussion—*brain injury*—*may occur.*

She pauses, and then says:

I think if I was your age, I might not know what the word "concussion" means. I might have heard the word before, but I do not use or read that word very often. I think it might be important because it is in italics.

Now that I have noticed a word I don't know, I need to look for clues. [Pauses. Whisper-reads sentence again as though thinking.] *I see that the author included the words "brain injury" in between dashes.* [Refers to her copy of the bookmark.] *I know that sometimes authors give me words that are similar in meaning to the word I don't know or a synonym. I think that might be the type of clue the author has given me. I know an injury is not good. A concussion must mean or be similar to a brain injury.*

The teacher pauses to draw a box around the word *concussion* and underline the words *brain injury*. Then she writes the word *synonym* in the margins.

There's another clue I noticed, too. The phrase "blow is hard enough." I think that you get a concussion when your head gets hit really hard. The hit or blow is the cause of a concussion. What type of clue do you think "blow is hard enough" is?

The teacher draws the students into a conversation about how the phrase *blow is hard enough* might be considered a general context clue or a clue that provides a description of what can cause the concussion. With the article still on the document camera, the teacher underlines *blow is hard enough* and writes "general clue" in the margins nearby.

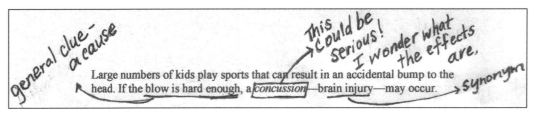

She also jots down a few words about what she is thinking, and then says:

Because I stopped and really thought about what the word "concussion" means, I realize that the author is talking about something very serious. This could be bad for your brain. I'm wondering what the effects of concussions are.

(continued)

FIGURE 10.6.

2. Practice with sections of the source.

The teacher draws the students into a shared think-aloud for the word *prone* that occurs in this sentence later in the article.

> This suggests that after brain injury, human men and boys also might be more prone to depression for months afterward, Raghupathi says. (Brookshire, 2015)

Together the group refers to the bookmark and then thinks through the clues that are in that sentence, as well several sentences just before the word to arrive at an idea of the meaning.

The teacher follows by asking students to reread the article in order to think about words they do not fully understand. When they notice an unfamiliar word (or a word they do not know really well), she encourages them to put a box around it and then try to figure out the meaning of the word by thinking about the types of context clues the author uses. She suggests they refer to the bookmark as a tool for thinking.

As the students work independently, the teacher confers with individuals and helps them problem-solve. If a student has *not* noticed an unfamiliar word, the teacher asks the student questions about particular words in the source: Do you know the meaning of this word? When a student falters, she assigns the student the task of looking for and making sense of clues.

3. Discuss.

The teacher closes by asking the students to talk with a partner about what they did to make sense of unfamiliar words and what they learned as a result. She leans in to listen to one pair share.

TEACHING Phase 3—Meet the Response

1. Introduce prompt for the response.

The teacher posts and briefly discusses the following prompt for writing:

> *Describe how you figured out the meaning of one word in this article. Be sure to include the type of clue you think the author used and why it is that type of clue.*

2. Plan and rehearse.

The teacher engages the students in writing a sample response for the word *concussion*. It looks like the following:

> I thought that the word *concussion* was tricky. Then I noticed that right after the word, the author used dashes to make the words *brain injury* stand out. I thought these words might be similar to or a synonym for the word *concussion*. When I thought about the words *brain injury*, I realized that *concussion* means that the brain has been hurt in some way. This could be serious!

The students look at their notes and choose one word they will focus on in their response. They talk with a partner about what they might write. The teacher confers with a few individuals who she knows will struggle. Then the students begin writing.

3. Write and confer.

The teacher supports individuals by asking questions like, "What did you do to figure out this word?" and "How can you say that in your response?" She notices that most of the students do not write about how they made sense of "general" clues, perhaps because they found it harder to describe. She will follow up on this in later lessons. When the students are done writing, she asks them to share in small groups.

FIGURE 10.6. *(continued)*

FIGURE 10.7. Planning guide for "Teaching Students How to Use Context Clues to Figure Out the Meaning of Unfamiliar Vocabulary."

PLANNING Phase 1—*Meet the Source*
1. Introduce and preview the source.
• Locate a source that has several potentially unfamiliar words with helpful context clues.   • Plan a purpose for reading the source a first time. The purpose might be answering questions like, *What is this article mostly about?* and *What did you learn that was new?*   • Plan an introduction to the source. (See Chapter 5 for suggestions.)
2. Read–view–listen and confer.
If the students will be watching a video, determine the point(s) at which you will pause and ask students to turn and talk about what they have learned.
3. Discuss.
• Plan to return to the purpose you gave students for reading or viewing.   • Think about a teaching point you might share with the students. This might emerge while you are conferring with students.

PLANNING Phase 2—*Meet the Strategies*
1. Explain and model strategic reading–viewing–listening.

• The students' purpose for reading closely will be to make sense of unfamiliar words.
 • Create an anchor chart or bookmark with the types of context clues you want to present. (See Figures 10.3 and 10.4 for examples of what you might include.)
 • Your think-aloud might include the following:
  ○ Stating the *what*, *why*, and *how* of using context clues (see Figure 10.1 for student-friendly language you might use).
  ○ Identifying an unfamiliar word in the source (or one a student might not know).
  ○ Thinking about the types of clues (by referring to the anchor chart or bookmark).
  ○ Rereading to look for and identify a clue.
  ○ Writing in the margins of the source or in your notes what you think that word means and why.

2. Practice with sections of the source.
Choose particular words you would like students to practice tackling, or plan to let students choose a few on their own.
3. Discuss.
• Plan a discussion question related to strategic processing. For example, you might ask, "What did you learn today about using context clues to figure out an unfamiliar word? Why is that important?"   • Create a prompt related to content learned from the source. For example, you might ask, "What part of this source did you understand better because you focused on making sense of a particular word? What did you learn?"

(continued)

PLANNING Phase 3—*Meet the Response*
1. Introduce prompt for the response.
Design a prompt for writing, for example: *Describe how you figured out the meaning of one word in this article. What information in the source did you understand better because you knew the meaning of this word?*
2. Plan and rehearse.
• Decide how students will plan or rehearse for writing. Possible options include choosing one word from their notes and talking with a partner about what they might write. • Plan for how you will help students who need extra support during writing. Possible options include writing aloud a sample response, sharing a sample response you wrote in advance, and/ or pulling a small group to work with more closely.
3. Write and confer.
What will you try to notice when you lean in to confer? (This will depend on the prompt for writing.)

FIGURE 10.7. *(continued)*

Phase 2, or another part of the day, I check first to make sure the student understands what she just read. I might start by saying, "Tell me a little bit about what you just learned in this part." If the student reveals a strong understanding of the content, then I check for her understanding of more difficult vocabulary in the part of the source she just told me about—especially if the student did not use this word to explain what she learned. If you suspect that the student does not know the meaning of a word or may need support in locating and thinking through clues, start by affirming the student's attempts at making meaning. Your comments might sound like one of the following statements:

- I noticed that you used the word _____ to explain what you learned.
- You seemed to have thought through the clues the author provides as to the meaning of this word.
- You paused when you read this word, as though you are monitoring for whether you understand that word.

Then determine a teaching move related to helping the student figure out the meaning of that word. Figure 10.8 on the next page includes scenarios you might encounter as students talk with you about an unfamiliar word, as well as suggestions for what you might say in response.

As you listen to students or read their written responses to informational sources, notice whether they are using vocabulary specific to the content area. For example, when I listen to a student, I notice whether he says, "This is about this guy who studies mice" or "This is about a *neuroscientist* who is studying the brains of mice." If he is using the specific word related to the content, then I observe for the control he has of this word. Does his use of the word convey an understanding of its meaning? Is he using the word easily? Or does his use of the word feel awkward? Figure 10.9 on page 205 is a continuum of stages or growth you might observe in students. The student who responds with "This

Scenario	How you can respond
The student has identified an unfamiliar word, but he is unsure of what to do next.	• Invite the student to look for clues with you. Together reread or view again that section of the source. When you find a clue, start to think aloud for the student. Use language like, "I noticed . . . and this made me think . . ." • Refer to the tool you created for students to use as a reference—a bookmark or an anchor chart. Ask, "How can you use this to help you?"

The student has identified and attempted to think through the meaning of a word. When she explains what she thinks the word means, she merely repeats the words that are in the source.	• Prompt the student to consider how she can explain the meaning of the word using her own words. Some examples of prompts include:
	  ○ *How can you put that in your own words?*
	  ○ *So, what does the author mean by that?*
	• Be prepared to step in and think aloud about how you would define the word, using your own words.

The student has used context clues to figure out a word, but he needs support in explaining what he has learned in the source related to this new word.	Possible prompts: • *So, what did you learn in this part? What does that make you think?* • *What do you understand better about the topic of this source because you know what this word means?*

FIGURE 10.8. Vocabulary: Conferring scenarios and suggestions for coaching.

is about a guy who studies mice" might fall in the attempting stage. The student who responds with "This is about a neuroscientist . . ." might fall in the meeting stage. Categorizing students by stage can help us think about what their responses should look like as their vocabulary grows and as their ability to make sense of unfamiliar words improves.

WHAT DOES FOLLOW-UP INSTRUCTION LOOK LIKE?

Recently I had a conversation with a teacher who introduced the types of context clues to a small group of students as part of an intervention implementing the three-phase guide for learning. She told me that she focused on the types of clues for *several* Phase 2 lessons before the students started looking for clues on their own, without her continuous prompting. The fact that it took a while for students to do this automatically on their own did not surprise me. Learning to be mindful of context clues and then thinking through these clues in a way that is productive takes time. For more support, see a brief guide for planning these types of lessons over the course of several lessons in Appendix A, page 236.

Stage	Characteristics of students' oral and written responses
Attempting	• The student notices when she does not know the meaning of a word. • If the definition is not clearly stated, the student needs additional support recognizing or thinking through other types of context clues. • In written responses, the student does not include new or less familiar vocabulary in explanations of what she learned.
Approaching	• Student initiates problem solving and can discuss attempts to determine context clues. • Student is starting to recognize and understand multiple types of clues. • With prompting, the student uses new vocabulary during conversations or as part of her writing. Her attempts at using a word may feel awkward, but it is clear she is beginning to grasp the meaning of the word.
Meeting	• The student is regularly aware of words he may not know and will share with others what he did to figure out the meaning of words. • The student uses domain-specific vocabulary (included in the source) to describe what he has learned. • The student experiences an "aha" moment when he notices new vocabulary in a context separate from the source in which he first noticed it.
Exceeding	• The student easily integrates new vocabulary into oral and written responses. • The student uses new vocabulary flexibly, in multiple contexts throughout the school day.

FIGURE 10.9. Stages of development in students' oral and written responses to "using context clues."

Figure 10.10 on the next page includes recommendations for instructional moves you might make as you observe students and notice particular strengths and needs related to this type. Some of these suggestions include ideas for how you can integrate conversations about vocabulary into the three phases—even when you have moved on to teaching another type of strategic processing during Phase 2. For example, you can make unfamiliar or key vocabulary the focus of the closing discussion during a Phase 1 lesson. In discussing the infographic "Traumatic Brain Injury in Kids" (NIH, 2017), a teacher might pose the question "What is a traumatic brain injury?" followed by "Why is it important for us to know about this type of injury?" For the article about how girls and boys may respond differently to head injuries (Brookshire, 2015), the teacher might ask, "What is a neuroscientist?" and then "What are neuroscientists learning about concussions?"

CLOSING THOUGHTS

While we do want to applaud students for using context clues to make sense of unfamiliar vocabulary, we also need to make sure we message why they are doing this. Learning the meaning of domain-specific vocabulary helps us learn and think critically about the content in a source. In the classroom discussed earlier, where the teacher had to provide

If . . .	Then . . .
Students are recognizing and using clues that clearly define words but are struggling to make sense of other types of clues.	• During Phase 2—Meet the Strategies, focus on thinking aloud about words that have general clues or other types of clues. Draw students into thinking aloud about how to make sense of these clues. • For the discussion question at the close of the Phase 1 lessons, ask students questions like, "What does the word _____ mean in this sentence?" and "How do you know?"
Students' oral responses do not include new vocabulary or vocabulary specific to a particular source.	• During Phase 2, focus on thinking aloud about how once you figured out the meaning of a word, you thought about how that word helped you understand the topic better. • When you close Phase 1—Meet the Source lessons, prompt students to use particular vocabulary when they discussed what they learned. Provide sentence stems as needed. If a student's use of the word sounds awkward, gently coach him on how to use the word correctly.
Students' written responses do not include new vocabulary or vocabulary specific to a particular source.	• During Phase 3—Meet the Response, when students plan for writing, generate a list of key vocabulary they think they might use in their response. Leave this list up for all students to refer to as they write. • Engage the students in shared writing of the first part of a response. During this experience, coach them in formulating sentences that integrate new vocabulary.

FIGURE 10.10. Suggestions for follow-up instruction.

several lessons on context clues, the focus on deciphering these clues did not override learning the content in the informational sources they were reading. The texts she used to teach the types of context clues were part of a set of sources on the characteristics of various biomes. The discussion questions she posed during Phase 1 and Phase 2 focused on the content learned and the bigger ideas in the texts. During Phase 3, the students wrote responses about what they learned regarding biomes. This teacher also looked for other authentic contexts during the school day to talk with students about unfamiliar vocabulary and what they were doing to make sense of these words. This is another important message for our students—we do not just learn new words during reading instruction. We do this all the time to make sense of the world.

CHAPTER ELEVEN

Synthesis of Information from Multiple Sources

When I was visiting a fifth-grade classroom one day, I remember talking to two students who excitedly shared that they were going to write a research report on hedgehogs. They delighted in saying that they had just finished reading several books about hedgehogs. When I asked them to tell me about the central ideas they were going to include in their report, however, their animated faces fell blank. They had no idea. I immediately realized that they had been reading broadly but without a specific purpose. They probably just thought that they would write about everything they read.

What might be a more efficient and productive approach for these students? What if these students had decided that they would only read or watch parts of sources that answered one or more of the following questions?

- What are the basic needs of the hedgehog?
- How has the hedgehog adapted to its environment?
- How is the existence of the hedgehog threatened?

Keeping these questions in mind might help the students determine which parts of sources are worthy of close reading or viewing. In a sense, these questions serve as a filter for determining what is important in multiple sources.

The students studying the hedgehog also did not appear to have a system for taking notes about the facts they learned from the book they had read and other sources. In their minds, they probably thought they would just look back at the sources as needed. What if these students also had a tool for note taking that provided room for the important details they gleaned from sources and that allowed the information from different sources to be seen all at once? With this type of tool, the students could have looked across the details they gathered, as they consulted a second and third source, to note similarities and differences in the information presented in these sources and to determine whether they needed to take additional notes. When they felt as though they had collected enough information, they could have also looked at all the details again to draw conclusions about what they had learned.

What does this approach look like in practice? This chapter explores helping students generate their own questions for research (or purposes for reading multiple sources) and introducing students to the inquiry chart, a simple tool for organizing their thinking.

WHAT DO WE MEAN BY "SYNTHESIS ACROSS SOURCES"?

What: Readers know that when two or more authors write about the same topic, they may include details that are similar or different to the others.'

Why: Noticing similarities and differences can help us compare and contrast the information in sources *and* combine information from multiple sources. Noticing similarities and differences can also help us evaluate the difference in authors' points of view.

How: Make sure you know what your purpose for reading multiple sources is. Read the first source and determine what is important. Then as you read each additional source, ask yourself this question:

- Is this information similar to or different from what I learned in the other source(s)?

FIGURE 11.1. Student-friendly explanation of what we mean by "synthesis across sources."

As described in Chapter 6, noticing connections or relationships between details and using our background knowledge to help us do so is what we mean by **synthesis**. Synthesis can happen as we think about the information in one source or as we think about information from multiple sources (see Figure 11.1 above). It involves noticing the differences and similarities in the information presented or how information is presented. This process may occur easily for proficient readers. Frequently, we have a specific purpose for looking at more than one source on a topic. Perhaps we are doing research about an illness that a friend is experiencing. Perhaps we are researching the types of plants that would be best suited for the climate in which we live. Perhaps we are concerned about an issue in our community, and we are wondering about the perspectives of other community members. As we look at sources we filter information, determining which details are important for answering our questions and which are not. As we determine what is important, we also begin to notice when authors are conveying the same information or when there are discrepancies between two sources. Noticing differences aids us in combining or integrating the information from multiple sources.

What does synthesis across sources look like? Pause momentarily to think back to the set of sources presented in Chapter 6 on main ideas: the book *The Wolves Are Back* (George, 2008), the infographic "Wolves Keep Yellowstone in Balance" (Earthjustice, 2017), and the video *Understanding the Ecological Roles of Wolves in Yellowstone*

National Park (NSF, 2015). There is a wealth of information in these three sources for students to digest regarding the role wolves play in a healthy ecosystem. What if our students' purpose for reading and watching was to answer only this question: What is the relationship between the wolves and the elk herds in a healthy ecosystem?

 With the book *The Wolves Are Back* (George, 2008), the students might notice text on page 15 that specifically addresses what happened to the elk population when the wolves were removed from and then returned to Yellowstone. Here is the text from this page.

> The [wolf] pup who had followed his father to eat heard a Vesper sparrow sing. This songster had not been in the Lamar Valley for almost a century.
>
> The vast elk herds had eaten grasses the little bird needed for food and nesting material. When the wolves returned, they frightened the elk up into the mountains. The grasses grew tall.
>
> The sparrows raised babies and sang.
>
> The wolves were back. (p. 15)

A reader can gather from this excerpt that in a healthy ecosystem, the wolves keep the elk from eating grasses that the sparrow needs to build its nest. They do this by scaring the elk up into the mountains. While not stated explicitly in the text, the reader can infer that wolves must be a predator of the elk and, therefore, the elk try to avoid them. This observation requires some background knowledge about the concept of ecosystems and the role of predators and prey in these systems.

 With the infographic "Wolves Keep Yellowstone in Balance" (Earthjustice, 2017), the student might identify two important details about the wolf and elk populations.

- [When the wolves were removed] Elk populations exploded without their primary predator, resulting in severe overgrazing of willows and aspen needed by beavers for food, shelter and dam building.
- After the wolf reintroduction in the northern range, elk numbers drop and beaver **colonies increase** from 1 to 12.

If a student has closely read and thought through the excerpt from *The Wolves Are Back* (George, 2008), as he reads the information in this infographic, he might notice that the author highlights a different animal impacted by the increase in the elk population: the beaver. Now the student can integrate this information with what he learned from the first source. Also, the author of "Wolves Keep Yellowstone in Balance" confirms what the student inferred from the details in the first source: that the wolf is a predator of the elk. The student can also add to this knowledge the fact that the wolf is not just one of many predators, but is the "primary" or main predator of the elk.

 The video *Understanding the Ecological Roles of Wolves in Yellowstone National Park* (NSF, 2015) presents a good deal of information that answers the question, "What is the relationship between the wolves and the elk herds in a healthy ecosystem?" For the purposes of our discussion, let's just think about the statistics stated by the narrator early in the video (at minute 1:15).

Today more than 4,500 elk graze Yellowstone's Northern Range. That's down from a peak of about 18,000 before the wolf reintroduction.

If a student listens carefully (maybe a couple of times) to this narration, his understanding of the elk's impact on an ecosystem should deepen. This statistic reveals how large the elk population was after the wolves had been absent from the park for several decades and how within just two decades the reintroduction of the wolves reduced the number of elk by thousands. (Wow!) Grasping this content does assume that the student recognizes this type of detail—a statistic—and understands numbers to some extent. He or she also has to recall when the government allowed the wolves to be exterminated from Yellowstone (i.e., the 1920s), when the wolves were reintroduced (i.e., 1995), and have some understanding of the role that time played in these events.

As revealed in this discussion, in order to think across multiple sources, our students have to tap a repertoire of skills and strategies, including the following:

- Generating a purpose for reading, viewing, or listening to multiple sources.
- Sustaining a focus on that purpose.
- Activating background knowledge (as needed) about the world and how sources work.
- Making connections between details or noticing similarities and differences.

If students are going to write in response, they may also have to be in control of supporting strategies, such as how to take notes and how to organize them.

DO YOUR STUDENTS NEED TO WORK AT SYNTHESIZING INFORMATION FROM MULTIPLE SOURCES?

What have your observations or formative assessments revealed? Do students need support in synthesizing information from multiple sources? What makes you think so? Consider the following series of questions as you determine if this is an area of need for your students.

During conferences with individuals or small groups:

- Do the students seem to have a clear purpose (or set of guiding questions) to drive their purpose for reading, viewing, or listening to multiple sources?
- Do they talk about everything they have learned on a subject without revealing insight into central or main ideas or connections between the details they have learned?
- Do they seem overwhelmed by all of the material they have encountered on the subject?

In evaluating students' written responses to a set of sources:

- Are they able to organize their learning into some type of organized note taking and then use those notes to write or create?
- Do they have a clear focus for their writing?
- Do they cite different sources easily?
- Does their writing reveal a synthesis or integration of information learned from multiple sources?

Your responses to these questions may reveal that students need more support in synthesizing information from multiple sources.

WHERE TO START? INTRODUCE INQUIRY CHARTS WITH GUIDING QUESTIONS

An inquiry chart (Hoffman, 1992), or I-chart, is a graphic tool that students can use to organize their notes as they record what they have learned from multiple sources. (See Figure 11.2 on the next page.) In the first row of the chart, the student writes the key questions to be answered across the top row (additional columns may readily be added). In the second row, the student summarizes his or her prior knowledge regarding answers to each question. In the next three rows (additional rows can be added for additional resources), the student writes the name of the resource in the first column and then in the following columns the answers provided by each resource for each question. The final row is a space for students to summarize what they have learned from all of the sources. The summaries often become the main or central ideas of a written response or research report.

This chart is not simply a fill-in-the-blank form. Instead, it should represent to students what they need to do to make sense of information from multiple sources. For example, students need to have a clear purpose or purposes for reading, viewing, or listening to multiple sources. There is space for these purposes (stated as questions) on the chart. The students need to also think about what they already know in response to these questions. It is acceptable for them to write "I don't know anything" or "IDK." The value of this row is that it reminds students that they need to be comparing what they already know with what they are learning from the sources. The row for each source, with space to respond to each question, supports students in staying focused on their purpose for reading. If a source lacks information to answer a question, then students can simply draw an X in that spot, which represents the strategic processing and determination that appropriate information was not present. The row at the bottom of the chart is a reminder that students need to look down each column of notes, to notice similarities and differences in information, to think about which details will be important to include in a summary, and to notice which details can be combined. When we introduce the inquiry chart, we need to message to students that this chart represents the strategic processing we need to engage in when thinking across sources.

FIGURE 11.2. Minimized blank I-chart.

	Question #1	Question #2	Question #3
Student's name			
What I already know about the topic			
Resource #1			
Resource #2			
Resource #3			
Summary			

HOW DO WE PLAN AND TEACH FOR LEARNING FROM MULTIPLE SOURCES?

Whether you are introducing students to the research process or you just want to start teaching reading with multiple sources on a regular basis, the three-phase plan for learning can be adapted for this use. One example of an adaptation might include phases that look like the following:

- Phase 1—Meet the Sources: Introduce an anchor source, usually the strongest source in a larger set of sources.

- Phase 2—Meet the Strategies: Introduce the inquiry chart and engage in close reading–viewing–listening to complete the chart for the first source. Then introduce additional sources and release responsibility for close reading and note taking to students.

- Phase 3—Meet the Response: Write in response to the set of sources.

In preparation for these lessons, you need to locate an anchor source on a particular topic the students can use to generate and answer key questions. Then you need to find additional sources with at least some content that overlaps with the content in the first source. For example, with one group of students studying severe weather, I chose a magazine article on thunderstorms that had enough useful content to answer several interesting questions students might naturally pose. This would be the anchor source. Then I looked for additional sources that addressed some of the same subtopics as those in the first article. For example, in the first article, there was a strong description of thunderstorms. A second source, an online article, had a similar description of thunderstorms, but the details varied just a bit. Figure 11.3 on the next page is an image of the notes I took about both sources in preparation for teaching. Notice that the second source did not address the benefits of severe weather. This difference in detail is okay, as it is an opportunity for students to notice that their questions are answered in some sources and not in others. These notes helped me think through the questions that students might ask and questions that I might need to guide them in asking. Students may not know how to ask strong questions up front. However, since you also want them to experience some success in locating answers to their questions, providing students guidance in asking good, relevant questions will more likely help them achieve it.

When I first introduce inquiry charts, I provide large pieces of paper on which students can draw a chart. See Figure 11.4 on page 215 for one example of a student's inquiry chart. When I model taking notes, I also write on a similar chart placed on a document camera so that all students can see what I write in my notes. Once students have an understanding of the purpose of these charts and how they work, you might encourage them to create the charts on a laptop or other type of device.

When you introduce the inquiry chart (during Phase 2 or whenever you plan to do this), there are three important steps (or sets of steps) you want to highlight for students.

1. Generating questions that will guide their close reading (or viewing or listening).

2. Skimming to identify important parts, closely reading, and then taking notes.

3. Synthesizing the relevant information in notes taken from these sources in order to write a summary of learning.

Early on you may need to model these steps for students or engage them in following these steps with you. This instruction might occur during one or more lessons that are part of "Phase 2" after students have had a chance to read the anchor source you have chosen during "Phase 1."

How do we teach students to generate questions for research or questions they can use as a guide while reading or viewing multiple sources? Figure 11.5 (pp. 216–217) is a description of what a lesson focused on generating questions might look like. Prior to the lesson described, the students read a *National Geographic Explorer* article titled "Storm Warning" (Brooks, 2010). Notice how the teacher leads the students into asking questions about thunderstorms by first making a connection to their everyday lives. (We always have questions that we may want to answer by looking at multiple sources.) Then as she leads them in generating questions related to thunderstorms, she coaches them on how to formulate questions by thinking about what they already know as a starting point.

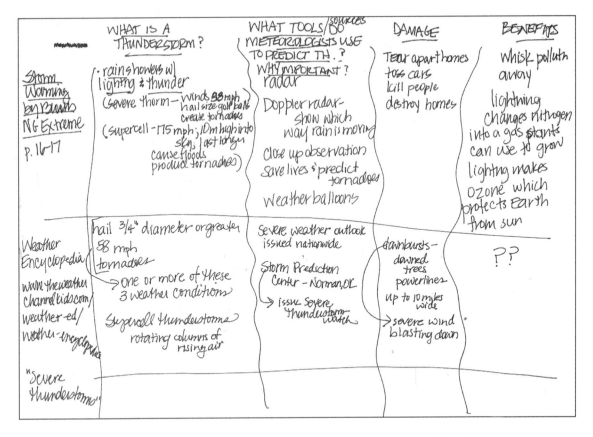

FIGURE 11.3. The notes I prepared for lessons with a group of fifth-grade students writing mini-reports on severe thunderstorms.

214

SEVERE THUNDERSTORMS NOTES	WHAT is a Severe Thunderstorm?	How can be safe in a Severe Thunderstorm	Beatrice I 5th How can a Meteorologist predict a severe Thunderstorm
What I Already (think) I Know	A servere thunderstorm is a really dangreous storm. There is lightning, rain lots of rain, dark clouds, and semetimes hale. And very high winds.	You can be safe in a severe Thunderstorm by going in a room that is surrounded by Walls with no windows. Also by going to your basement because they are undergrand. Also you can go in a ditch.	• They can tell because they Know all the signs that a severe thunderstorm is coming.
National Geogrphic Magizine	• Rain showers with lightning and Thunder. winds (58 miles) Per hour or Faster. Hail the size of golf balls. Create some tornatos. A super cell is a serve Thunderstorm. Some place get fist size balls of ice clobber the ground. It can cause Floods.		• With radar • Radio wave into the sky • They observe the strom • Weather tools • There is a storm perdiction in Norman, Oklahoma. • local office of the national weather service
Online Web page Weatherencylopedia	• Straight line Winds • When its warmer that means that the storms are getting stronger. supercell • Are capable of maintaining severe thunderstorm strengh for hours		• Four times daily, a severe weather outlook • They observe surface and upper air. • Radar's and satelites track the storms. • They use a severe thunderstorm watch.
WeatherWizkids.com			
AlliantEnergyKids.com		• listen to radio and television latest infomation and instructions • Watch, possible • Warning, taking place in area • Out doors look at the sky for flashes of lightning, darkening skies, or increasing winds • Struck by lightning — call 9-1-1 • Indoors — Do not use electricity. • keep a storm safety kit • Stay inside all times	

FIGURE 11.4. Isabella's I-chart.

She also engages them in discussion about how to analyze whether a question is worthy of researching.

Once students have generated questions for research, how do we help them tackle multiple sources? The introduction to inquiry charts is usually followed by a palpable sense of relief. Students feel liberated by the idea that they only have to determine what is important in responding to a few questions and that they do not have to remember and write about every detail in every source. The lesson described in Figure 11.5 also includes an introduction to inquiry charts.

If you have provided instruction related to identifying key details in one source (as described in Chapter 8), closely reading the first source to identify key details that answer a particular set of questions should feel familiar. Examining the second source is the point at which the process may get tricky for some students because they have to identify what is important in that source, *and* they have to compare that information to

FIGURE 11.5. Example of a lesson focused on generating questions.

Lesson: Generating Questions

1. Introduce the concept of generating questions for research with a real-life example.

At the beginning of the lesson, the teacher introduces the concept of "doing research" with a real-life example.

> *Sometimes when we want to know more about a topic we are interested in or we have a question about a particular topic, we engage in research. I know that when I have questions, I search for sources on the Internet that might help me answer this question. For example, when my family decided to get a second cat, I had a lot of questions. One was, "How do you introduce a kitten to an older cat?" Has anyone ever had a question or a topic they were curious about?*

Several students raise their hands. The teacher asks them to turn and talk with someone nearby about a topic or a question for which they have searched for more information. She leans in to listen to a few pairs share their thoughts. When the students regroup, the teacher gets at the purpose of this discussion by saying the following:

> *Usually when we have a question, it is about a topic we already know a little bit about. We may have already read something on the topic. In my case, I had seen how cats do not always get along when I visited an animal shelter once. There were two cats in nearby cages hissing at each other. So, I had a little bit of background knowledge that I could use to generate a question—enough to know that they do not always get along and I need to find out more.*
>
> *How does this approach to research apply to what we learned about thunderstorms in the article we read yesterday? Let's review what we learned and then generate questions we would like to learn more about.*

2. Brainstorm questions with a shared think-aloud and shared writing.

The teacher continues by asking the students to turn and talk with a partner about the source on thunderstorms they had read the previous day. She prompted conversation by asking, "What did you learn about thunderstorms from the article?" She leans in to listen to a few partners and chimes in with her own response to the question.

Next, the teacher places a blank piece of paper on the document camera and says:

> *What did we learn about thunderstorms that we might want to learn more about by reading other sources? Let's generate some questions together. I'll start with one I have: "What is a severe thunderstorm?" I know there is information in this article to help me answer this question, but I also want to see what other authors have to say.*

She pauses to write the question down on the blank paper. Then she calls on volunteers to share a question. She encourages them to think about questions that are answered in the article and that might be worth finding more sources in which to look for answers. As students offer suggestions, she coaches them to notice whenever a question is redundant, that is, it solicits the same information as an earlier question; whenever a question may not require much research (e.g., "yes" or "no" questions); or whenever questions should be grouped together because they are related in some way. The group finishes with a list of questions similar to those in the list in the image that follows. Notice the question *What is a severe thunderstorm?* and the arrow down to the question *How does a thunderstorm develop?* The teacher and students discussed how these two questions might be closely related.

(continued)

> *What is a severe thunderstorm?* ☆
>
> *Where do most thunderstorms occur?*
>
> *How can we be safe in severe thunderstorms?* ☆
>
> *How can a meteorologist predict a thunderstorm?* ☆
>
> *How does a thunderstorm develop?*
>
> *What kind of damage do these storms do?*

3. Determine key questions to research.

The teacher moved forward by saying the following:

> *When we are looking through multiple sources for information, it is helpful to narrow our list of questions to two or three and then look for answers to just those questions.*

The teacher chooses the first question the group will research because she knows the students will be able to find answers in the anchor source. She will also be demonstrating how to do this in the following lesson, so she wants the source to have answers she can locate. Together they choose the last two questions, and the teacher marks each with a star.

4. Create inquiry charts.

Then the teacher introduces the inquiry chart.

> *Sometimes if we decide to look for answers in more than one source, the information we can gather can be too much to remember. Organizing that information in notes of some sort is helpful. One way to do this is to draw an inquiry chart that helps us in organizing what we are learning about a topic of interest.*

She leads the students in folding an 11″ × 17″ sheet of blank paper so that there are four columns and six rows. She provides directions for where to write the questions and the name of the first source.

On the board, she writes the following question for students to discuss in small groups: *Why do you think this chart would be helpful if we are reading multiple sources on a topic?* She leans in to small groups to listen.

5. Close with a discussion of the process.

The teacher wraps up this lesson by asking, "What steps did we take to start the research process today?" Students share responses like, "We thought about what we already knew about a topic and what we wanted to know more about" and "We listed questions and then chose a few to focus on when we look at sources."

FIGURE 11.5. *(continued)*

the previous source's information, *and* finally they have to decide how we can state what we have learned in short notes on the inquiry chart. Unpacking this process for students is another lesson or shared experience that we need to plan and implement. Figure 11.6 is a description of what this lesson might look like. The teacher draws the students into a shared think-aloud as they skim the first source to identify an important part and then closely read and take notes. This is followed by the teacher bringing the students back together to talk about what readers do when they read a second source. She posts a helpful question for them to consider, "Is this information similar to or different from what I learned in the other source(s)?" She engages them in a shared close reading, and through conversation they begin to notice details that are similar and different before she nudges them to take responsibility for doing this on their own.

Do not hesitate to integrate numerous types of sources into this experience. The question about similarities and differences between sources can be applied to any type of source. If you have taught students how to identify key details in video and infographics, they should be able to apply the skills they developed to thinking across a variety of sources.

Once students fill in the answers to the question on the inquiry chart, I have found that they still need help in synthesizing the information to summarize their learning. When students attempt to write summaries of their learning by using the notes on the inquiry chart, they tend to start at the top of the notes and proceed to write a sentence for each bulleted item. Instead, they need to read through all of the notes for one question and figure out which points or observations go together.

Figure 11.7 on page 221 is an example of how one teacher uses a student's notes to generate a summary during a lesson. She thinks aloud about how she noticed similarities in some of the details from the two sources and then draws the students into a discussion about how to combine those details into one sentence.

As they compose the rest of the paragraph, the teacher takes advantage of numerous opportunities to highlight the thinking students need to do when they are writing from their notes. For example, in the paragraph they compose together, notice that there is a detail that is *not* included in Isabella's notes—"hail can be ¾ of an inch." When the teacher called on a student to create a sentence aloud for the paragraph, he added this fact. The teacher and students discuss that this fact was not in the notes but had been included in one of their sources and was relevant. They decided that this detail was an appropriate one to include in that sentence at that point in the paragraph.

Toward the end of the shared writing experience, the students realized that they had not included every detail from Isabella's notes in the paragraph they had composed. Again, the teacher took a moment to discuss this point. They had a conversation about how as they consider what is in their notes and what they want to say in a piece of writing, they may determine that some notes are not that important and do not have to be included.

Students can do more than write summaries of their learning with the information they have gathered using the inquiry chart as a tool. There is value in writing these summaries because doing so requires students to look for details from multiple sources that are similar and could be combined in some way. Students also have to determine which notes are important to include and which are not. Once they get the hang of writing

FIGURE 11.6. Example of a lesson on teaching skimming, close reading, and note taking.

Lesson: Skimming, Close Reading, and Note Taking

1. Review the purpose of the inquiry chart.

The teacher begins the lesson by asking students to turn and talk in trios in response to this question: "How does the inquiry chart help you organize your thinking?"

2. Prompt students to activate background knowledge and write notes.

The teacher starts by saying:

Remember that we are always thinking about what we already know about a topic as a way to help us make sense of the information in a source. The second row on the inquiry chart serves as a reminder to do this. Take a moment to fill in the spaces with information you already know or think you know. If you feel like you do not have any background knowledge to answer a particular question, it is okay to simply write, "I don't know."

The students spend a few minutes jotting down what they already know. The teacher leans in to help those students who hesitate.

3. Explain the purposes of first skimming and then closely reading. Demonstrate and then begin to release responsibility.

The teacher places her copy of the inquiry chart on the document camera. The three questions the students chose to research during the previous lesson are listed across the top of the chart:

- What is a severe thunderstorm?
- How can a meteorologist predict thunderstorms?
- How can we be safe during severe thunderstorms?

Now that we have questions regarding what we want to know more about, we have to return to the first source and look for answers. When we do this, do you think we should reread the whole article? [Pauses for responses.] Probably not, huh? Do you think reading the section headings might help us determine which sections will have the answers we are looking for? [Pauses for responses.] That's right. We can skim the section headings and make predictions about whether we will be able to answer one of our questions. Let's try this together.

The teacher places the article on the document camera and leads the students in thinking through the first heading "Birth of a Thunderstorm" in the article "Storm Warning"" (Brooks, 2010). The students determine that this section might have information relevant to the first question. (They also remember this from their first read.) The teacher reviews what it means to "determine what is important" by referring to the pasta analogy taught in previous lessons. (See Chapter 8 for more information.)

The teacher and students engage in a close reading of this particular section in the article. As they determine which words or phrases are important in answering the question *What is a severe thunderstorm?*, the teacher models writing these details on her own copy of the inquiry chart.

> - Rain showers with lightning
> - Winds at 58 miles per hour or faster
> - Hail the size of golf balls

The students copy her notes or write their own; then, with a partner, they closely read the rest of that section, identifying additional details they want to include in their notes. Releasing responsibility, the teacher encourages the students to continue skimming the article for important

(continued)

sections and then closely reading to identify key details for their notes. The students begin to locate answers to the other two questions on the chart. The teacher confers.

As they closely read and take notes, some of the students make comments about the difference between what they thought they already knew and the new information they are recording on their charts. For example, one student wrote that she already knew thunderstorms "had high winds." When she wrote down "winds at 58 miles per hour or faster" in her notes for the first source, she turned to a partner and said, "I knew the winds were fast, but I didn't realize how fast the winds can be. That's almost as fast as a car drives on the highway."

4. **Introduce strategic processing of a second source. Engage the students in guided practice.**

Once the students have taken significant notes with the first source, the teacher introduces the second source, a website the students locate on classroom laptops. She provides time for the students to read this article. Then she asks them to regroup and says the following:

> *As you read this source, did you notice any details in it that would help you respond to one of our questions? [Pauses for responses.] I agree. This source might be helpful. What did we do with the last source that we can do with this one? [Pauses for responses.] Yes! Let's begin to skim, to locate a relevant section.*

The teacher and students determine which section is important, and then the teacher says:

> *Readers know that it is important to notice the similarities and differences in information presented in multiple sources. As we read, we need to ask this question: "Is this information similar to or different from what I learned in the other source(s)?" Asking this question helps us compare and contrast information in the sources and decide what we want to include in our notes. Let's try this together.*

The teacher leads the students in closely reading the section they had just identified. As they read, they begin to identify details that are new or different from what they learned in the previous source. There is a conversation about how "different" may mean that some details that are in one source are not in another source. These are the details they write in their notes on the inquiry chart.

5. **Encourage independent or partner practice with additional sources. Continue to coach as needed.**

As pairs or individuals exhaust the information in the second source, the teacher encourages them to find a third source. She refers them to a Google doc with a link to additional websites that might be helpful. (While she was planning this lesson, she located and vetted these sites.) She continues leaning in to confer with students as they read and then skim and closely read these sources.

6. **Close with a discussion of the process and content learned.**

The teacher asks the students in small groups to lean in and discuss the strategic processing they engaged in during the lesson as well as the content they learned. She writes these questions on the dry-erase board for the students to consider as they talk: *What is new information you learned about thunderstorms today?* and *What did you do as readers to make sense of multiple sources?*

FIGURE 11.6. *(continued)*

Lesson: Using Notes to Summarize Learning

1. Begin to explain how to think *across* notes on the inquiry chart.

The teacher begins by saying the following:

> *In the past few days, you have generated questions and read or watched several sources to locate answers to these questions. Now we are going to think about how you can use your notes to write a summary of what you learned. Isabella gave permission for me to do this with the notes she took for the first question, "What is a severe thunderstorm?"*

The teacher projects Isabella's notes on a smart board. (Prior to the lesson, she scanned the notes and dropped them into appropriate software so she could project them.)

SEVERE THUNDERSTORMS NOTES	What is a severe thunderstorm?
What I already know?	A severe thunderstorm is a really dangerous storm. There is lightning, lots of rain, dark clouds, and hail. And very high winds.
National Geographic article "Storm Warning" (Brooks, 2007)	• Rain showers with lightning and thunder • Winds (58 miles per hour) or faster • Hail the size of golf balls • Create some tornados • A super cell is a severe thunderstorm • Some places get fist size balls of ice that clobber the ground • It can cause floods
Internet site Weather Encyclopedia	• Straight line winds • When it's warmer that means the storms are getting stronger • Supercells are capable of maintaining severe thunderstorm strength for hours

> *Let's take a moment to read through her notes.* [Provides several seconds for students to read quietly.] *If Isabella was going to summarize what she learned, she could just start at the top and write a sentence for each bulleted note.* [Points to the first bullet on the notes from the article and, in a monotone voice, starts listing sentences for each bulleted note.] *There are rain showers with lightning and thunder. Winds are 58 miles per hour or faster. Hail is the size of golf balls.* [Pauses as though to stop and think about what she has just done.] *This does not sound very good, huh? I am all over the place. I don't have a clear direction. What can I do instead?*

Through discussion and close reading of Isabella's notes, the students arrive at the idea that many of the details Isabella has written reveal how dangerous thunderstorms can be. They decide to make the severity of thunderstorms the focus of the summary.

(continued)

FIGURE 11.7. Example of a lesson on using notes to summarize learning.

2. Engage in shared writing with continued coaching on how to think across notes.

With the teacher as a scribe, the students collaborate to compose a summary paragraph (written on the dry-erase board next to Isabella's projected notes) in response to the question, *What is a severe thunderstorm?*:

> A severe thunderstorm can be a dangerous thunderstorm. A severe thunderstorm has rain showers, lightning, straight-line winds, and thunder. It can produce hail the size of a golf ball at 3/4 of an inch. It has strong winds that can reach the speed of 58 miles per hour or more, and it can even create tornados. If the weather gets warmer, that means that the storm is likely getting stronger, and some thunderstorms, like a super cell, can stay strong for hours.

As they compose this paragraph, the teacher coaches them on how to combine details from different sources. For example, after they compose the first sentence, the teacher begins to think aloud and says:

> As I look at Isabella's notes, I notice that there are several details about the physical features or parts of a thunderstorm. [Points to specific details in Isabella's notes.] For the first source, Isabella has written "rain showers with lightning and thunder" by the first bullet. For the second source, she has written "straight line winds." I think we should combine these details into one sentence. Who wants to give that a try?

3. Release responsibility.

When they have finished the shared writing, the students return to their own notes and, using laptops, compose summaries of learning for the second and third questions on the inquiry chart. The teacher leans in to coach students.

4. Close with a discussion of the process.

The teacher asks the students in small groups to lean in and discuss how they used their notes to summarize their learning. She closes by asking the students for a thumbs-up, thumbs-down, or thumbs sideways in response to this question, *Do you think you could talk with someone at home tonight about severe thunderstorms?* She prompts them to turn and tell a partner what they would say.

FIGURE 11.7. *(continued)*

summaries or at least some familiarity with it, I would recommend increasing the complexity of the tasks we ask them to complete as far as writing in response to their learning. For example, one group of students used inquiry charts to research a historical figure. They were not required to fill in the last row on the I-chart to summarize their thinking. Instead, they were asked to write an obituary for this figure. Based on the information they had gathered, they had to draw conclusions about the person and explain their reasoning.

As students determine what is important in a second and third source, it is important that we confer with individuals or small groups to get a sense of their strategic processing. Are they clear about their purpose for reading or viewing these additional sources? Are they noticing similarities and differences between information in the source they are currently reading and a previous source they read? Usually, when I first lean in to confer, I start by saying, "Tell me a little bit about what you are learning from this source." If the student's response reveals that he is understanding the content in that source, then I say, "So how is the information in this source (or this part of the source) similar to or different from what you learned in the last source?"

As the student responds, I begin to formulate an affirmation I can share. This might sound like one of the following statements:

- The purpose for reading (or watching) these sources seems to be clear in your mind.
- It sounds like you are understanding what you have read in this part.
- Your comments reveal that you are actively comparing and contrasting the information in these two sources.

If appropriate, I follow with a teaching point. Figure 11.8 on the next page includes examples of what you might notice and suggestions for how to respond. As you confer with students, be prepared to think aloud about how you noticed similarities and differences in the sources they are reading or viewing. Do not worry about knowing all of the sources inside and out. Instead, trust the process of keeping a clear purpose in mind, skimming to identify important parts, and then closely reading those parts. If you follow this process with two sources, most likely, similarities and differences will surface for you, and you will be able to highlight what you noticed for the student.

Another opportunity to assess students' synthesis of information from multiple sources is in analyzing their written responses. Figure 11.9 on page 225 includes suggestions of what students' written responses might look like at different stages. The purpose of this tool is to help you frame where students are on a continuum of learning that you can revise or build on as needed. I highly recommend asking students to partner with you in creating assessment tools or criteria for written responses because they may be more aware than you are of the energy they put into thinking across sources (Cummins, 2018). You might use the descriptions in the continuum as a starting point for a conversation with students, encouraging them to decide which descriptors are appropriate and which descriptors should be added. Based on this conversation, they can collaborate with you in creating a rubric or checklist of sorts.

Scenario	How you can respond
The student shrugs or seems unclear when asked how the information in the source he is currently reading is similar to information in previous sources.	• With the student, identify a section in the new source that may help him respond to his purpose for reading. Together closely read one sentence at a time. Coach the student to stop and think about what he learned in that sentence and then how the information in that sentence is similar to or different from the information in the previous source. • Be prepared to model how you noticed a similarity or difference in details. Modeling may include noticing that a detail or piece of information in a second source is not present in the first source.
The student's response reveals a surface-level understanding of similarities in two sources. For example, she might say, "They are both about turtles."	• Remind the student of her purpose for reading or refer to the questions listed on the inquiry chart and say, "What have you learned from both sources that helps you answer this question?" • Refer to previous lessons on types of details authors of informational sources include to help the student explain her learning. This exercise may involve thinking about details in both sources that reveal *where*, *when*, *how*, and *why*. (See Chapter 8, Figure 8.9 for more information.)
The student refers to what she learned in one source and then in another source, but not in a way that integrates the information from both sources.	Possible prompts: • *If you were talking to someone about what you learned, how could you integrate this information into one or two sentences?* • *How are these details from the sources similar, or what do they have in common? How would you write about their similarities in a sentence?*

FIGURE 11.8. Multiple Sources: Conferring scenarios and suggestions for coaching.

WHAT DOES FOLLOW-UP INSTRUCTION LOOK LIKE?

Lessons like the ones I have described in this chapter do not have to be reserved for times when students are completing "research reports." While there is value in time spent on these bigger projects, reading multiple sources on a topic a few times a year is not enough practice for students to master the skills required to synthesize information from these sources (Cummins, 2017). They need regular opportunities to engage in this type of thinking. My recommendation would be to make reading or viewing multiple sources on a topic a *regular part* of your instruction. Working with multiple sources

Stage	Characteristics of written responses
Attempting	• Student attempts to answer the question or respond to the purpose for reading. • Student is clearly trying to draw from more than one source. • With support, the student is beginning to integrate information from multiple sources into written responses.
Approaching	• Response is brief and mostly relevant. • With support, the student is beginning to draw conclusions based on information from multiple sources. • Details may not be presented in an integrated fashion. Writing may feel "listlike" (e.g., I learned this from "Source A." I learned this from "Source B").
Meeting	• Student is drawing accurate conclusions based on information from multiple sources. • With minimal support, the student is beginning to include reasoning that refers to details from more than one source. (This response may include analyzing authors' points of view and critiquing discrepancies in sources.) • Student is beginning to integrate information easily into response formats other than "learning summaries."
Exceeding	• Student's written response has a seamless, well-informed quality. • Student is able to integrate information easily into multiple types of response. • Reasoning reveals critical thinking about how and why the sources differ.

FIGURE 11.9. Stages of development in students' written synthesis of information from multiple sources. Adapted from Cummins (2018).

does not have to be done in pursuit of completing a larger project, and students' written responses might be quick and short.

What does this type of instruction look like in the classroom over an extended period? I worked closely with an intermediate-grade teacher for 2 years to make this a regular part of her practice. We started by just asking, "What are we teaching next week?" and "How can we incorporate more than one source?" With practice, we began to look at entire units in social studies and science, identifying points in the curriculum that would lend themselves to reading multiple sources. By the end of the second year, reading multiple sources became just second nature for this teacher every time she tackled a new topic with her students. Another colleague, a reading specialist who pulls students from multiple classrooms for small-group instruction, made this shift, too. She chose high-interest topics, like the sinking of the *Titanic*, and always made a point of locating multiple sources on each topic. Again, this just became a part of how she operated.

As students engage in reading multiple sources, we need to keep an eye on where they are developmentally and continuously use this information to plan follow-up instruction. Figure 11.10 on the next page provides suggestions for lessons you might implement based on what you have noticed. These opportunities can easily be implemented during Phases 2 and 3 of the three-phase plan for learning.

If . . .	Then . . .

Students are struggling to integrate information.	• Post sentence stems students can use while they talk about multiple sources. Some examples include:
	  ○ *Both sources include information about . . .*
	  ○ *I noticed a similarity in details about . . .*
	  ○ *The first source did not include information about . . .*
	• Provide colored pencils students can use to circle details on their inquiry chart that belong together. Use one student's chart to demonstrate what this exercise looks like.

Students are restating what they learned from multiple sources, but not necessarily drawing conclusions.	• Review the types of details authors of informational sources frequently include (see Figure 8.9 on p. 145). This review might help students notice the similarities between details (e.g., *these details are all <u>physical characteristics</u> of . . .* or *these details all explain <u>why</u> . . .*). • During a Phase 2—Meet the Strategies lesson, think aloud for students about how you used your background knowledge and details in multiple sources to draw a conclusion (e.g., *When I thought about the details in both of these sources, I decided that this historical figure must have been brave because . . .*).
Students are drawing conclusions, but they are struggling to explain their reasoning.	• Provide opportunities for groups of students to discuss in detail the conclusions they have drawn as a result of consulting multiple sources. Lean in to coach students as they explain their reasoning. • Engage the students in shared writing experiences, with you as the scribe and coach, that focus on explaining their reasoning.

FIGURE 11.10. Suggestions for follow-up instruction.

CLOSING THOUGHTS

If teaching with multiple sources is not a regular part of your practice, consider making this shift. I would not wait for "just the right time" or for the "perfect set of sources." Just give it a go. In Appendix A, page 238, you will find a one-page guide that can aid you in planning these lessons. Once you begin implementing these lessons, what you see, as far as student growth, may amaze you. Students *love* engaging with multiple sources because they develop a depth of knowledge on a topic or issue. They can speak at length. They can share what they have learned more easily with others. Learning becomes easier, too. They understand what they are reading in new sources *because* they have read other sources on the topic.

Lessons for Phase 2—
Meet the Strategies

	Phase 2—Meet the Strategies Lessons	Page
1	Synthesis and Identifying Main Ideas Using the Framed Photo Analogy	229
2	Monitoring for Meaning Using the Coding Strategy	230
3	Identifying Key Details Using the Pasta Analogy	231
4	Recognizing the Types of Details Authors Use	232
5	Explaining Key Details with "Explode to Explain"	233
6	Recognizing a Source's Structure	234
7	Learning from the Features in a Source	235
8	Using Context Clues to Figure Out the Meaning of New Vocabulary	236
9	Identifying an Author's Purpose	237
10	Synthesizing Information from Two Sources	238

The purpose of this appendix is to give you a quick view of lessons you might provide as part of a *whole-class lesson* or as part of a small-group *guided-reading lesson*. While the series of lessons is listed in a general order in which you might teach them, you should pick and choose particular lessons according to the needs of your students. Each series of lessons may occur over several periods and with multiple sources.

Generally, students should be given an opportunity to read or view a *whole* source before they engage in closely reading or viewing the source or parts of the source. Therefore, the lessons described are appropriate as part of a *second* lesson (or read), after the students have already heard the text read aloud (during a whole-class lesson) or read the text on their own (during a Phase 2 lesson).

The lessons described *do not* include how to help students write in response (Phase 3). Writing a response benefits the students in many ways, though, and should be incorporated into lessons that follow. The notes that students take during the lessons described can easily be used to plan for a written response.

Please consider the following as you read through suggestions for instruction:

- Each lesson includes language about the *what, why,* and *how.* The *what* describes what readers know about how sources work or how a reader goes about making sense of a source. The *why* explains the purpose or benefits (to the reader) of this type of strategic processing of a source. The *how* explains the strategic processing readers must engage in to make sense of the source.

- The *what, why,* and *how* can be used as an introduction to your lesson and can easily be turned into helpful anchor charts. Revise or modify this language to meet the needs of your students.

- There are several points at which the directions suggest that you "think aloud" for students. It is recommended that you prepare for this think-aloud in advance. Students need to hear and see what you are doing to make sense of a source. Plan for what you will say and how you will show the students what you are writing on a text excerpt.

- If you are using a text you have read aloud, when you think aloud, make sure you project the text in some way or have copies available so students can view the text.

- Materials for lessons include:
  - Anchor charts and/or bookmarks
  - Copies of excerpts from the source or hard copies of the source that students can write on or place sticky notes on
  - Pencils

- For each series of lessons, there is a reference to chapters in this book that provide further explanation. For some lessons, there is also a link to a resource posted at my website, *www.Sunday-Cummins.com.* If you need more information on what Phases 1 and 3 might look like for these lessons, see the sample lessons in Chapters 6–11.

1 Synthesis and Identifying Main Ideas Using the Framed Photo Analogy

What: Readers know that a *main idea* is the most important point or thought in a source or a section of a source. A main idea may be stated clearly by the author, or the main idea may be revealed in important details the author includes.

Why: Identifying the main idea can help you remember what you read, heard, or saw in a source that is important. This knowledge can help you change or add to what you already know about the world.

How: You can figure out an author's main idea by asking yourself three questions as you read, view, or listen to a source:

- *What are important details in this source?*
- *How are all these details connected?*
- *How does this information help me figure out the author's main idea?*

You might have to use information from the source and your background knowledge about the world to help you answer these questions. This process is called *synthesis*!

Tip: Sometimes when we are trying to identify the author's main idea, it is helpful to think about a framed photograph. The details in the source are the photograph, and the frame is the author's main idea. As we are thinking about how the details are connected, we can ask ourselves, Why would the author write or *frame* this source?

For more information, see Chapter 6, pages 89–91, or visit a blog entry I wrote at *https://bit.ly/2sp9lq2*.

Series of Phase 2 Lessons

1. **Model and guide.** Share the *what* and *why* of identifying main ideas. Introduce the framed photograph analogy. You might use a framed photo you have and say something like, "What do you notice in this framed photograph? Why do you think I framed this photograph?" Give students a chance to respond and provide an explanation of who or what is in the photograph and why you framed this particular one. Then you might say:

   We call what you just did "synthesis." You looked at all of the details in the photograph and thought about how they are connected. You used the details you noticed and your background knowledge to infer this information. Then you thought about why this photograph is important enough to frame and put on my desk. When we read, view, or listen to a source to identify a main idea, we engage in the same process. The key details are the details in a photograph, and the main idea is the frame.

   Read aloud a text and then lead the students in discussing one of the main ideas and the important details in the source that reveal this idea.

2. **Provide a main idea statement and sections of a source to closely read or view.** After students read or view a source, provide a main idea statement. Direct student partners to read specific sections of the source (that you selected in advance) to look for key details. Coach students as they list possible supporting details for the main idea you presented. Ask probing questions like, "What makes you think this detail supports this idea?"

3. **Collaborate with students to identify a source's main idea.** After reading a source, engage students in generating a list of possible main ideas on a piece of chart paper. (Have a few ideas ready in case the students hesitate.) Then circle one of the ideas and coach students as they look through the source for details that support that idea. Lead a shared writing of the details they find. As needed, provide stems to help students explain their thinking:

   - *I think this detail is important because . . .*
   - *This detail made me think about the main idea because . . .*
   - *This detail is connected to that detail because . . .*

4. **Coach students as they engage with a source independently.** Provide paper for students to draw a frame around the edge in which to write a main idea statement and then to illustrate or write (in the center) details from the source that support this idea.

2 Monitoring for Meaning Using the Coding Strategy

What: Readers know that we need to think about our thinking or *monitor for meaning* as we read or view a source. This idea means that we notice when we do and do not understand information in a source.

Why: Monitoring for meaning will help you notice when you need to stop and figure out a tricky part of a source so that you understand the rest of the source better.

How: You can help yourself monitor for meaning by reading a chunk of a source or watching a clip of a video and by asking yourself these questions:

- *Is this new information?*
- *Do I already know this information?*
- *Do I understand this information?*

Tip: Sometimes, to help us start paying closer attention to a source, we might stop and "code our thinking" by writing down one of these codes and jotting down a note about what we are thinking.

Let's Code Our Thinking

* I already knew this information.

+ This is new information to me.

? I don't understand.. I wonder...

! Wow. I understand this and it's cool!

To download this bookmark, visit *www.guilford.com/cummins-materials*.

For more information, see Chapter 7, pages 113–115, or visit a blog entry I wrote at *https://bit.ly/2Ed550p*.

Series of Phase 2 Lessons

1. **Model and guide.** Share the *what* and *why*. Display a few pages of a source and an anchor chart with the codes. Explain that proficient readers of nonfiction sources "self-monitor" for meaning while they read. Remind students that self-monitoring means they think about questions like the following:

   - *Did I already know this information?*
   - *Is this new information?*
   - *Did I understand what I read?*

   Think aloud about a section of the source and which code you will use. An example of a think-aloud is:

   > *I just learned that a chameleon's tongue is as long as its body. I did not know this. I'm going to put a + in the margin and jot down a few words to help me remember this fact.*

   Have the students work with a partner to read a sentence or paragraph, discuss their thinking, and then code and jot on their texts or a sticky note independently. Confer with students.

2. **Engage students in coding and jotting notes.** Engage the students in closely reading a part of the source and thinking about their thinking. Encourage them to jot codes and notes that will help them remember their thinking. If needed, be prepared to model again. Close with a discussion about how thinking carefully about this part of the source helped them understand the source better. You might ask:

   - How did coding and note taking help you remember the details better?
   - Or make sense of those details?

3. **Prompt partners to think together about self-monitoring and coding.** Ask partners to read and jot notes independently before leaning in to discuss how they self-monitored and to share their notes. Lean in to confer. Language stems you might provide include:

   - *I was confused when I read . . .*
   - *This was new information to me . . .*
   - *I didn't know that . . .*

4. **Ask students to identify a difficult section of a longer source.** Ask students to each identify a section of the source they found to be tricky and to reread and code the source as a way to help them understand it better. Lean in to confer. Close by asking partners to share what they did to make sense of the tricky part of the source and what they understand better as a result.

3 Identifying Key Details Using the Pasta Analogy

What: Readers know that informational sources have lots of details and that some details are more important than others. We can figure out which details are important by thinking about our purpose for reading (e.g., What is new information that I am learning about this topic?) and then looking for bits of information that help us respond to our purpose. These pieces of information are *key details*.

Why: You can use key details to help you remember what you learned from a source, to compare what you learned to information in other sources, and to think critically about why the author wrote or created this source.

How: You can identify key details by asking questions like these:

- *What is my purpose for reading?* (e.g., to answer a question, to learn new information, to identify details that support a main idea)
- *What are words or phrases (or bits of information) that help me respond to my purpose?*

You may have to use your knowledge about the world and about how sources work to help you.

Tip: Sometimes it helps to think about pasta when you are trying to determine what is important. When you make pasta, you do not eat the water the pasta is boiled in, right? You want to eat just the pasta! When you are reading, some words or phrases are pasta, worthy of thinking about and remembering. Other words are not as important, or are like the water you boil the pasta in.

For more information, see Chapter 8, pages 138–141, or visit a blog entry I wrote at *https://bit.ly/2CvXJEW.*

Series of Phase 2 Lessons

1. **Model and guide.** Share the *what* and *why* of identifying key details. Display a photo of pasta and explain the analogy. You might say:

   When we make pasta, we drain the water and just eat the pasta. When we read, some words or phrases are more important than others. Those are the pasta words. As we think about our purpose for reading, let's think about pasta words that help us understand the text better.

   Post a section of a text for all students to view. State a purpose for reading the text (e.g., "We are going to read to find out about . . ." or "We are going to read to look for answers to this question . . ."). Read aloud a sentence. Then think aloud about which words, phrases, or images are worthy of remembering (or that help you respond to the purpose for reading) and why. Ask the students to work with a partner to identify key words and phrases, graphics, or images in a few additional sentences or in a short part of the source. Model for students how to use their list of words and phrases to summarize orally. To model for students, you might say, "I am looking at the key words I listed in my notes. Listen to me try to use the words to summarize what I learned." Engage students in taking turns with a partner to orally summarize by using the key words in their notes.

2. **Engage students in determining what is important and then listing key words/phrases as notes.** State the purpose for reading (e.g., *to answer the question* [insert question] or *to learn new facts about . . .*). Review the pasta analogy. Coach students in stopping after each sentence in an excerpt of text to think about important details that might help them respond to the purpose. Show them how to list those details or key words in their notes.

3. **Coach individuals.** Ask students to identify important sections or parts of a source and then to closely read, identifying pasta words or phrases and jotting these down in a list on a sticky note. Coach as needed. Provide time for partners to use the words as they summarize aloud what they learned. These key words and phrases can be used to plan and write a response.

4 Recognizing the Types of Details Authors Use

What: Readers know that authors use different *types of details* to describe the topic or explain what happens or to tell a true story. Examples of types of details are where, when, how, and why.

Why: If you can recognize that an author is sharing a particular type of detail, like where something happened or how something works, then you will understand the source better and be able to remember what you learned. This can also help you explain what you learned in your own words.

How: When you identify a key detail or piece of information in a source, stop and ask yourself:

- *What type of detail is this?*
  and
- *What did I just learn?*

Types of Details
• Where or location
• When or duration
• Why or cause–effect
• How something behaves
• How something works
• Function or purpose
• Physical attributes (color, shape, size, number, texture, construction)
• Statistic (fact or data stated in numbers)
• Definition
• Synonym
• Comparison
• Real-life examples

For additional types of details, see Figure 8.9 on page 144.

For more information, visit a blog entry I wrote on teaching students what we mean by *example* at *https://bit.ly/2HoaHdv.*

Series of Phase 2 Lessons

1. **Introduce and guide.** Share the *what* and *why*. Post an anchor chart with *how* and a list of selected types of details. (An alternative option is to generate a list with students as they "discover" types of details.) Hand out copies of an excerpt from the source. Guide the students in identifying key details and then thinking about which types of details they are. You may need to think aloud, saying something like the following:

   This phrase jumped out at me. I'm going to underline this and think about what type of detail this is. [Pauses.] *I think the author is trying to tell me where this event took place because this word is a location. So, I just learned where _____ happened. It happened in _____.*

   Once the excerpt has been closely read and annotated, model for students how you can use the annotated text to help you explain what you learned. Then coach students in sharing aloud about what they learned.

2. **Coach partners as they closely read, annotate, and discuss.** Provide a copy of an excerpt for students to annotate with a partner. Language stems you might provide to support their conversation include:

   - *I think this word is worth underlining because . . .*
   - *This detail tells me* [fills in type] *. . .*
   - *I'm going to write . . . in the margins because . . .*

   Close by asking partners to explain what they learned using their annotated excerpts.

3. **Coach individuals as they identify types of details independently.** Provide a copy of an excerpt or ask students to locate an important part of a source on their own. As you lean in to support students, continue to provide language stems as needed. Close by asking students to turn and talk with a partner about what they learned, using their annotated excerpts as a reference.

5 Explaining Key Details with "Explode to Explain"

What: Readers know that sometimes we need to slow down and think carefully about important details in a source if we want to be able to explain what we have learned.

Why: Being able to explain what we learned (in our own words) can help us explain evidence in the source that supports a main idea or an important point that we want to make.

How: Locate one sentence or short section to closely read. As you read,

- Underline important words or phrases.
- Jot notes about what those words mean or make you think about.
- Finish by asking two questions while you look back at your annotations:
  - *What did I learn that I can explain to someone else?*
  - *Why is this important?*

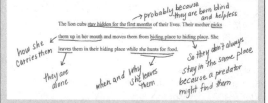

For more information, see Chapter 8, pages 142–145, or visit a blog entry I wrote at *https://bit.ly/2EKTRQJ.*

Series of Phase 2 Lessons

1. **Model and guide.** Share the *what* and *why* of being able to explain what we learned from a source. Post an anchor chart with the suggestions for *how*. Ask the students to think back to the source (that they read during Phase 1) and help you generate a main idea statement. Once you have this statement, ask the students to help you choose one sentence or part of the source that reveals this idea. Write this sentence on chart paper for all students to view. Think aloud about the first part of the sentence. What words jump out at you as important? What kind of information do they provide? What does this information make you think? Underline words and jot notes that reveal your thinking. Then draw the students into doing this with you for the next part of the sentence and so forth. Refer back to the steps on the anchor chart as needed. Close by asking the students to explain to a partner what they learned. Help them refer to the underlined words and annotations. If needed, model how to do this.

2. **Coach partners as they closely read, annotate, and discuss.** Ask pairs to choose an important sentence (or you might decide on the sentence as a group) and write the sentence on a blank piece of paper. Prompt them to review the steps on the anchor chart before they start. Language stems you might provide to support their conversation include:

   - *I think this detail is worth underlining because . . .*
   - *This makes me think . . .*
   - *I think the author means that . . .*
   - *This is important because . . .*
   - *I'm going to write . . .*

   Close by asking partners to explain what they learned and why it is important (or supports the main idea) with another pair of students.

3. **Coach individuals as they explode to explain independently.** Ask individuals to choose a sentence from a source to think through and mark on their own. Provide support as they annotate and then discuss with a partner.

6 Recognizing a Source's Structure

What: Readers know that an informational source has a structure or that the details are organized in a certain way. Examples of structures include descriptive, sequence, comparison, cause–effect, and problem–solution.

Why: Noticing the structure of a source can help you determine what is important. For example, if you notice that a source has a problem–solution structure, then you are more likely to look for or notice problems the author poses and possible solutions.

How: As you read or watch a source, you need to *notice* and *name* the source's structure. You can do this by keeping the types of structures in mind and by noticing clues the author provides.

Structure	Student-friendly explanation
Descriptive	An author introduces a topic and then several related subtopics that describe or explain the main topic.
Sequence/ Chronology/ Narrative	An author describes a series of steps in a process or events over time or tells the story of a person, group, or event.
Comparison	An author examines how two or more people, places, things, or ideas are alike or different.
Cause– Effect	An author explains why something happens or occurs.
Problem– Solution	An author identifies a problem and then explains how the problem was solved or could be solved.

Tip: Sometimes authors use more than one structure. While the source may have an overall or *macro-structure,* one part of the source may be in a different structure or have a *micro-structure.* For example, an author might describe the life cycle of a butterfly using a sequence structure for most of the text. In one part of the text, though, the author might compare and contrast the butterfly with the moth.

For more information, see Chapter 8, pages 145–149, or visit a blog entry in which I describe a lesson I gave introducing the problem–solution and description structures at *https://bit.ly/2Lgp41Y*.

Series of Phase 2 Lessons

1. **Introduce and guide.** Share the *what* and *why* of text (or source) structures. Post an anchor chart with kid-friendly definitions for two of the structures. Ask the students to think back to the source (that they read during a Phase 1 lesson). Guide them in a discussion about which structure the author uses for the source. Engage the students in closely reading a part of the source that reveals its structure. Regroup. On a piece of chart paper, generate a list of details (or features) in that part of the source that are clues to the structure (e.g., *The author poses a problem, The author explains why _____ happened, The heading says _____ and that makes us think _____*). Ask the students to closely read another section, and on a sticky note jot down clues that reveal the source's structure. Close by brainstorming what a graphic organizer for that source might look like; draft one together.

2. **Coach partners as they closely read and discuss.** Introduce a third structure. With a different source (that the students have already read), ask partners to determine which of the three structures the source fits in (mostly). Encourage them to return to the source for clues and to have a conversation. As needed, provide language stems for support, such as:

   - *In this section the author describes . . .*
   - *The author poses a problem when he writes that . . .*
   - *I noticed the author is comparing . . .*
   - *I think the author is explaining why something happened because . . .*
   - *It seems like the author is telling the story of . . .*

   Close by asking the students how noticing a source's structure helps them remember what they learned.

3. **Coach partners as they determine what is important and create a graphic organizer.** With the same source or a new one, coach students as they discuss which structure the author used, citing details from the source. Support students as they create a graphic that reveals the source's structure and then take notes. Close by asking them to use the notes in the organizer to help the partners share what they learned from the source.

7 Learning from the Features in a Source

What: Readers know that informational sources have lots of features that we need to pay attention to and learn from as we read, view, or listen to them. Examples of *features* are titles, headings, maps, photographs, diagrams, charts, and graphs.

Why: Paying attention to some features like titles and headings can help us locate information in a source or make predictions about what we will be learning about. Carefully reading or looking at features, like photographs, maps, and diagrams, can help us learn more about the topic of that source and understand the rest of the source better.

How: You can make sense of a feature by asking questions like these:

- *What is the purpose of this feature?*
- *What am I learning from this feature?*
- *How does this feature help me understand other parts of the source?*

You may have to use your knowledge about the world and what you already know about features to help you.

Feature	Purpose
Photographs, Illustrations	Shows an example of what the author (or narrator) is describing in the source.
Diagrams	A drawing with labels that helps the reader visualize what is being described in the source.
Graph	A graphic that shows how two or more things are related.
Inset or Close-Up	A picture that gives the reader an up-close view of a small part of a bigger picture.
Map	A drawing of a location or place that gives the reader more information about that place.
Table	A display of data or information in rows and columns that provides the reader with an easy way to look at the information.
Timeline	A graphic that shows the reader the order of a series of events.

For more information, see Chapter 9, pages 168–174.

Series of Phase 2 Lessons

1. **Model and guide with two questions.** Share the *what* and *why* of features. Post an anchor chart with the first two questions listed under *how*. Share with the students that these are questions that they can ask themselves when they closely read a feature. Ask the students to find a particular feature in a source they have already read like a photograph and caption. Think aloud for students about this feature.

   Your think-aloud might sound like the following:

   > *I noticed a picture of _____. I know that the purpose of a picture in an informational source is to _____. So, I think the author wants me to know _____.*

   > *Then I noticed the caption _____. When I read this, I realized that _____.*

   In front of the students jot down a few notes on a sticky note or in the margins of the source about what you learned from the feature. Then guide students in thinking through another similar feature in the source and taking notes.

2. **Coach partners as they closely read and discuss.** Ask partners to choose a feature, like a photograph and caption or a diagram, in the source to closely read. Confer with partners. As needed, provide sentence stems like:

   - *I noticed that . . .*
   - *The purpose of this feature is . . .*
   - *In this feature, the author is showing me . . .*
   - *I learned that . . .*

   Ask students to each write their own notes about what they learned.

3. **Coach individuals as they closely read and jot notes.** Allow students to identify a visual image they find challenging. Support them as they make sense of the feature and jot notes about their learning.

4. **Guide students in making connections between features and text.** Add the third question under "how" to the anchor chart. Model for students how you made a connection between information in the main part of the source and a particular feature. Ask students to locate an additional feature, to reread the text, and then to closely read the feature. Coach them in sharing the connections they make between the two.

8 Using Context Clues to Figure Out the Meaning of New Vocabulary

What: Readers know that sometimes there are words in a source for which we do not know the meaning. We also know that authors sometimes provide context clues to help us figure out the meaning of a word. There are certain types of clues authors use like definitions, synonyms or antonyms, examples, general clues, and visual images.

Why: Figuring out what a new word means can help you recall details in the source. This may also help you understand a part of the source better or the big ideas in the source.

How: You can figure out the meaning of a word by asking yourself these questions:

- *What type of clue do I notice?*
- *What does this make me think the word means?*

> ### 5 Types of Context Clues Readers Can Use To Figure Out Tricky Words
>
> 1. **Definition:** the author **explains the meaning** of the word right in the sentence or in that part of the source.
>
> 2. **Synonym:** the author uses a word **similar in meaning.**
>
> 3. **Example:** the author provides one or more **example words or ideas.**
>
> 4. **General:** the author provides several words or statements that **give clues** to the word's meaning.
>
> 5. **Visual Cues:** the author provides a **visual image** or graphic that gives an explicit or implicit clue to the meaning of a word or phrase in a source.

To download this bookmark, visit *www.guilford. com/cummins-materials*.

For more information, see Chapter 10, pages 195–197, or visit a blog entry I wrote at *https://bit. ly/2LcPVvz*.

Series of Phase 2 Lessons

1. **Model and guide.** Share the *what* and *why* of using context clues to figure out the meaning of unfamiliar words. Post a chart or provide a bookmark with the types of clues. In some way, project, for all students to see, part of a source they have already read or ask them to locate that part on their own copy of the source. Model for students noticing a word in the source that seems unfamiliar (to you or the students); draw a box around this word. Then demonstrate looking for a clue to help you figure out the meaning and underlining the clue in the source. Jot notes in the margins about the type of clue and what it makes you think the word means. As you do this, refer to the types of clues on the bookmark or chart. Assign another unfamiliar word in the source for students to each draw a box around (on their own copy of the source) and then practice making sense of it by looking for context clues with a partner, then underlining and annotating. As students finish, encourage them to locate other tricky words and engage in the same strategic processing.

2. **Think aloud about how you make sense of (harder) general clues.** Follow a similar routine as described for "Model and Guide," but focus primarily on the types of clues you have noticed that students are still struggling to make sense of while reading.

3. **Ask partners to identify three to four unfamiliar words and problem-solve collaboratively.** Partners identify and draw boxes around unfamiliar words. Then they look for clues together. Provide sentence stems to support student conversations such as:

   - *A clue I noticed is . . .*
   - *That clue made me think about . . .*
   - *I think this word means . . . because . . .*

4. **Ask individuals to prepare a think-aloud for a small group of peers.** Tell students they will be teaching their peers how to make sense of harder context clues. Advise them as they select a word and related clues, and then plan for how they will "think aloud" or make clear what they did to make sense of the clue in front of a small group of peers. Later, when they present, encourage each student to talk about how the word he chose helped him understand the ideas in the source better.

9 Identifying an Author's Purpose

What: Readers know that authors have a reason or purpose for writing an informational source (in which they have PRIDE). Authors' purposes include to instruct (or teach us), to tell a true story, to explain, to describe, and to persuade.

Why: Identifying an author's purpose can help you think about what is important in a source. For example, if you notice that an author seems to be instructing or teaching you how to do something, then you will be looking for specific steps or directions you can follow.

How: As you preview and then read a source, look for clues as to the author's purpose. Try to *notice* and *name* the author's purpose. You can do this by keeping the types of authors' purposes in mind.

Tip: Sometimes an author has more than one purpose!

Anchor Chart

Purpose	Student-Friendly Explanation
Persuade	The author wants to persuade you to do something or believe something. In other words, the author may have an opinion on a particular topic!
Recount	The author wants to tell you a story (that really happened) about a person or event.
Instruct	The author wants to teach you how to do something.
Describe	The author wants to report on, or describe, the physical features or behaviors of a thing or group of things.
Explain	The author wants to make clear how something works, how something is made, or why something occurs or occurred.

For more information, see a blog entry I wrote at *https://bit.ly/2G2Gr8G*.

Series of Phase 2 Lessons

1. **Introduce and guide.** Share the *what* and *why* of the author's purpose. Post an anchor chart with kid-friendly definitions for two of the purposes. Ask the students to think back to the source they already read or viewed during Phase 1. Engage them in a discussion about which purpose the author has for the source they read. Engage the students in closely reading a part of the source that reveals the author's purpose. On a piece of chart paper, generate a list of details (or features) in that part of the source that are clues to the author's purpose (e.g., *The author describes _____, The author gives steps for how to _____*). Ask the students to closely read another section and on a sticky note jot down clues that reveal the author's purpose. Close by asking students to talk with a partner about what they noticed in the source that makes them think the author has a particular purpose.

2. **Coach partners as they closely read and discuss.** Introduce a third purpose. With a different source (that the students have already read), ask partners to determine which of the three purposes the author has for this source. Encourage them to return to the source for clues to discuss. As needed, provide language stems for support such as:

   - *In this section the author provides steps for how to . . .*
   - *The author tells the story of . . .*
   - *I noticed the author is describing the features of . . .*
   - *I think the author is explaining how . . .*
   - *It seems like the author wants me to believe that . . .*

   Close by asking the students how this discussion about authors' purposes helps them think about what is important. You might say:

   > *If you notice the author wants* [insert author's purpose], *how does that help you think about what is important in a source? Or what will you look for as you read?*

3. **Coach partners as they determine key details.** With the same source or a new one, coach students as they discuss the author's purpose, citing details from the source. Support students as they take bulleted notes like the following:

   - Author's purpose for writing the source
   - Detail from the source that reveals the purpose

   They can use these notes to write about the author's purpose during Phase 3.

10 Synthesizing Information from Two Sources

What: Readers know that when two or more authors write about the same topic, they may include details that are similar or different to the others.

Why: Noticing similarities and differences can help you compare and contrast the information in sources *and* combine information from multiple sources. Noticing similarities and differences can also help you evaluate the authors' points of view.

How: Make sure you know what your purpose for reading multiple sources is. Read the first source and determine what is important. Then as you read each additional source, ask yourself this question:

> *Is this information similar to or different from what I learned in the other source(s)?*

Tip: Remember that "different" can just mean that some details found in one source are not in another.

Example of Inquiry Chart

	Question #1	Question #2	Question #3
What I already know			
Source #1			
Source #2			
Source #3			
Summary of What I've Learned			

For more information, see Chapter 11, pages 211–212.

Series of Phase 2 Lessons

1. **Model and guide.** Share the *what, why,* and *how* of synthesizing information from multiple sources. Review how reading with a clear purpose helps us determine what is important in a source. Provide a purpose or help students generate a purpose for reading two sources. After they read and identify key details in a first source, introduce a second source and ask them to read. Ask the students if they noticed any similarities and differences among the sources. Then demonstrate for them how you thought about specific similarities and differences in details while reading one sentence or short part of the second source. Engage the students in noticing how you did this as they read another sentence or short section with you. Then assign partners to think through another section in the second source. Lean in to coach as needed.

2. **Introduce the inquiry chart.** Instruct the students on how to create the organizer (e.g., fold the chart so that there are six rows and four columns). Return to the first two sources and help the students generate three questions they should be able to answer with information from these sources; prompt them to write these questions on the top row of the chart. Demonstrate skimming the first source to find a part that may have relevant details and closely reading that part to identify key details to be written on the chart. Coach students as they skim the second source, closely read the relevant parts, and take notes on the chart in response to the three questions. Remind them to ask questions about how the details in the sources are similar or different. Introduce a third source and guide students as they engage in a similar process. Close by asking students to share what they learned with a partner.

3. **Guide students in looking across notes and identifying details to combine.** Provide students with colored pencils. Project one student's inquiry chart for all the students to view. Think aloud about how you noticed that particular details from each source belong together in some way. (The details might all be causes, effects, physical characteristics, functions, locations, etc.) Demonstrate circling each of these details with the same colored pencil. Guide students in trying this out with their own notes. Close by asking them to share the details they noticed should go together with a partner.

4. **Guide students in writing learning summaries.** Project one student's inquiry chart. Use the notes for one question to lead students in a shared writing of a learning summary. Support students as they engage in using notes on their own inquiry charts to write summaries.

Study Guide

This study guide has been created to enrich your understanding of the instruction presented in this book. Although as individuals each of you may find this guide helpful, the suggestions I make are primarily geared to professional learning communities (PLCs) of any kind, including grade-level and cross-grade-level teams with specialists, schoolwide teams, district-based teams, and groups of graduate students. Recommendations for instructional exercises and prompts for conversations are included for each chapter and can be followed in a sequence, or one may skip forward to particular chapters. The chief objective of this guide is simply to nurture conversations helpful to members' everyday practice. As part of this endeavor, each section of the guide suggests bringing your own teaching artifacts, instructional materials, and student work samples to the PLC meetings.

CHAPTER 1. Strategic Close Reading of Informational Sources

1. Before reading this chapter, chart what members of the group think *close reading* means. The chart could be a list or a graphic of some sort. After reading this chapter, return to the chart and add or revise details about what is meant by *close reading*. If there are big differences between the before and after, what are the shifts you may need to begin to consider in what *close reading* means or entails?

2. Read the section in this chapter on "close viewing" of a video on pages 9–11. Consider the following questions:
   - What kind of lessons are you currently giving that teach students how to strategically process the content in a video?
   - What do you need to consider adding?

3. Reread the section in this chapter on "close reading" of an infographic on pages 11–12. Consider the following questions:
   - What kind of lessons are you currently giving that teach students how to strategically process the content in infographics?
   - What do you need to consider adding?

CHAPTER 2. A Repertoire of Strategies Needed for Close Reading

1. After reading this chapter, individually or with the members of your PLC, locate several informational sources that are available in your instructional setting. Engage in a close reading or viewing of selected sections of the sources. As you read, consider the following questions:

   - What skills are required for a reader to understand this source in depth?
   - How do the features and the main source collaborate in supporting each other?
   - What obstacles might interfere with a student's understanding this source well?

2. As a group or individually, set goals for teaching or observing close reading with students. Consider the following questions:

   - How can teaching close reading be better integrated into content-area units of study?
   - What should integrating literacy and content-area instruction "look like" when teaching close reading?
   - How can teams of teachers plan instruction that supports close reading throughout the day?

   Visit my website (*www.Sunday-Cummins.com*) for examples of sets of sources that have been grouped thematically for content-area units of study in science and social studies. These sets of sources include texts for reading aloud, excerpts of texts intended for close reading, and texts that can be made part of the classroom library (i.e., for general reading). Consider examining these sources as a way of developing conversations about how best to integrate literacy instruction with content-area instruction.

CHAPTER 3. An Assessment-Driven, Three-Phase Plan for Learning

1. Read and discuss Chapter 3 with members of your PLC. As you read this chapter, reflect on how the instruction described compares with your own. Consider the following questions:

   - What have you observed your students doing as close readers?
   - How do you scaffold instruction in close reading when teaching with informational sources?
   - What do you do to prepare in advance for this instruction?
   - What, if anything, is missing in your instructional practices?

2. Meeting as a PLC, have a conversation about the instructional practices described in this chapter. Additional questions to consider include:

   - What might the three-phase plan for learning look like in your classroom?
   - What types of support do you and your colleagues need to enhance your teaching with informational sources that you are not already receiving?
   - How can you best support one another?

3. Locate a video of an educator teaching for strategic processing of information in a source or develop a video in which one member of the PLC teaches strategic processing. As you view the video with the other members of your PLC, take three-column notes as follows:

What is the teacher saying? What actions does the teacher take?	How does the teacher's language and actions serve to support the students?	How does this practice resonate with my practice? What are questions that I have?
Example of notes about language: The teacher says, "When I tackle a source like this, I start by previewing the whole source. Let me show you how I do this."	*Example of notes about language:* The teacher is putting herself or himself out there as a reader—stating aloud for students to hear what is going through her mind as a reader. First she said . . . Then she said . . .	*Examples of notes:* I usually am explicit about what the student should be doing as a reader, but I am telling the student what a reader does. I am not saying what *I* do as a reader. I wonder if that makes a difference.
Example of notes about actions: The teacher places the excerpt from the source on a document camera. As she talks, she draws arrows next to the features she has previewed.	*Example of notes about actions:* Students can actually see how she previews the source when she marks on the source.	*Examples of notes:* I don't always have the source projected in some way for all the students to see. When I do, I point to the source, but I do not mark on the source as a visual for what a reader needs to do. I need to think about doing that.

After viewing the video clip, debrief. Consider the following questions:

- What connections could be drawn between the group members' observations?
- What themes were apparent in the purposes of the scaffolding described?
- What instructional changes might you need to consider implementing?

CHAPTER 4. Selecting Sources

1. Create a list of informational sources available to members of your group. This exercise may include hunting for sources in your building or searching the sites recommended in Figure 4.3 on page 59.

2. As members of the PLC, dialogue with one another about various types of sources (e.g., printed texts, videos, infographics) that you have access to and determine which sources are better suited for close reading, viewing, or listening. Use the recommendations in Chapter 4 to guide your discussion.

CHAPTER 5. Introducing Sources and Teaching Students to Make *Informed* Predictions

1. Browse through informational sources that you might use for instruction, including a few videos. Based on your students' strengths and needs, what might you need to include in the introduction to each source? Use the suggestions in Chapter 5 as a guide.

2. Individually or with your PLC, practice using the THIEVES approach to previewing and predicting with a text that your students will likely be reading in the near future. After previewing the text systematically, read the text. Discuss the following questions:

   • What did you notice about yourself as a reader after you previewed the text strategically?

   • How might this approach be helpful to your students?

   • What might this approach look like with a video or infographic?

3. Plan and implement a lesson by introducing the THIEVES mnemonic. If you have already taught your students a previewing strategy, consider how you might review this strategy for more effective use by the students. (See Figure 5.9 on page 75 for an example of a teacher's introduction.) After the lesson, reflect as follows on your own or with a group:

   • What did you notice during the lesson? What about after the lesson, when you looked at students' responses?

   • How will you address these observations during the next lesson? (See Figure 5.12 on page 80 for suggestions for follow-up instruction.)

CHAPTER 6. Synthesis and Identifying Main Ideas

1. Individually or as members of the PLC, locate and read (or watch) several high-quality informational sources available in your school. Consider these questions:

   • What are the authors' main ideas? What evidence in each source supports these ideas?

   • What would you say during a think-aloud about your synthesis of each source or a part of the source?

2. Individually or with support, plan for and implement an interactive read-aloud, introducing the students to synthesis by means of the framed picture analogy. (For more information on selecting sources to read aloud, see Chapter 4, pages 55–57.) If you have already been reading aloud informational sources to your students and talking about synthesis, use your experience to consider the specific ideas elaborated in this chapter. What does the chapter content offer that you might want to consider introducing into your own practice? Plan and implement a lesson based on your reflection of your particular instructional practices.

3. Bring the text from a lesson and any related teaching artifacts or student writing samples to your PLC meeting. Consider engaging in the following experiences:

   • Have a conversation about the lessons that individual members have implemented. What went well? Which aspects of your own instructional practices might benefit from modifications?

   • Take time to look through your own students' work using the four stages of development described in the chapter (see Figure 6.10 on page 99) to assess your students' responses. What do you notice? What might a future small-group or whole-class lesson look like based on your observations (see Figure 6.17 on page 106)?

   • Consider making a commitment to return to the PLC later with additional teaching artifacts and student responses from a subsequent lesson. The following protocol, "Looking at Your Students' Work" (based on the work of Blythe, Allen, & Powell, 2008), can be used to guide these discussions.

Looking at Your Students' Work

Prior to this meeting, each member will have selected one student's work to share with the group. One person in the group agrees to keep track of the time and to help the group stay focused on following the schedule and agenda. The description below includes the recommended steps, the suggested questions to help direct what is shared and discussed, and the recommended time allowance for each step. Groups should feel free to modify this protocol to best meet their individual needs.

Protocol

1. **Teacher presents.** What has the teacher already noticed about this student? What was the assignment? What did the teacher notice in the student's written work? (2 minutes)
2. **Group analyzes.** What is the student doing well? What does the student need to work on? (5 minutes)
3. **Group brainstorms.** What instruction might help this student? (5 minutes)
4. **Teacher plans.** When and how will this happen in the classroom? (2 minutes)
5. **Group draws conclusions.** How might a similar approach work for student(s) in other members' classrooms? (5 minutes)

CHAPTER 7. Monitoring for Meaning

1. Read and discuss Chapter 7 with your PLC colleagues. Consider these questions during your dialogue:

    - What have you noticed during interactions with your students that reveals whether they are self-monitoring while reading informational texts?
    - What have you already done to teach them how to self-monitor? What have you noticed as a result?
    - Based on the content of this chapter, what might be missing from your assessment of students' self-monitoring? From your own instruction?

2. Locate informational sources your students may be reading as part of a science or social studies unit of study. As you skim the sources, notice which parts are more complex than others.

    - What makes those parts harder for students to understand?
    - How might a lesson on coding and using fix-up strategies support them?

3. If your students need to work on self-monitoring, plan and implement a lesson on how to use the coding method. (See Figures 7.7 and 7.9 on pages 117–119 and 122–123 for support.) Plan specifically to confer with your students during the Phase 2—Meet the Strategies lesson. Use Figure 7.10 on page 124, which describes several common conferring scenarios, as a reference for what you might notice and say during conferences with your students. As you meet with them individually, take anecdotal notes about your conversations.

    - What did they say?
    - What did you say to prompt their thinking?
    - How did this exchange move the student forward (or not)?

    Bring your anecdotal notes to your PLC meeting. Dialogue with your peers about what you observed and said during the conferences.

    - What seemed to be helpful?
    - What was still puzzling?
    - What do you need to continue to do when conferring with students?
    - What do you need to do more of when conferring with students? What do you need to do less of?

CHAPTER 8. Identifying and Explaining Key Details

1. Locate a few short informational sources and practice identifying key details. Use the "How" in Figure 8.2 (page 134) to support you. Based on this experience, what do you need to consider when preparing a lesson on how to identify key details?

2. Video yourself teaching a lesson on determining what is important on the basis of the ideas in Chapter 8. (See Figures 8.13 and 8.14 on pages 151–153 and 155–156 for support.) Then, after watching the video by yourself or with a partner, ask yourself:

   - What do you observe yourself doing that makes clear to students what a proficient reader does to determine what is important?

3. Share a 3- to 5-minute video clip of your instructional techniques with your PLC. Agree as a group in advance what you will be looking for in each member's clip, whether it's how one interacts with the visually accessible images of the text or what one says during the think-aloud portion of the mini-lesson. Engage with members in a nonevaluative dialogue about each video clip; it might include members reading from their notes, asking one another questions, or sharing anecdotes from their own practice. The objective would solely be to affirm and broaden the group's collective practice experience. The protocol described earlier can be modified for these conversations.

CHAPTER 9. Learning from a Source's Visual Images and Other Features

1. As a PLC, read and discuss Chapter 9. Extend this discussion by examining the layout and design of the features in sources you locate in your school or on the Internet. Consider the following questions:

   - How should the reader deal with the typical one- or two-page spread? Reading from top to bottom? From left to right? Or clockwise?
   - How do the features support the main part of the source?
   - How does the information provided in the features individually and in the running text (or, in the case of video, spoken narrative) work to support and reinforce one another?

2. Individually or with colleagues' support, plan a lesson or cycle of lessons focused on close reading of visual images (e.g., photographs, maps, diagrams) and their supporting print features (e.g., captions, labels), based on the ideas in Chapter 9. Implement the lessons and collect the resulting instructional artifacts and the students' responses.

3. Acting collectively as a PLC, have a conversation about the lesson(s) implemented. Consider these questions:

   - How did the individual members of the PLC make a visually accessible image for the students to see during the think-aloud?
   - What was the flow of each member's think-aloud like? Did the students want to join in a shared think-aloud? How did the members maintain an ongoing dialogue with their students?
   - In the artifacts, what are the students revealing about their understanding of the visual image? What do they include that connects to the information in the main part of the source? (See Figure 9.11 on page 182 for support.)

CHAPTER 10. Using Context Clues to Make Sense of Unfamiliar Vocabulary

1. Locate a few sources on content-area topics that students might find engaging to read or watch. Take time to read or watch the source. As you do, notice vocabulary that may be unfamiliar to students. What are the context clues the author provides? What type of clue are they? Use Figure 10.3 on page 196 as a reference.

2. Plan and implement a lesson introducing the types of context clues. (See Figures 10.6 and 10.7 on pages 199–201 and 202–203 for guidance.) Afterward when you reflect on your observations during the lesson, consider these questions:

   - How did your think-aloud or demonstration go? What makes you think so?
   - What types of clues did you notice students understanding? What types did they seem to struggle to make sense of?
   - What might follow-up instruction look like? (See Figure 10.10, page 206.)

3. Plan another lesson and focus specifically on the conferring you do with your students during the Phase 2—Meet the Strategies lesson. Use Figure 10.8 on page 204, which describes several common conferring scenarios, as a reference for what you might notice and say during conferences with your students. As you meet with them individually, take anecdotal notes about your conversations.

   - What did they say?
   - What did you say to prompt their thinking?
   - How did this exchange move the student forward (or not)?

   Reflect on and discuss your notes with the PLC. What needs to happen as part of follow-up instruction? Use Figure 10.10 on page 206 as a guide.

CHAPTER 11. Synthesis of Information from Multiple Sources

1. With colleagues, spend time reading or watching several sources on the same topic. Develop a set of sources (from the larger collection you looked at) that could be used in a series of lessons that introduce the inquiry chart.

2. Meet as a PLC several times during this series of lessons. Consider bringing any relevant instructional artifacts and student work samples to the group's meetings to reference during the discussions. The likely topics for discussion include:

   - What type of instruction best helps students generate questions for research.
   - What students reveal in their I-charts about their skills in determining what is important (you should review Chapter 8, on identifying and explaining key details, before undertaking this topic).
   - How students should combine notes from multiple sources in developing their summaries and how instruction can best be shaped to support students in this task.

3. Make a commitment to return to the PLC in the future with instructional artifacts and students' work from any additional lessons. Each member should bring whatever evidence best shows that his or her students are continuing to make progress in close reading and synthesizing of the most relevant information from multiple sources.

References

ACT, Inc. (2006). *Reading between the lines: What the ACT reveals about college readiness in reading.* Iowa City, IA: Author.

ACT, Inc. (2017). *The condition of college and career readiness.* Iowa City, IA: Author.

Adler, D. A. (2015). *Simple machines: Wheels, levers, and pulleys.* New York: Scholastic.

Afflerbach, P. (2012). *Understanding and using reading assessment, K–12* (2nd ed.). Newark, DE: International Reading Association.

Afflerbach, P., Pearson, P. D., & Paris, S. G. (2008). Clarifying differences between reading skills and reading strategies. *The Reading Teacher, 61*(5), 364–373.

Allington, R. (2009). *What really matters in response to intervention: Research-based designs.* New York: Allyn & Bacon.

Allington, R. L., & McGill-Franzen, A. (2017). Comprehension difficulties and struggling readers. In S. E. Israel (Ed.), *Handbook of research on reading comprehension* (2nd ed., pp. 271–292). New York: Guilford Press.

Anderson, T. H., & Armbruster, B. B. (1984). Content area textbooks. In R. C. Anderson, J. Osborn, & R. J. Tierney (Eds.), *Learning to read in American schools: Basal readers and content texts* (pp. 193–226). Hillsdale, NJ: Erlbaum.

Armbruster, B. B., McCarthey, S. J., & Cummins, S. (2005). Writing to learn in elementary classrooms. In R. Indrisano & J. R. Paratore (Eds.), *Learning to write, writing to learn: Theory and research into practice* (pp. 71–96). Newark, DE: International Reading Association.

Ash, G. E., & Baumann, J. F. (2017). Vocabulary and reading comprehension: The nexus of meaning. In S. E. Israel (Ed.), *Handbook of research on reading comprehension* (2nd ed., pp. 377–405). New York: Guilford Press.

Associated Press. (2014, January 26). Barges pulling up all sorts of trash from Rio's polluted bay. Associated Press via Newsela (Ed. Newsela Staff. Version Lexile 720). Retrieved from *https://newsela.com/read/rio-garbage/id/2496*.

Baker, L., DeWyngaert, L. U., & Zeliger-Kandasamy, A. (2015). Metacognition in comprehension instruction: New directions. In S. R. Parris & K. Headley (Eds.), *Comprehension instruction: Research-based best practices* (3rd ed., pp. 72–87). New York: Guilford Press.

Beck, I. L., McKeown, M. G., & Kucan, L. (2013). *Bringing words to life: Robust vocabulary instruction* (2nd ed.) New York: Guilford Press.

Bishop, N. (2008). *Frogs.* New York: Scholastic.

Blythe, T., Allen, D., & Powell, B. S. (2008). *Looking together at student work*. New York: Teachers College Press.

Brooks, H. (2010). Storm warning. *National Geographic Explorer! Extreme, 3*(6), 12–17.

Brookshire, B. (2015, October 28). Males and females respond to head hits differently. Retrieved from *www.sciencenewsforstudents.org/article/males-and-females-respond-head-hits-differently*.

Brummett, B. (2010). *Techniques for close reading*. Thousand Oaks, CA: SAGE.

California Department of Education. (n.d.). California assessment of student performance and progress (CAASPP) system. Retrieved from *www.cde.ca.gov/ta/tg/ca*.

Cincinnati Children's Hospital. (n.d.). Injury prevention in youth and teen sports [Video file]. Retrieved from *www.cincinnatichildrens.org/service/s/sports-medicine/research*.

Clay, M. M. (1993). *Reading recovery: A guidebook for teachers*. Portsmouth, NH: Heinemann.

Collard, S. B., III. (2005). *The prairie builders: Reconstructing America's lost grasslands*. Boston: Houghton Mifflin.

Cummins, S. (2011). Using choice words in nonfiction reading conferences. *Talking Points, 22*(2), 9–14.

Cummins, S. (2013). What students can do when the reading gets rough. *Educational Leadership, 71*(3), 69–72.

Cummins, S. (2015). *Unpacking complexity in informational texts: Principles and practices for grades 2–8*. New York: Guilford Press.

Cummins, S. (2017). The case for multiple texts. *Educational Leadership, 74*(5), 66–71.

Cummins, S. (2018). *Nurturing informed thinking: Reading, talking, and writing across content-area texts*. Portsmouth, NH: Heinemann.

Cummins, S., & Stallmeyer-Gerard, C. (2011). Teaching for synthesis of informational texts with read-alouds. *The Reading Teacher, 64*(6), 394–405.

Earthjustice. (2017, February 23). Infographic: Wolves keep Yellowstone in balance. Retrieved April 19, 2018, from *https://earthjustice.org/features/infographic-wolves-keep-yellowstone-in-the-balance*.

Echevarría, J., & Graves A. (2015). *Sheltered content instruction: Teaching English learners with diverse abilities*. Upper Saddle River, NJ: Pearson.

Echevarría, J., Vogt, M., & Short, D. J. (2017). *Making content comprehensible for English learners: The SIOP model*. New York: Pearson.

Englert, C. S., Mariage, T. V., & Dunsmore, K. (2006). Tenets of sociocultural theory in writing instruction research. In C. A. MacArthur, S. Graham, & J. Fitzgerald (Eds.), *Handbook of writing research* (2nd ed., pp. 208–221). New York: Guilford Press.

Finkelman, P. (2006). *The Constitution*. Washington, DC: National Geographic Society.

Fisher, D., & Frey, N. (2009). *Background knowledge: The missing piece of the comprehension puzzle*. Portsmouth, NH: Heinemann.

Fleming, C. (2016). *Giant squid*. New York: Roaring Brook Press.

Fountas, I. C., & Pinnell, G. S. (2017). *Fountas & Pinnell Benchmark Assessment System 2: Grades 3–8, levels L–Z*. Portsmouth, NH: Heinemann.

Free School (Producer). (2015, July 22). 3 states of matter for kids (solid, liquid, gas) [Video file]. Retrieved from *www.youtube.com/watch?v=wclY8F-UoTE*.

Fu, D. (2009). *Writing between languages: How English language learners make the transition to fluency, grades 4–12*. Portsmouth, NH: Heinemann.

Geiger, B. (2010a). Active earth. *National Geographic Explorer! Pathfinder, 10*(1), 8–13.

Geiger, B. (2010b). Thirsty planet. *National Geographic Explorer! Pathfinder, 10*(2), 18–23.

George, J. C. (2008). *The wolves are back*. New York: Dutton Children's Books.

Gibbons, P. (2015). *Scaffolding language, scaffolding learning: Teaching English language learners in the mainstream classroom.* Portsmouth, NH: Heinemann.

Graham, S., Harris, K. R., & Chambers, A. B. (2016). Evidence-based practice and writing instruction: A review of reviews. In C. A. MacArthur, S. Graham, & J. Fitzgerald (Eds.), *Handbook of writing research* (2nd ed., pp. 211–226). New York: Guilford Press.

Guthrie, J. T., & Wigfield, A. (2000). Engagement and motivation in reading. In M. L. Kamil, P. B. Mosenthal, P. D. Pearson, & R. Barr (Eds.), *Handbook of reading research* (Vol. 3, pp. 403–422). Mahwah, NJ: Erlbaum.

Headley, K. (2008). Improving reading comprehension through writing. In C. C. Block & S. R. Parris (Eds.), *Comprehension instruction: Research-based best practices* (2nd ed., pp. 214–225). New York: Guilford Press.

Hoffman, J. V. (1992). Critical reading/thinking across the curriculum: Using I-charts to support learning. *Language Arts, 69*(2), 121–127.

Hoyt, L. (2008). *Revisit, reflect, retell: Time-tested strategies for teaching reading comprehension.* Portsmouth, NH: Heinemann.

Illinois State Board of Education. (n.d.) Assessment PARCC. Retrieved from *www.isbe.net/Pages/PARCC-Place.aspx.*

International Literacy Association. (2017). Literacy assessment: What everyone needs to know. Retrieved from *https://literacyworldwide.org/docs/default-source/where-we-stand/literacy-assessment-brief.pdf?sfvrsn=efd4a68e_4.*

Jenkins, S., & Page, R. (2008). *What do you do with a tail like this?* New York: Houghton-Mifflin.

Johnson, R. L. (2002). *Global warming.* Washington, DC: National Geographic School.

Johnston, P. H. (2004). *Choice words: How our language affects children's learning.* Portland, ME: Stenhouse.

Johnston, P. (2010). Teachers as evaluation experts. In P. Afflerbach (Ed.), *Essential readings on assessment* (pp. 13–16). Newark, DE: International Reading Association.

Kids Discover. (n.d.-a). States of matter. Retrieved June 17, 2018, from *https://online.kidsdiscover.com/infographic/states-of-matter?ReturnUrl=/infographic/states-of-matter.*

Kids Discover. (n.d.-b). Volcanoes inside and out. Retrieved April 19, 2018, from *https://online.kidsdiscover.com/infographic/volcanoes.*

Manyak, P. C., & Bauer, E. B. (2009). English vocabulary instruction for English learners. *The Reading Teacher, 63*(2), 174–176.

Manz, S. L. (2002). A strategy for previewing textbooks: Teaching readers to become THIEVES. *The Reading Teacher, 55*(5), 434.

Massachusetts Department of Elementary and Secondary Education. (2017). English language arts and literacy: Grades pre-kindergarten to 12. Retrieved from *www.doe.mass.edu/frameworks/ela/2017-06.pdf.*

May, S. (2015, June 5). A day in space. National Aeronautics and Space Administration via Newsela (Ed. Newsela Staff. Version 840). Retrieved from *https://newsela.com/read/elem-sci-day-in-space/id/25651.*

Mesmer, H. A., & Rose-McCully, M. M. (2017). A closer look at close reading: Three under-the-radar skills needed to comprehend sentences. *The Reading Teacher, 71*(4), 451–461.

Missouri Department of Elementary and Secondary Education. (n.d.). Missouri learning standards. Retrieved from *https://dese.mo.gov/college-career-readiness/curriculum/missouri-learning-standards.*

Moss, B. (2003). *Exploring the literature of fact: Children's nonfiction trade books in the elementary classroom.* New York: Guilford Press.

Moss, B., & Loh-Hagan, V. (2016). *40 strategies for guiding readers through informational texts.* New York: Guilford Press.

National Aeronautics and Space Administration. (2015, March 6). #suitup for safety—infographic. Retrieved from *www.nasa.gov/content/suitup-for-safety-infographic.*

National Aeronautics and Space Administration. (n.d.). What is a sounding rocket?—infographic. Retrieved from *www.jpl.nasa.gov/infographics/infographic.view.php?id=11445.*

National Council for the Social Studies. (n.d.). College, Career, and Civic Life (C3) Framework for Social Studies State Standards [Scholarly project]. (2017, June 12). Retrieved from *www.socialstudies.org/c3.*

National Geographic. (n.d.-a). Cobra vs. mongoose. Retrieved April 19, 2018, from *https://video.nationalgeographic.com/video/cobra-vs-mongoose-predation.*

National Geographic. (n.d.-b). Volcanoes 101. Retrieved April 19, 2018, from *https://video.nationalgeographic.com/video/101-videos/volcanoes-101.*

National Governors Association Center for Best Practices & Council of Chief State School Officers. (2010). *Common Core Standards for English language arts and literacy in history/social studies, science, and technical subjects.* Washington, DC: Authors.

National Institutes of Health. (2017, December 30). Infographic: Traumatic brain injury (TBI) in kids: Causes and prevention strategies. Retrieved from *www.nichd.nih.gov/newsroom/digital-media/infographics/TBIinKids.*

National Science Foundation. (2015, August 31). Understanding the ecological role of wolves in Yellowstone National Park. Retrieved April 19, 2018, from *www.nsf.gov/news/mmg/mmg_disp.jsp?med_id=80849.*

National Science Foundation. (2016, October 24). Food and fear: Modeling animal tradeoffs shaped by landscape complexity. Retrieved from *www.nsf.gov/news/special_reports/science_nation/foragingrabbits.jsp.*

NGSS Lead States. (2013). *Next Generation Science Standards: For states, by states.* Washington, DC: National Academies Press.

Paris, S. G., & Winograd, P. (1990). Self-regulated cognition: Interdependence of metacognition, attributions, and self-esteem. In B. F. Jones & L. Idol (Eds.), *Dimensions of thinking and cognitive instruction* (pp. 15–44). Hillsdale, NJ: Erlbaum.

Paris, S. G., & Winograd, P. (2001). *The role of self-regulated learning in contextual teaching: Principles and practices for teacher preparation.* Commissioned paper for the project Preparing Teachers to Use Contextual Teaching and Learning Strategies to Improve Student Success in and Beyond School, U.S. Department of Education, Washington, DC.

Pearson, P. D., & Cervetti, G. N. (2017). The roots of reading comprehension instruction. In S. E. Israel (Ed.), *Handbook of research on reading comprehension* (pp. 12–56). New York: Guilford Press.

Pearson, P. D., & Gallagher, M. C. (1983). The instruction of reading comprehension. *Contemporary Educational Psychology, 8,* 317–344.

Peppas, L. (2013). *How do we measure matter?* St. Catharines, ON, Canada: Crabtree.

Pigdon, K. (2012). *Side by side.* South Yarra, Victoria, Australia: Eleanor Curtain.

Pressley, M. (2000). What should comprehension instruction be the instruction of? In M. L. Kamil, P. B. Mosenthal, P. D. Pearson, & R. Barr (Eds.), *Handbook of reading research* (Vol. 3, pp. 545–561). Mahwah, NJ: Erlbaum.

Pressley, M., El-Dinary, P. B., Gaskins, I., Schuder, T., Bergman, J. L., Almasi, J., et al. (1992). Beyond direct explanation: Transactional instruction of reading comprehension strategies. *Elementary School Journal, 92*(5), 513–555.

Public Broadcasting Service. (2015, October 26). Infographic: All about snowy owls. Retrieved

April 19, 2018, from *www.pbs.org/wnet/nature/magic-of-the-snowy-owl-infographic-all-about-snowy-owls/7962.*

Reid, R., Lienemann, T. O., & Hagaman, J. L. (2013). *Strategy instruction for students with learning disabilities* (2nd ed.). New York: Guilford Press.

Richardson, J., & Walther, M. P. (2013). *Next step guided reading assessment: An assess-teach system built for the Common Core.* New York: Scholastic IMPACT Professional Development & Resources.

Ruane, M. E. (2010). KABOOM! *National Geographic Explorer! Pathfinder, 10*(2), 10–17.

Saner, E. (2016a, May 12). Fighting wildfires with fire in Alberta, Canada. Retrieved from *https://newsela.com/read/alberta-wildfire/id/17510.*

Saner, E. (2016b, May 9). How do you stop a wildfire? Retrieved from *www.theguardian.com/world/shortcuts/2016/may/09/wildfire-alberta-canada.*

Short, D. J. (2002). Language learning in sheltered social studies classes. *TESOL Journal, 11*(1), 18–24.

Simon, S. (2018). *Icebergs and glaciers.* New York: HarperCollins Childrens Books.

Springer, S. E., Dole, J. A., & Hacker, D. J. (2017). The role of interest in reading comprehension. In S. E. Israel (Ed.), *Handbook of research on reading comprehension* (pp. 519–542). New York: Guilford Press.

Stevens, A. P. (2016, October 21). A new "spin" on concussions. Retrieved from *www.science-newsforstudents.org/article/new-spin-concussions.*

Sturm, J. (2012). *Understanding biomes.* Vero Beach, FL: Rourke.

Swanson, H. L., & Hoskyn, M. (2001). Instructing adolescents with learning disabilities: A component and composite analysis. *Learning Disabilities Research and Practice, 16*(2), 109–119.

Swanson, H. L., Kehler, P., & Jerman, O. (2010). Working memory, strategy knowledge, and strategy instruction in children with reading disabilities. *Journal of Learning Disabilities, 43*(1), 24–47.

Swanson, H. L., & Sachse-Lee, C. (2000). A meta-analysis of single-subject-design intervention research for students with LD. *Journal of Learning Disabilities, 33*(2), 114–136.

Turbill, J., & Bean, W. (2006). *Writing instruction K–6: Understanding process, purpose, audience.* Katonah, NY: Owen.

Vocabulary.com. (n.d.). Balance. Retrieved from *www.vocabulary.com/dictionary/balance.*

Vygotsky, L. S. (1978). *Mind in society: The development of higher psychological processes.* Cambridge, MA: Harvard University Press.

Westrup, H. (2015, January 9). Invasion of the drones. Retrieved July 20, 2017, from *http://magazines.scholastic.com/news/2015/01/Invation-of-the-Drones.*

Wiggins, G., & McTighe, J. (2005). *Understanding by design.* Upper Saddle River, NJ: Pearson.

Woollett, L. A. (2015). *Big top burning: The true story of an arsonist, a missing girl, and the greatest show on Earth.* Chicago: Chicago Review Press.

Wright, T. S., & Cervetti, G. N. (2016). A systematic review of the research on vocabulary instruction that impacts text comprehension. *Reading Research Quarterly, 52*(2), 203–226.

Index

Note. *f* following a page number indicates a figure.

Accuracy, selection of sources and, 49*f*, 50–51
"Active Earth" (Geiger), 149
Advanced readers, 45
Appeal of sources, 49*f*, 52–53
Approaching stage of development. *See* Stages of development
Appropriateness, selection of sources and, 49*f*, 51
Assessment
    context clues to figure out unfamiliar vocabulary and, 194–195, 198, 203–204, 204*f*, 205*f*
    continuous, 35–36
    key detail identification and, 137, 154, 156, 157*f*, 158*f*, 159*f*, 160*f*
    main idea identification and, 88, 97–99, 98*f*–99*f*
    monitoring for meaning and, 112–113, 121, 124*f*, 125*f*
    selection of sources and, 47–48
    source features and, 178, 180–181, 181*f*, 182*f*, 183*f*
    synthesis across multiple sources and, 210–211, 223, 224*f*, 225*f*
Attempting stage of development. *See* Stages of development
Audio clips, 16, 69–70. *See also* Strategic close reading–viewing–listening
Authority, selection of sources and, 49–50, 49*f*
Author's purpose, 134, 136, 237

B

Background knowledge. *See* Prior knowledge
Big Top Burning (Woollett), 49
Bookmarks
    with the coding strategy, 113, 114*f*, 230
    with context clues, 195, 197*f*, 236
    THIEVES bookmark, 72*f*, 73–74

C

Cake-baking analogy, 184
Cause–effect structures, 23, 146*f*, 234. *See also* Structure of sources; Text structures
Chronology structure, 146*f*, 234. *See also* Structure of sources
Coaching. *See* Conferring and coaching
Cobra vs. Mongoose (National Geographic), 133, 135, 136, 141, 150
Coding strategy, 113–116. *See also* Monitoring for meaning
College, Career, and Civic Life (3C) Framework for Social Studies and Standards (National Council for the Social Studies), 64. *See also* Standards
Comparison context clues, 196*f*

Comparison structure, 146f, 147f, 234. *See also* Structure of sources

Conferring and coaching
   context clues to figure out unfamiliar vocabulary and, 194, 198, 203–204, 204f
   continuous assessment and, 36
   key detail identification and, 137, 154, 156, 157f
   main idea identification and, 88, 98f
   monitoring for meaning and, 112, 124f
   source features and, 167, 180, 181f
   synthesis across multiple sources and, 210, 223, 224f
   THIEVES mnemonic and, 76, 77f, 80f
   three-phase plan for learning and, 35–36
Connection of details. *See* Synthesis of details
The Constitution (Finkelman), 25–27, 27f, 29
Content areas, 44
Content objectives, 64–65
Context clues, using with unfamiliar vocabulary
   assessing students' need for support with, 194–195, 198, 203–204, 204f, 205f
   follow-up instruction regarding, 204–205, 206f
   introducing vocabulary and, 66–67
   lesson planning for, 197–198, 198f, 199f–203f, 236
   monitoring for meaning and, 24–25
   overview, 191–194, 191f, 193f
   sample lesson plans for, 199f–203f
   types of, 195, 196f, 197f, 198f, 236
   See also Vocabulary
Continuous assessment. *See* Assessment
Contrast context clues, 196f

D

"A Day in Space" (May), 53–54, 58, 60
Decoding skills, fix-up strategies for, 130f
Definitions as context clues, 67, 68f, 196f, 197f
Descriptive structure, 23, 146f, 147, 148f, 149, 234.
   See also Structure of sources; Text structures
Development, stages of. *See* Stages of development
Disabilities, learning, 42–44

E

Engagement, student, 82–83
English learners, 44–45
Enumerative structure, 146f, 147. *See also* Structure of sources
Examples as context clues, 196f, 197f

Exceeding stage of development. *See* Stages of development
Explode-to-explain strategy, 142–145, 142f, 143f, 145f, 233

F

Features, source. *See* Source features
Fix-up strategies, 24–25, 115, 128–129, 130f–131f. *See also* Strategies
Food and Fear (NSF video), 9–11, 10f, 50, 51, 52
Framed photograph analogy
   coding strategy and, 120–121, 120f
   overview, 89–90, 90f, 91f
   sample lesson plans utilizing, 93f–97f, 229
Frogs (Bishop), 8–9

G

General context clues, 196f, 197f
Giant Squid (Fleming), 50, 52
Global Warming (Johnson), 184–188, 185f
Goals for reading. *See* Purposes for reading–viewing–listening
Guided practice, 38–40

H

How Do We Measure Matter? (Peppas), 163f, 164–165, 169, 180–181
"How Do You Stop a Wildfire?" (Saner), 55

I

I charts. *See* Inquiry charts (I charts)
I statements, 38
Ideas, main. *See* Main idea identification
Identification of key details. *See* Key detail identification
Identification of main ideas. *See* Main idea identification
Informed predictions. *See* Predictions
Injury Prevention in Youth and Teen Sports (Cincinnatic Chidlren's Hospital), 194
Inquiry charts (I charts)
   examples of, 214f, 215f, 238
   form for, 212f

introducing to students, 213–215, 217*f*, 218, 223

lesson planning for, 238

synthesis across multiple sources and, 211

See also Question generating

Interactive read-alouds, 55–56. *See also* Read-alouds

Introducing sources to learners, 36–37, 61–62, 62*f*, 63–71, 66*f*, 67*f*, 68*f*, 69*f*, 81. *See also* Source selection

K

"KABOOM" (Ruane), 108, 110, 116, 119–120, 121, 123

Key detail identification

assessing students' ability for, 137, 154, 156, 157*f*, 158*f*, 159*f*, 160*f*

explode-to-explain strategy and, 142–145, 142*f*, 143*f*, 145*f*

follow-up instruction regarding, 156–157, 161*f*

lesson planning for, 149–154, 151*f*–153*f*, 155*f*–156*f*, 231–234

noticing a source's structure, 145–149, 146*f*, 148*f*

overview, 132–133, 134–137, 134*f*, 158

pasta analogy approach and, 138–141, 139*f*, 140*f*, 141*f*

sample lesson plans for, 151*f*–153*f*, 155*f*–156*f*

Key vocabulary. *See* Vocabulary

Kid appeal, 49*f*, 52–53

Knowledge, prior/background. *See* Prior knowledge

Knowledge construction, 14–15

L

Language objectives, 64–65

Learning disabilities, 42–44

"Leveled" sources, 54–55

M

Macrostructure of texts, 23. *See also* Text structures

Main idea identification

assessing students' understanding of, 97–99, 98*f*–99*f*

follow-up instruction regarding, 99–100, 103–106, 103*f*, 104*f*, 105*f*

framed photograph analogy and, 89–90, 90*f*, 91*f*

key detail identification and, 136

lesson planning for, 92, 93*f*–97*f*, 229

overview, 84–88, 84*f*, 87*f*, 106–107

sample lesson plans for, 93*f*–97*f*

strategic close reading–viewing–listening and, 8–9, 10, 11

student needs regarding, 88

synthesis of details and, 28–30

Meeting stage of development. *See* Stages of development

Microstructure of texts, 23. *See also* Text structures

Modeling

English learners and, 45

THIEVES mnemonic and, 80*f*

written response and, 40

See also Guided practice; Scaffolding

Monitoring for meaning

assessing students' use of, 112–113, 121, 124*f*, 125*f*

coding strategy and, 113–115, 114*f*, 115*f*, 116*f*

explaining and modeling, 37–38

follow-up instruction regarding, 121, 123, 126–129, 126*f*, 128*f*, 130*f*–131*f*

lesson planning for, 116–121, 117*f*–119*f*, 120*f*, 122*f*–123*f*, 230

overview, 24–25, 109–112, 110*f*, 111*f*, 129

sample lesson plans for, 117*f*–119*f*

think-alouds and, 108–109, 109*f*

See also Coding strategy

Multiple sources, synthesis of information from. *See* Synthesis across sources

N

Narrative structure, 146*f*, 234. *See also* Structure of sources

National standards. *See* Standards

Next Generation Science Standards (NGSS Lead States), 64. *See also* Standards

Noticing structure strategies, 145–149, 146*f*, 148*f*. *See also* Structure of sources

P

Pasta analogy

key detail identification and, 138–141, 139*f*, 140*f*, 141*f*

sample lesson plans for, 151*f*–153*f*, 155*f*–156*f*, 231

The Prairie Builders (Collard), 56, 100, 103

Predictions

developing prior knowledge and, 20, 22

introducing sources and, 71

Predictions *(cont.)*
    purposes for reading–viewing–listening and, 18
    THIEVES mnemonic and, 72–81, 72*f*, 73*f*, 74*f*,
        75*f*, 77*f*, 78*f*–79*f*, 80*f*
    topic of the source and, 65
Previewing
    introducing sources and, 71
    THIEVES mnemonic and, 72–81, 72*f*, 73*f*, 74*f*,
        75*f*, 77*f*, 78*f*–79*f*, 80*f*
    topic of the source and, 65
Prior knowledge
    development of, 20, 22
    English learners and, 44
    introducing sources and, 37, 51, 68, 69*f*
    key detail identification and, 136
    main idea identification and, 85
    related to how sources work, 22–23
    related to the topic of the source, 19–22, 21*f*
    source features and, 168
    strategic close reading–viewing–listening and, 11
    students reading above grade level, 45
    synthesis and, 29, 215
    THIEVES mnemonic and, 73
    types of, 20
    unfamiliar vocabulary and, 190
Problem–solution structure, 146*f*, 234. *See also*
        Structure of sources
Purpose, author's, 134, 136, 237
Purposes for reading–viewing–listening
    continuous assessment and, 36
    determining what is important and, 25–28, 27*f*
    introducing sources and, 70–71
    key detail identification and, 134–135, 136,
        149–154
    overview, 4–5, 17–19
    selection of sources and, 53–54
    strategic close reading–viewing–listening and, 8,
        13
    topic of the source and, 65

Q

Question generating, 214–215, 216*f*–217*f*. *See also*
        Inquiry charts (I charts)

R

Read-alouds, 55–57, 57*f*
Research projects. *See* Synthesis across sources

S

Scaffolding
    context clues to figure out unfamiliar vocabulary
        and, 198
    English learners and, 45
    guided practice and, 39
    three-phase plan for learning and, 33
    See also Visual scaffolds
Selecting sources. *See* Source selection
Self-monitoring, 24–25. *See also* Monitoring for
        meaning
Sequence structure, 23, 146*f*, 234. *See also*
        Structure of sources; Text structures
Side by Side (Pigdon), 70, 132–133, 134, 136, 142,
        144, 145, 150, 156–157
Simple Machines (Adler), 27–28
Skimming, 219*f*–220*f*
Source features
    assessing students' need for support with,
        167–168
    follow-up instruction regarding, 188, 189*f*
    introducing to students, 168–174, 170*f*–173*f*, 174*f*,
        175*f*
    learning from, 164–167, 164*f*, 165*f*, 166*f*
    lesson planning for, 174–178, 176*f*–178*f*, 179*f*–180*f*,
        235
    overview, 162–163, 163*f*, 188
    prior knowledge regarding, 22–23
    sample lesson plans for, 176*f*–178*f*, 179*f*–180*f*
    types of, 170*f*–173*f*, 235
    See also THIEVES mnemonic
Source selection
    criteria to guide, 48–53, 49*f*
    go-to resources, 58, 59*f*
    "levels" of sources and, 54–55
    overview, 47–48, 58, 60
    purposes for reading–viewing–listening and,
        53–54
    read-alouds and, 55–57, 57*f*
    three-phase plan for learning and, 36–37
    See also Introducing sources to learners
Special education, 42–44
Stages of development
    coded notes and monitoring for meaning and,
        125*f*
    context clues to figure out unfamiliar vocabulary
        and, 205*f*
    key detail identification and, 158*f*, 159*f*, 160*f*
    main idea identification and, 99*f*, 100*f*, 101*f*, 102*f*
    previewing and prediction and, 78*f*–79*f*

source features and, 181, 182*f*, 183*f*

synthesis across multiple sources and, 225*f*

Standards, 1, 64–65

"Storm Warning" (Brooks), 214

Strategic processing

explaining and modeling, 37–38

overview, 3, 16–17

Structure of sources

introducing sources and, 69–70

lesson planning for, 234

noticing, 145–149, 146*f*, 148*f*

See also Text structures

Students with learning disabilities, 42–44

Summarizing

sample lesson plans for, 221*f*–222*f*

synthesis across multiple sources and, 218, 221*f*–222*f*, 223

THIEVES mnemonic and, 79–80

Synonyms as context clues, 196*f*, 197*f*

Synthesis across sources

assessing students' need for support with, 210–211

follow-up instruction regarding, 224–225, 226*f*

I charts and, 211, 212*f*

lesson planning for, 213–222, 214*f*, 215*f*, 216*f*–217*f*, 219*f*–221*f*, 238

overview, 28–30, 207–210, 208*f*, 226

Synthesis in general, 28–30, 208

Synthesis of details

follow-up instruction regarding, 99–100, 103–106, 103*f*, 104*f*, 105*f*

overview, 28–30, 84–88, 84*f*, 87*f*, 107

strategic close reading–viewing–listening and, 11

See also Details in informational sources

T

Teacher-determined purposes, 18–19. *See also* Purposes for reading–viewing–listening

Text features. *See* Source features

Text selection. *See* Source selection

Text structures

fix-up strategies for, 131*f*

introducing sources and, 69–70

key detail identification and, 136, 145–149, 146*f*, 148*f*

prior knowledge regarding, 23

See also Structure of sources

THIEVES mnemonic

bookmark for, 72*f*, 73–74

introducing, 71, 72–74, 75*f*

lesson regarding, 72–74, 72*f*, 73*f*, 74*f*, 75*f*

overview, 72, 72*f*, 73*f*

source features and, 168

Think-alouds

context clues to figure out unfamiliar vocabulary and, 197–198

English learners and, 45

explaining key details in a source and, 144

fix-up strategies for, 130*f*–131*f*

guided practice and, 39

monitoring for meaning and, 108

source features and, 184, 186

synthesis across multiple sources and, 218

THIEVES mnemonic and, 73, 74*f*, 79

"Thirsty Planet" (Geiger), 18, 76–77, 79–80, 123

3 States of Matter (Free School), 165, 174

Three-phase plan for learning overview, 32–45, 32*f*, 34*f*, 41*f*

U

Understanding Biomes (Sturm), 114

Understanding the Ecological Roles of Wolves in Yellowstone National Park (NSF), 85, 209

V

Visual artistry, 49*f*, 51–52

Visual features as context clues, 196*f*, 197*f*. *See also* Source features

Visual scaffolds, 61–62, 62*f*, 198. *See also* Scaffolding

Vocabulary

developing prior knowledge and, 22

fix-up strategies for, 130*f*

introducing, 66–67, 66*f*, 67*f*, 68*f*

main idea identification and, 90, 91*f*

overview, 190

See also Context clues, using with unfamiliar vocabulary

W

What Do You Do with a Tail Like This? (Jenkins & Paige), 56

The Wolves are Back (George), 55–56, 82–83, 83*f*, 84–85, 89, 92, 93*f*–97*f*, 99–100, 103, 208–209

Written response
    coded notes and monitoring for meaning and, 124*f*, 125*f*, 126*f*, 127*f*
    context clues to figure out unfamiliar vocabulary and, 195
    continuous assessment and, 36
    examples of, 83*f*, 100*f*, 101*f*, 102*f*, 103*f*, 104*f*, 105*f*, 183*f*
    key detail identification and, 137, 154
    main idea identification and, 97, 99*f*
    monitoring for meaning and, 113
    source features and, 168, 180–181, 183*f*
    synthesis across multiple sources and, 210, 223, 225*f*
    THIEVES mnemonic and, 80*f*
    three-phase plan for learning and, 32*f*, 33, 40, 41*f*

Z

Zone of proximal development, 33, 35